DANCING IN THE DARK

Also by Barbara Lazear Ascher

Landscape Without Gravity
Playing After Dark
The Habit of Loving

DANCING
IN THE DARK

Romance, Yearning, and the
Search for the Sublime

BARBARA LAZEAR ASCHER

Cliff Street Books
An Imprint of HarperCollinsPublishers

HarperCollins books may be purchased for educational, business, or sales promotional use. For information please write: Special Markets Department, HarperCollins Publishers, Inc., 10 East 53rd Street, New York, NY 10022.

FIRST EDITION

Designed by Nancy Singer Olaguera

Ascher, Barbara Lazear.
    Dancing in the dark : romance, yearning, and the search for the sublime / Barbara Ascher.
       p. cm.
    Includes bibliographical references.
    ISBN 0-06-017442-0
    1. Life. 2. Romanticism. I. Title.
BD431.A73 1999
141'.6—dc21   98-51506

99 00 01 02 03 ❖/RRD 10 9 8 7 6 5 4 3 2 1

This book is dedicated with love and gratitude to the memories of
Jacqueline Kennedy Onassis
and
Ken McCormick
Beloved friends, inspired editors, true romantics

DANCING IN THE DARK
TILL THE TUNE ENDS.
WE'RE DANCING IN THE DARK
AND IT SOON ENDS.
WE'RE WALTZING IN THE WONDER
OF WHY WE'RE HERE.

Howard Dietz

CONTENTS

ACKNOWLEDGMENTS

Thank you, Bob and Dotsy Lazear, for dancing in the dark of the kitchen each night. As your child, it was inevitable that I would grow up believing in the power of romance.

Thank you, Becky Lazear Okrent, first dance partner, great sister, and cheerleader.

Thank you, Bob Ascher, for signing every available space on my dance card and, above all, for being a great kisser.

Thank you, Rebecca Ascher-Walsh, for introducing me to the exquisite romance that exists between mother and daughter.

Thank you, Joel Upton, for opening my eyes to the romance of art, and, Arthur Zajonc, for opening my mind to the science of the sublime.

Thank you, Maurice Tempelsman, king of romance, and his daughter-in-law Cathy Tempelsman, for dazzling research assistance.

Thank you, Nancy Newhouse, for keeping the faith all these years.

Gail Eisenberg, thank you for running my life, although you're capable of running the country.

And to those brave souls, the early readers of very early drafts, Marilyn Johnson, Helen Houghton, Elizabeth Berg, and Jeannette Watson Sanger. Thank you for being available, large-hearted, smart, and fearless.

Thank you to those on call day and night: Judith Clurman for musical and Craig Townsend for theological insights; Jennifer Brown for Insights in General; Nancy McCartney for gracious hospitality at the New York Society Library.

And dear Diane Reverand, Joy Harris, Leslie Daniels, and Kassandra Duane for your radiant attention and divine enthusiasm. "Thank you" seems too slight, but it's all we've got.

Margot Wilkie and Xenia Rose, you showed up just in the nick of time. What a blessing.

INTRODUCTION

Romance is structured yearning. In the romantic moment, we gather and focus that yearning in order to connect with something outside ourselves, believing against all odds that such connection is possible, knowing paradoxically that romance is born in the space between our reach and our grasp.

Historically, the term "romance" was applied to stories written in the Romance languages that evolved in the former provinces of the Roman Empire. These tales were characterized by derring-do, noble acts, and worthy love, all unfolding against a backdrop of poetic landscape. Given this definition, twentieth-century critic Jacques Barzun writes that it is impossible to tell "by the mere use of 'romantic' applied to a person whether he is a hero, a lover, a fairy prince . . . or a mountain climber."

All that and more. Romantics are those who, sensing themselves to be part of a larger whole, and yearning for an intuited harmony with the universe, embark on the ageless quest to discover who they are, who you and I are, and what we're all doing here together. They believe the answers are just around the corner. If not this one, then the next. They are ready and willing to be amazed and to give expression to that amazement.

The romantic quest can be embarked upon solo. It doesn't call for a significant other, great beauty, pulsating sexuality, a new dress, or complex planning. Its only requirements are the courage of an available heart and freedom of imagination.

Members of the nineteenth-century European Romantic Movement (called variously by scholars Romanticists or Romantics, and referred to herein as Romanticists), made this clear with the often achingly lonely and always passionate thrust of their poetry, prose, painting, and music. Defined by their creative responses to the challenges of their time, Berlioz, Beethoven, Constable, Byron, Wordsworth, Shelley, Keats, and Victor Hugo were among those considered Romanticists. So crucial was imagination to their undertakings that they were responsible for introducing the term into common usage. They honored it with reverence and a capital *I* as though it were a god walking among them. Imagination was their source of divine inspiration and the safeguard of intuition. It salvaged these life-giving qualities they believed had been stifled by both the Enlightenment and the repressive formalities of eighteenth-century classicism. For them, truth was to be found in the unpredictability of beauty rather than rigid standards of learning, behavior, design, and decorum.

This is not to say that the Romanticists shunned the Age of Reason or science. They did not check intellect at the door and throw themselves on the mercy of passion. They simply believed, as Aristotle did before them, that poetic truth is sometimes truer than history. Their pursuit of this truth, an awareness of the interconnectedness of unlike things, demanded equal reverence for history and experience, fact and fancy.

They took on faith what today's quantum physicists know, that things are more than they appear. That to be enlightened scientifically and spiritually requires the courage to suspend disbelief. For physicist and romantic alike, the fact that strange and wondrous things are occurring just out of sight is a source of awe rather than frustration.

Expect the unexpected. Better yet, don't expect at all, and certainly don't expect to explain, urged physicist, philosopher, and Nobel prize winner Werner Heisenberg. "You must have felt this too," the man whose uncertainty principle overthrew classical physics said to Einstein, "the almost frightening simplicity and wholeness of the relationships which nature suddenly spreads out before us and for which none of us was in the least prepared." The Romanticists called this the sublime.

Like romance, quantum physics is richer in implications than in explanations. The physicist knows that matter can turn into energy, that energy can turn into matter, and energy never dies. But he can't explain it. The Romanticists knew that love is capable of moving the stubborn human heart and can endure forever, but couldn't explain it. But they could sing it. Like the nature of light, love is its own thing, mysterious, beyond explanation, a source of awe and exaltation.

The Romanticists didn't invent romance any more than the physicist invented the atom. They both gave us languages to express what is essentially beyond language. They gave us the tools for the struggle that has engaged us ever since our earliest ancestors turned their backs to the night and told stories or lowered themselves into caves to paint experience on stone walls, ever since we first sensed the existence of the sublime.

Although Romanticism is limited to a historical time and a cultural movement, romance is not. Romance is ageless, as pedestrian as it is exotic, widely available rather than exclusive. It can be found in Notre Dame or Central Park, at the table of a pastry chef or in the classroom of a gifted teacher. It is Plato's divine enthusiasm, a state of being "possessed by a God."

The inspiration for romance is particular to an individual, but the resulting romantic moment bears certain common elements. The full enthusiastic response to experience, be it rapturous or mournful, eases isolation, blurs the boundaries between self and other, present and past. It sharpens the senses at the same time that it confuses them. A visual memory can evoke a flavor tasted, a line of Bach heard can cause the heart to ache as though a new lover's hand had enfolded one's own. In the romantic moment, we are saturated with eternity.

Only our defenses bar us from this enchantment. Concerned about how we appear to others, we move in secrecy and hide vulnerability from the light of day. We tend to be on guard and watchful, not for experience but for imagined attack.

Such scurrying for safety makes us sentimental. The sentimentalist hordes passion, the romantic is compelled to share it, to make us see what she sees by giving inspiration a shape we can comprehend—a story, a song, a poem, a cathedral. How much easier to ride the highs and pathos of emotion and leave it at that, rather than to admit our loneliness, to declare our need for larger connection, to proclaim its beauty, and to put our hearts on the line. The romantic is aware that the heart might be broken, but trusts that it will break open.

The sentimentalist shares neither this optimism nor courage. Romance challenges, sentimentality soothes. The aftertaste of romance is longing, precisely what created the hunger in the first place. Sentimentality is rewarded with emotional satiation. Who wouldn't prefer it?

Coleridge wouldn't. Nor would Shelley, Keats, Byron, Blake, or Goethe. Not Frank Lloyd Wright. Not the ancient painters of the Ardèche caves. Not Beethoven, Berlioz, or Brahms. Not Bach. Not the anonymous builders of Chartres Cathedral. Not Shakespeare.

Nor, at fifty, would I. Sentiment served me well in adolescence, but in middle age, a time when real life can become plain old life, I needed romance. A long marriage, independent children, a body set on being contrary, and a mind tuned to the rush of time all conspired to inform me that I required passionate connection, something beyond love affairs and official business. Loneliness necessitated a journey out of the self with senses fully alive and defenses down. I needed to throw myself into experience with the wonder of a beginner. To enter it fearlessly and come back with whatever truth it had to reveal. To live as intensely as the Romantics who had lived not just in the nineteenth century but across all time.

What was there to lose? My daughter's respect, it seemed, as I began trailing after Central Park birders. My husband's companionship as I went in search of Northern Renaissance art that failed to move him. But romance served the purpose of reassuring me that I was not alone. "Grace is everywhere," wrote Georges Bernanos in *Diary of a Country Priest*. My idiosyncratic romantic quest, which took me to unexpected places, revealed that he was right.

Romance is everywhere, alive even in this technological time of low trust and high cynicism. There is something eternal in our desire for connection and exaltation, for a sense of wonder and our compulsion to give it expression. Romance is the salvation that E. M. Forster's Margaret saw "latent in the souls of everyman," even in the soul of *Howards End's* obtuse Mr. Wilcox, who "simply did not notice things." She held steadfast to her belief that a "rainbow bridge" could be built to "span their lives with beauty." All that was required was to connect. "Only connect! That was the whole of her sermon. Only connect the prose and the passion, and both will be exalted, and human love will be seen at its height. Live in fragments no longer."

Romance endures. It survives ages of reason, space, and technology. Romance survives in spite of our defenses against its power and our natural preference for answers over mystery. Romance survives because it is in our nature to enter singing. The romantic lives the song and exits on its wings.

DANCING
IN THE DARK

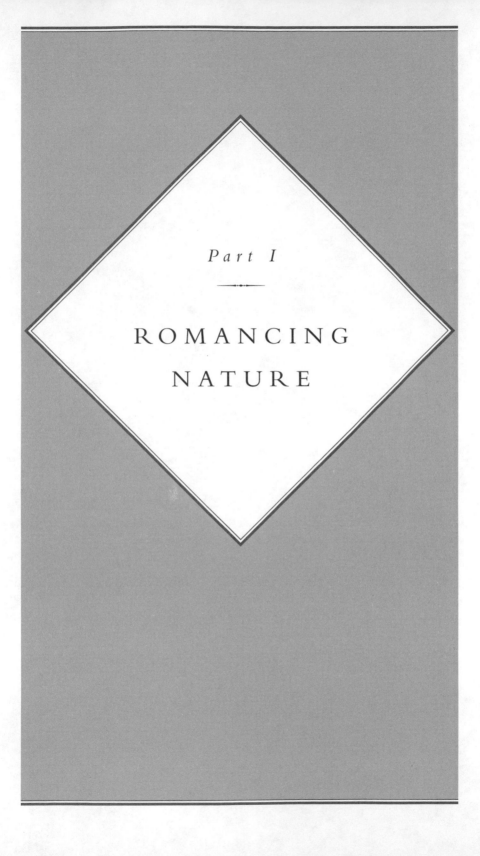

Part I

ROMANCING NATURE

1

BIRDERS

Central Park

Wordsworth took to the lakes, Keats to Rome, Shelley to Lake Como, Byron to Venice, and Thoreau to the woods. My first stop in the romantic quest was Central Park.

"*Puleese*," says my twenty-seven-year-old daughter, Rebecca, giving the word syllables and disdain it was never meant to have.

I've made the mistake of telling her ("rhapsodizing," she says) about birds. I'm uncertain whether it is the subject or the dreamy look on my face that elicits her response.

"For the book," I quickly add. "I'm studying them for the book."

She suggests an espresso at Sant Ambroeus rather than this proffered walk in Central Park. With her mother. With her mother who's taken to sporting binoculars and sturdy brogues (the better for brambles).

She looks up from her book long enough to mutter that she first saw signs of my becoming "a freak" when I immersed myself in Henry David Thoreau and determined to test his theory that "It takes a man of genius to travel in his own country, in his native village; to make any progress between his door and his gate. But such a traveler will make the distances which Hanno and Marco Polo and Cook and Ledyard went over ridiculous." That, she informs me, is truly ridiculous.

I admit that at first it seemed extreme. After all, given the choice, I'd rather go Cook's distance. To Tahiti, for instance. Getting an assignment that would pay my way there, now that would take genius. And, with all due respect, traveling "widely in Concord" did not have the romantic appeal as, say, traveling widely on the *Concorde*. But those weren't options and Central Park was, since that's where I walked my dog, Gabriel, a large, jubilant, black standard poodle possessing particular enthusiasm for such outings. So that was the first stop on the quest, where I went, waited, and watched for romance.

I began to notice a group of regulars who showed up with binoculars. That is, except in spring, when they showed up with telescopes and appeared to focus them on Woody Allen's Fifth Avenue apartment. Another dog walker, who had also taken note of this activity and found the group entirely odd, whispered to me, lest Woody hear from his duplex penthouse fifteen stories above, half a block of oaks, London Planes, and one model-boat pond away, "I'll bet you anything they're watching Woody. I mean, look at that. Those telescopes are facing his bedroom on the top floor of the penthouse." She nodded discreetly in the general direction. "That's Woody's bedroom." Pause. "You know, Woody and Soon-Yi." Be still my heart.

By early winter, when these same people were cheerfully and consistently appearing in the park after sunset when the cautious would have deemed it unwise, I popped the question. After all, Manhattan is a city of citizens who believe that satisfying curiosity is an inalienable right.

"May I ask what you're looking at?"

Manhattan is also a city in which responses vary. Sometimes it's silence and a turned back. At others, a simple "Oh, nothing," and you're left feeling as nosy as you are. And on certain occasions the response turns out to be the beginning of high romance.

"The long-eared owl." One of the six turned and smiled at me. "He just flew out of his tree." The rest joined in eager descriptions of the flight.

"First he stretched as though waking from a long sleep."

And then, "He hopped to a lower branch."

"And then," another said, laughing with pleasure, "then he swooped low, right here across the grass in front of us." By the time I had joined them the bird had gained distance and altitude and was lost to the night.

They explained that they had been gathering at this spot in front of a twenty-five-foot blue spruce tree every evening for a month since the owl was first sighted. There is something about an owl, they said. The myths and fairy tales. Its appealing combination of furry-pet appearance and mysterious, unknowable, nocturnal ways. Its eyes—wise old owl—hat appear to take everything in without being taken in. Its persistent remove. Even its call is infrequent. Not for the owl the profligate chatter of finches, the crude cawing of crows, the devil-may-care loud-mouth quality of flickers. The birders were attracted to the owl precisely because of its "otherness." Humans rarely keep their own counsel, venture fearlessly into the night, or restrain the instinct to put on a show, to be noticed and heard.

People choose partners for less valid reasons, reaching out to bond with another who will be what they long to be.

I got up the nerve to ask them what they watched when they appeared to be watching Woody. "And in the spring. With the telescopes?"

"Red-tailed hawks in a nest on a Fifth Avenue apartment building."

It gave me pause. Maybe I'd been wrong about bird-watchers. I'd accused Rebecca of being small-minded in her notion that the majority of the twenty-five million bird-watchers in America were bony-kneed, retired Yalies scrambling through the under-brush with zinc oxide on their noses. In truth, I'd never sought out their company, invited one home for dinner, to a birthday party. Though I find it all a marvel now, my friends and I were unanimous in our childhood opinion that the little girl who regularly went bird-watching with her older brother was "queer." Why wasn't she doing normal stuff, like playing marbles and reading movie magazines? I'll bet you anything that Teddy Roosevelt and H. D. Hudson weren't the most popular kids. Stuffing dead birds instead of playing baseball? Are you kidding?

So how to explain it all to Rebecca, who within the month

of that first meeting with the owl watchers was accusing me of
going bird crazy? "Mom, you look deranged."

I was puzzled. "What do you mean?"

"Look at you. Like some kind of voyeur, like some kind of
pervert." I looked down at myself. Same old jeans, same old dog
at my side. Looked like the same old me to me.

"Do you go *everywhere* with binoculars around your neck?"

"Not when I'm dancing Giselle with the New York City
Ballet."

"Mom, I *mean* it. You're going over the edge."

I found myself growing a bit defensive. Unwise tactic with
adult children. Did I actually stammer, "Well, not everywhere." I
mentally began to assemble a list that would make me appear more
stable, more Ordinary Upper East Side and thus perhaps less threat-
ening to one who counts on a certain degree of parental sanity and
decorum. "Not out to dinner. Not to the library . . . well, unless I've
just come from the park and forget I have them on."

"That's exactly what I mean. You forget you have them on."

"O.K., so I won't come to your office with them around my
neck. O.K.? I won't meet you downtown for lunch and have them
around my neck. O.K.? If I run into any of your friends, I'll say
I've just been to the opera and forgot to take off my glasses. O.K.?"

"Whatever."

WhatÆvver. So many syllables. So many inflections and
innuendoes.

Maybe I do wear them just about everywhere. When do the
tables turn and our children obtain the power to make us doubt
ourselves? When do we decide that the better part of family peace
is achieved by living a secret life just as they did in adolescence?
When did she become the Classicist and I the Romanticist?

I was slow to admit that I had enthusiastically attached myself
to this group she called "weird." That I was honored they let me tag
along. That they had become somehow dear to me. That I had
taken to standing with them in dark sleet in case an owl showed up.

How to tell her that there was romance here? That, given a
choice between freezing while looking nervously over my

shoulder in a darkening Central Park and going with her to the Bra Smyth for a new lace Italian thong, I'd choose the former. "Is this another menopause thing?" she'd taken to asking whenever my perceived eccentricities made her nervous. How could I tell her, "Actually, no, it's a romance thing."

She was making *me* nervous. In her presence I felt as awkward as a lovesick girl talking about a suitor she knows the listener finds unsuitable. "What do you see in *him*?" Nonetheless, I kept talking, compelled to continue until she understood my ardor. But how to say, "I've fallen for an owl."

And so I didn't tell the truth for a while. Like other parents of my generation, I get confused sometimes about which of us is the grown-up around here. Intimidated, I hid behind those I knew, she, a former college art-history major, respected. Like Cézanne. When she rolled her eyes as I responded to her question "Where are you going?" I told her as I headed out the door for the park, "You know, Cézanne's son, Paul, could never understand why his father kept returning to Mont Sainte-Victoire, to paint it over and over again." And for good measure added, "And aren't we glad he did?" Noting a touch of grandiosity, I explained, "So Cézanne told his son that, by returning to the same place and simply changing his angle of vision, he was seeing new things all the time and eventually becoming 'clear-sighted before nature.' And isn't that the whole point of life? Clear sight?"

"Whatever," she repeated, picking up her Proust.

Gabriel and I were dismissed.

What I was learning was that clear sight is the whole point of bird-watching in particular and romance in general, and maybe I couldn't have known that before fifty. Certainly I didn't have a clue at Rebecca's age. I had not guessed that clear sight eventually makes sense of the heart's intuitions. Cézanne's tool was a brush, the birders' binoculars. Common to both is the persistent and patient faith that nature holds secrets worth waiting for. It's hard to wait in your restless twenties and thirties, when the future seems a fickle thing and the present intones, "Thank you for holding. Please wait for the first available operator."

During the next two years, all of this was slowly revealed as I became used to traipsing after people who seemed to speak in tongues.

"Hear that, 'Tsee-tsee-tsee-tsee-titi-wee'? Yellow warbler."

"Ahh! Listen! 'Zoo zee zoozoo zee.' Green warbler."

"Yellow rumps in phragmites!"

The bird-watchers' journeys between their doors and gates—that is, their apartments and the wooded trails of Central Park, did not fulfill Thoreau's lofty premise that Marco Polo's voyage would, by comparison, appear ridiculous. But theirs began to appear noble to me as I watched them bring to familiar terrain the same bold and optimistic gaze that explorers bring to the horizon.

I found the group romantic precisely because they were engaged in a Wordsworthian quest *not* in an expansive pastoral setting but within the boundaries of the power, greed, grime, and glory of Manhattan. Here was wilderness enough for their imaginations. And here, in this temporary haven within a major metropolis, not a hermit's permanent retreat, they sought and occasionally satisfied that ageless desire and Greek ideal to be at home in nature.

No matter that the idyll could be interrupted at any moment by the bearded man with three garbage bags on his back lurching past and yelling, "You bird-watchers! You should be watching Jesus!" Or by the less benign park habitué: "You got the time? How about money?"

The idyll, that fleeting romantic perception of harmony and interconnection, is heightened by its very precariousness. Poussin's painting of Virgil's greeny Arcadia is bordered by the distractions and seductive corruptions of Rome and the marshes of ominous wilderness. Annie Dillard's Tinker Creek was within a twenty-minute stroll of suburbia, and Thoreau's Walden was walking distance from his mom.

These are not sentimentalists, these birders, painters, and scribes, who prize truth over easy tears, clarity over rose tint. Rather than take satisfaction in a superficial semblance of "brotherhood," they seek connection between unlike things. Proust believed that this was the essence of the writer's task. For the romantic, it is the essence of being fully alive.

2

OWL

December

Most of them are here. Shy Merrill Higgins, whose duties as pay-roll clerk at Riker's Island prison limit his Central Park visits to vacations and weekends. Marie Winn, author of Red Tails in Love, a winning account of the secret lives of Central Park's birds, beasts, beetles, and butterflies. Shuffling, silent Margaret O'Brien, whose small face is barely visible behind thick, smudged glasses that cling to the last remnants of failing sight. Long, elegant Charles Kennedy, who shows up daily, bicycling some hundred blocks from his SoHo loft to keep track of the park's bird life. A surprise legacy from an aunt makes his life as voyeur possible. Green-eyed Noreen O'Rourke, who moves with the deliberate, alert grace of a heron. And there is a newcomer who seems lonely but for the company of birds and those who watch. A disparate group bound by common passion.

They pull scarves tighter around their necks and wait for another turn at Merrill's telescope, set in front of the blue spruce. Fifth Avenue is at their backs and the ornate spires of Central Park West loom above the hill and trees before them.

"Look at his ears! Oh, my God, he's so cute!"

"Look at his gorgeous breast feathers!"

"You should see how beautiful he is when he flies out of here at six."

Two hours to go and it's not likely that many of us will be here for what the regulars refer to as "the flyaway." It's twenty-two degrees; the cold northeast wind is damp and scented with snow. We stamp our feet and blow into our hands, attempting to warm them with inadequate breath.

They tell me that last year they kept this same vigil dusk after dusk for three weeks and then were left standing at the altar. The owl simply disappeared. They were surprised by and then mocked themselves for their resulting sense of loss. "It was only natural," Charles explains. "It's a primary dream we all have, that we can connect with something so exquisite." They had wanted the owl to stay, and that desire was drawn from a deep well of human yearning. From the earliest recorded artists, through the Celts, Pythagoreans, Orphics, Romantic poets, and transcendentalist philosophers to these spurned birders, we as a species have intuited and longed for a kinship between man and beast, a reciprocity with nature.

Stubbornly, and at times against our better judgment, we cling to the dream. Even unto death, writes Howard Nemerov in his poem "Elegy for a Nature Poet," for a man who died of exposure, not having the sense to come in out of the rain or romantic reverie. "Rude Nature, whom he loved to idealize / And would have wed, pretends she never heard / His voice at all."

The birders refused such rude indifference, and with the obsession of stalkers spent ten days peering into the empty tree, circling its base, staring into other openings, other branches, until their hands grew cold and darkness blurred their vision. They searched the wooded area around the Azalea Pond, checked every conifer in the Ramble, and wandered up to the Harlem Meer. They spent days in relentless pursuit. But nothing.

After I've been brought up to date on this sad history, I ask if the bird might have flown to Canada. Had it been disturbed by constant staring and commentary?

Maria Ramirez, a lovely park maintenance worker and over-seer of the grounds, who sometimes joins the group, assures me that this had not been the case. She'd spent last winter working in the area of the owl's accustomed spruce, "And he seemed unfazed by the commotion of electric clippers, trimmers, mowers."

It seems to me astonishing that the owl had ever been sighted in the first place. "Look at the ground below evergreens," the bird books advise, "and keep a sharp eye for pellets." Pellets are, to put it succinctly, owl throw-up, the undigested bones, fur, or feathers of prey regurgitated after a hearty meal. Just another example of nature tending to the details. Pellets were out of view beneath this particular tree, which had been fenced off from pedestrian traffic in order to protect newly seeded lawn. Even so, the owl was discovered deep within dense spruce boughs, snug up against a trunk the same color as its feathers.

When the news spread, the group formed, wooing ensued, and then the bird was gone.

"Left without so much as a good-bye," commented one of the birders.

Careless lover. Rude nature. I find their sense of betrayal perfectly normal. After all, we expect to be loved in return. We dream that nature will answer our call as the woods echoed Virgil's shepherd's flute. The birders had made the leap that scientists warn against: They had imagined they and the bird had connected. They figured that they had kept their part of an elusive bargain. Acting on the notion that nature is divine, that it requires a human response, they responded. Well, they wondered, so where's nature's response? Could their beloved be indifferent? Unmoved? Why, it was straight out of a courtly love poem.

"But wait until you hear this . . ." they tell me. This year, the owl returned as silently as it had left. The curtain rose on the second act and the set hadn't even been changed. Same tree. Same branch. Same bird. Merrill was the first to spot him, and as word got out, the group reunited with all the renewed innocence, enthusiasm, and expectancy of jilted lovers offered a second chance. How easily they are seduced and persuaded to resume the courtship.

This December, I regularly join them for the "flyaway" as darkness gathers and the owl comes forth to ride it. At first we hear a large rustling against branches, surprising for a bird so small. Not surprising when someone gasps, "There it goes!" and this cuddly FAO Schwarz creature spreads its formidable wings and takes off, dips to skim the ground, then rises over distant treetops and heads for prey that will fall victim tonight to unsuspected power. The flight is stealthy and silent, the result of nature's grand design—wing feathers with hairlike edges that provide noiseless passage through the air and surprise attack on the ground.

There is a sense of great good fortune among those who catch this glimpse of glory. The flyaway lasts no more than four seconds, as the owl forfeits its hiding place and claims another, but it's enough. The birders are buoyant. They are hungry for more.

"Where do you think it goes?" I try to sound professional. "It" rather than "he." Then I wonder, professional what?

"Up into the Ramble."

"How do you know?"

"Several of us formed a chain. From this tree up the hill to the next tree that he regularly flies to and then on up the path."

The bower-burdened Ramble is deep in shadow even on bright summer days. Like Fontainebleau Forest's 42,000 acres of former royal hunting grounds surrounding Fontainebleau palace in France, it appears wilder than it is and, like its French cousin, is a direct response to Voltaire's contention that the classic restriction of Le Nôtre's revered symmetry starves the romantic imagination, which demands, "*Les vastes forêts . . . la nature libre et hardie . . . Irrégulière dans ses traits.*"

When Calvert Vaux and Frederick Law Olmsted, leader of the nineteenth-century parks movement, designed Central Park in 1857, they sought to tame nature without visual constrictions, to maintain Voltaire's ideal of vastness and irregularity. The result was 843 acres of Virgilian *res rustica* and nineteenth-century European romantic ideal adapted to an American romance with wide-open spaces. Home on the range meets Arcadia.

The creation of this "natural" effect required 20,000 laborers, 10 million one-horse cartloads of topsoil, 4 to 5 million trees and shrubs, and time—fifteen years for the basic park and forty for the greensward effect to grow into itself. Such is the nature of romance. Sometimes it requires a lot of earth moving to create an atmosphere in which we can learn what we knew in the first place.

The Ramble is a favorite resting place for migrating birds. Following Fontainbleau's picaresque history it is also a favorite hangout for the twentieth-century, urban equivalent of highwaymen. I prefer to go there in the company of large men and dogs, and even then my nerves are on edge. What's behind that tree? That rock? What's that sound? You proceed at your own risk. Or with birds on the brain.

Merrill, generally self-effacing and slow to speak, now stands next to his telescope with the expansive expression and proud posture of a new father. He is surprised by his sighting. "I don't know why I found it and the regular, weekday birders didn't," he says, beaming. Easy. He listens and watches. He is a solitary man yearning for this particular connection.

Like all romantics, he keeps showing up, sometimes against all odds. He's the guy who stares at Keats's lovers on the Grecian urn and senses the romance in the eternal space between them. "Bold lover, never, never canst thou kiss, / Though winning near the goal."

The romance is in the quest. That a hand may never close on the object of desire or that facts learned do not necessarily reveal answers sought doesn't dissuade. The romantic, undeterred by mystery, enters it with enthusiasm and reverence as though entering a cathedral.

We conscientious tourists go with our guidebooks, take a seat in a pew, huddle against the cold, and read of the history and mechanics of columns, vaults, volutes, and stained glass. But the romantic enters empty-handed, sits and waits for the cathedral to reveal itself. He has faith that it will.

For him, mysteries begin to unfold through surrender, although surrender is among the most frightening of human endeavors. Imagine the courage required of Keats, for instance, to surrender to experience, burdened by pain and the fear of imminent death. He believed that vulnerability was the only means of freeing the imagination, which in turn had the power to transcend suffering and to reveal truths beyond the limiting facts of physical disability and disease. And he was right. We cannot read his odes without sharing glimpses of the realms of gold into which his imagination's journeys released him.

His was a generosity endemic to romantics; the beauty is to be shared. "You come, too," wrote Robert Frost. Not a tender young Englishman, but a grouchy old New Englander, just like me. Just like a lot of us. But Frost's art, like Keats's, was a means of sharing his romantic soul that reached beyond pain and fear to urge us, as the birders do, Look up! Take note! Don't miss it! Don't blink!

Since it is more common for birders to share beauty in stories told rather than poetry written, they prefer to travel in groups. They want an immediately available ear to heed the plea to listen, an eager eye to respond to "Hey, will you take a look at that!"

Lucky for a beginner like me that romantics like Merrill are eager to include the rest of us. Generous with his knowledge, enthusiasm, and equipment, he offers a look through his telescope to people who walk by with their dogs, to nannies with sticky-fingered kids in tow, to adolescents whose world view is determinedly turned inward, to briefcase toters who could care less.

"There's a long-eared owl in this tree. Would you like to look?" His own guilelessness is rarely met by theirs. "Ummm, no thanks," says a teenaged girl, who turns to her companion and rolls her eyes. They giggle and hasten down the path.

O.K., Rebecca's right, we're weird. A bunch of red-nosed grown-ups standing in dimming light making large ecstatic exclamations about a bird.

It's like this almost every winter afternoon as we gather to peer into a small opening in the branches near the top of the tree and feel somehow triumphant that the owl is precisely where "we left him." His (some expert determined that it was male) eyes are closed, his chest covered with dappled brown and beige feathers. His pointed ears give him the air of a dandy, as though he'd styled them himself. Just a block to the north, traffic races across the Seventy-ninth Street transverse through the park. Another block east buses belch and groan as they stop to take on more passengers headed down Fifth Avenue. Taxi horns honk and brakes shriek. Children squeal as they head home from the playground. The owl sleeps on.

He sleeps in spite of the intrusion of our probing, peering eyes, our words of love and admiration, our desire to press closer, to make him ours. He stirs, preens, and sleeps again. The still point of our delight. His is a peace as complete unto itself as that I've seen in Northern Renaissance nativity paintings, in which sanctified space exists in the midst of rough and tumble mundanity.

"Would you like to look at the owl?" Merrill asks a passerby with business on his mind and a camel-hair coat on his back. The man looks at Merrill, and seems to wonder whether there's a charge for this. He takes our measure: two short, thin women in middle age; one tall, skinny, hollow-cheeked guy who looks like a benevolent hippie; portly, ruddy-faced Merrill; and a white-haired, slightly stooped lady with smudged glasses. Seems safe. "Sure. Why not?" He lowers his briefcase to the ground, pins it between his legs, and leans toward the eyepiece. "Hey! Will you look at that! My, my." He steps back and looks at us as though he suspects a trick, as though we're about to laugh and say, "Ha! Gotcha, buddy! It's fake!" He expects this, but it doesn't happen. "Well, hey, thank you. Thank you very much." His accent is patrician, that of a dying class of New Yorkers who learned anglicized vowels and silent *r*'s in the laps of nannies. He wasn't ready for this. For this change in routine, for the slightest stirring of a sense of wonder as he walked from his Midtown office to his home on the Upper East Side. An owl in his path.

Once I've reached home, I take out the bird books and turn to "Owls." I need knowledge to buffer my emotion. This is nuts, falling in love with a bird. I determine that scholarship is safer and saner. I read what John Bull has to say in *Birds of the New York Area*: "Long-eared owl (*Asio otus*). Range: Holarctic species, the race *Wilsonianus* breeds south to Virginia. Status: Uncommon to locally fairly common winter visitant. Rare and local breeder perhaps overlooked."

There. Some interesting facts to enrich the experience of looking at the bird, to make the entire experience less suspect. Puleeze, as my daughter would say, a crush on a bird? Thoughtfully distanced and armed with the results of my research, though uncertain of what it means to be "uncommon to locally fairly common," I rejoin the birders the following evening. They aren't particularly interested. Although they have read and reread the same books, they do so because they, like poets, are enamored of facts. But none of them says that birding is reading about birds. I watch them more closely to determine just what it is about. It appears to be an act of inspiration in which observer sees, identifies, classifies, and is then moved by an awareness beyond the noted facts.

Paul Gauguin wrote in his journal that Courbet, while painting a landscape, was approached by a woman who wanted to know what he was thinking. "I am not thinking, madame," he responded, "I am moved."

My guess is that the response would be similar should I approach a birder peering through binoculars and pose the same question. His is the eye of an artist, the quest of a European Romantic poet, and the sensibility of a New England transcendentalist, all bound by the shared yearning to sense harmony and oneness with the world, the determination to adhere to a faith that such unity exists and the compulsion to give that yearning form. So how to answer "What are you thinking?"

Lofty thinkers of the two nineteenth-century movements Romanticism and Transcendentalism, like the birder, were inspired to approach experience with open minds, sharp eyes, uninhibited imaginations, and available souls. They came to nature in order to discover their own. They heeded the cry of their mentor Goethe, whose Faust, finding himself imprisoned by intellect, sought experience as an escape from institutional learning into vaster knowledge. "You must escape from this confining world!" Go out the door, "wander in the highest hills . . . read the courses of the stars and take from Nature your instruction." Nature, echoed Ralph Waldo Emerson, is "emblematic" and reveals eternal truths not immediately apparent in its surfaces. "Every natural fact is a symbol of some spiritual fact."

If the stated facts about owls are also symbols, then they are emblematic of possibility sensed but just out of sight, insight and discovery just around the bend. It is this element of romance that inspires those who walk forests, fields, and urban parks, their ears and eyes alert to facts and, oh yes, pellets.

This is the anticipatory watchfulness we bring to the first stages of romantic love, when, riveted by facts, we idealize and expand upon them. "Tell me everything about yourself," the lover pleads. Your history: "Tell me about your childhood." "Who were your friends?" "Were you the kid chosen first or last for the team?" "Were you shy?" "Did you like school?" "What were your parents like?" Your heart: "Who was your first love?" "Do you like your work?" "If you could do whatever you wanted, what would it be?" We long to ask the question asked by the new lovers in the movie *The English Patient* as they bathe together after lovemaking. "What do you love?" And naturally, in the end, what we really want to know is "What do you think of me?" Lover, owl, tree, life.

We look as eagerly into each other's hearts as the birders look through pine boughs. Slowly, over time, urged on by our relentless need to know, to connect through that knowledge, we become intimates. Naturally there are the secrets, history held back out of kindness or self-protection. Nevertheless, we gain a sense of one another through stories shared and behavior observed. We are working our way toward a oneness, to fulfilling the lover's dream of merging with the beloved. We have embarked on Plato's romantic quest, the search for the missing half of ourselves.

It is the same with the birders. They watch, they wait, in order to connect. Not just with a bird, but through the bird to the heart of nature. They press closer, sensing that connection might make them whole. Marie Winn, savvy Upper West Sider, translator of Czech and Ancient Greek, purveyor of *les bons mots*, not one given to sentiment or spiritual flippancy, tells me, "When you engage in watching birds, your lives intersect. You become part of a larger mystery." A part of something divine, Emerson claimed and believed that such moments of intersection were revelations of divinity existing within ourselves and throughout the universe.

Every once in a while we are saturated with this divinity. The trick is to be there when it happens. The romantic, inspired but not held back by facts of time and space, is able on occasion to achieve a sense of timelessness. Through the unblinking awareness of an instant, she may catch a glimpse of what seems to be eternity.

It takes a lot of nerve for those of us to whom my grandmother referred as "smarty pants" to take off those pants. And that's exactly how vulnerable I feel when I dare, like Courbet, to be "moved" as well as to think, to learn from institutions and books and then, like Goethe, to walk away.

Keats referred to this derring-do, the romantic's ability to immerse himself "in uncertainties, mysteries, doubts, without any irritable reaching after fact and reason . . ." as "negative capability." He urged us to use reason as a sword rather than a shield, a tool to pierce rather than protect us from life's passions.

"Why is the owl here?" an approaching stranger asks. "I don't know," a woman responds, and lowering her binoculars smiles. "Maybe word's gotten out that we're good to birds around here."

ENTIRELY POSSIBLE

Years ago my husband, Bob, while viewing an exhibition of heraldic shields, was particularly impressed by one emblazoned with the words "Why Not?" It's become his life's motto. A good piece of armor to carry into battle against the legions of Not Likelys, Impossibles, and Well, I've Never Seen It Dones. To *know* is less important to the romantic than to entertain possibility. To know is to contain something neatly within boundaries, while to wonder is boundless. The romantic is Schubert's Wanderer, the transatlantic single-hander navigating by wave and star, the nomadic Laplander crossing frozen borders without visa or passport or a backward glance.

Or the two elderly ladies, neither more than five feet tall, who shyly approach the birders in front of the spruce. One of them wears a pink beret and blue wool coat, the other wears rose. Both sport sensible walking shoes shined to a high polish and firmly tied with symmetrical bows. "What do you see?" asks one. "An owl," answers a young man who's just arrived after hearing about the bird from someone in his office. "I was at the water cooler and a guy was talking about this bird, and I went and got my coat and came up here." He smiles at the thought of such recklessness, of leaving unfinished business on his desk and no excuse in his wake. "Here, have a look." He lowers his binoculars, lifts their strap over his tousled brown hair and hands them to the lady in the pink beret. As she raises them to her eyes, he quietly describes exactly where to look and then stands back, eagerly anticipating her response. She doesn't disappoint. "Oh, isn't he fine! My, how lovely." She sucks in her breath. "Oh, my. How perfectly marvelous. Gladys, you must have a look." She hands the binoculars to her companion and turns to smile at each of us. "What a handsome fellow he is."

I find myself nodding in eager agreement. I'm suddenly part of a motley fan club happy to expand and welcome new enthusiasts. I feel a rush of that old camaraderie experienced in our fifth-grade Annette Funicello fan club.

"Don't you love it when she . . ."

"She's growing breasts!"

"She has a *great* figure."

"I wish I had hair like hers."

"You do! You sort of look like her . . ."

"Nah . . ."

"No, really . . ."

Friends for life.

I can see how my daughter, so long out of fifth grade and so far from fifty might find this peculiar. I think of Linda Parquette whose response to our third-grade nature walks was a dismissive "It's just walking through a bunch of cow plops." We never could see what our sixty-year-old teacher was seeing. We had lost that particular vision and hadn't regained it yet.

I hold out my binoculars to a woman who pauses with a well-coiffed bichon frise. She takes the glasses but has trouble focusing, gives up and hands them back. "As if I haven't seen owls before," says she. "I know, isn't it exciting?" I, caught up in the contagious enthusiasm of the group, am oblivious of her sarcasm, continue, "I'd always wanted to see an owl." She looks at me for about four seconds, the time it takes to register whether the person who speaks is dealing with a full deck, sighs and says, "I was being sarcastic."

"You're *certainly not* one of us," I think to myself. How quickly we become tribal. Then I attempt to recapture the expansive generosity of the romance she has just interrupted. I'm relentless. I give her one more chance.

"You've seen others?"

"The day of the blizzard last year I saw three."

Show-off. Refraining from responding with the playground challenge "Oh, yeah? Wanna bet?" I ask where and how. "I'm trying something new," she tells me. "I count how many sounds I can hear when I walk in the park. So I heard the hooting and looked up. There they were." Another tough New Yorker seduced by birds. She marches off, ears opening like morning glories.

Three twelve-year-old boys, coatless and careless of the cold, shuffle past, walking on the backs of their loafers. They wear the required navy blue blazer of a boys' private school a few blocks south. "What do you see?" one asks. "A long-eared owl," Merrill answers. "Want to look?" Without answering the kid drops his backpack to the ground and steps up to the scope. "Man! Oh, wow!" His friends shove against him, using elbows, hips, and shoulders to move him out of the way. "C'mon, let us look." Stepping away, he asks one question about the bird. "Who owns it?"

Indeed.

We bring who we are to the wild. To wildness. We roll our eyes at the remark, but it's not an invalid question. We have all staked our claims.

Moments later, I overhear Marie murmur to Charles, "There's trouble in Paradise." Something about next year's hawk count. Hawk count? I glance around to assure myself that Rebecca's nowhere within hearing distance. "They want you to get your chair out of there." Chair? I don't know what they're talking about, and I don't want to. In this respect, I am sentimental rather than romantic. I'm like the new bride who thinks divorce can't be far away when the honeymoon is interrupted by the first fight and tears. I don't want the trouble, only the Paradise. A true romantic knows that Paradise exists only momentarily in the midst of a heap of trouble and that one does not negate the other. At first, as a newcomer to this group, I don't want the whole truth, which is that as soon as two or three are gathered together noble ideals are challenged by jealousy and fear. Centuries of religious wars attest to that.

I want everyone in the group to be as unself-conscious as the object we have come to adore. I try to ignore another conversation behind me. Two men, not regulars, have appeared and raised their binoculars. "So, Peter," says one to the other, not taking his eye off the owl. "What'd you buy today?"

"Actually, I bought more mutual funds," says the acquaintance, lowering his own binoculars and heading off into the night.

"Remove my chair? Are you kidding?" Charles asks Marie.

"He wants you to get it off the terrace where we stand to count the hawks."

"He's . . ." Charles lowers his voice.

"It's political."

I have not been unaware that such passions are at work, I have simply struggled to hold them at bay. Gentle Noreen had recently told me that last spring she was reprimanded by a member of the group because she revealed the location of a mallard's nest to her two wide-eyed and grateful young nephews. "That was a secret!" she was scolded.

I know that there are those who become as territorial as the birds themselves. They squabble over who first spied which species and assert, "That doesn't sound right, she couldn't have seen that thrush, she's not a regular." On the other hand, meticulous, silent Tom Fiore, who tracks birds with the grace of an Indian scout, writes voluminous pages in the "Nature Book," a loose-leaf binder filled with park visitors' observations and left in the park's lakeside boat house for all to read. Tom sees the most birds, yet I hardly ever see him. It's as though he travels in camouflage. But he's been here. Page after page bear his firm-handed script detailing birds' names, markings, and gender.

Similarly, Charles, in spite of the brief upset over a chair, has his complete attention on birds. Modest and quiet, he engenders love without saying or doing much. It's that way with many of the birders. They tell you where the birds are to be found. They show you pictures. They describe their calls. Charles says that the song of a wood thrush breaks his heart. Thoreau must have felt the same, describing it as a song of "immortal beauty" which "deepens the significance of all things."

"It sounds like an oboe," says Charles, who also loves Antonin Dvorak's *New World Symphony* "because he integrated the song of

a redstart into the music." He grows quiet. His reverie reminds me
of Thea's in Willa Cather's, *The Song of the Lark* when she heard
that same symphony for the first time. "[S]he knew what she
wanted was exactly that. Here were the sand hills, the grasshoppers
and locusts, all the things that wakened and chirped in the early
morning. . . . There was home in it, too; first memories, first mornings long ago; the amazement of a new soul in a new world; a soul
new and yet old, that had dreamed . . . something glorious, in the
dark before it was born." Like Thea or Wordsworth, I think
Charles and his birding buddies are all set on homecoming, a journey less about spotting birds than returning to a place familiar
long ago, to an ancient wisdom. Call it wonder.

"How?" I ask Charles, interrupting his dream. "What instruments did Dvorak use?"

"You think I know anything about music?" He raises his
binoculars because he's seen movement among the branches
and calls out, "There he is."

We look up like so many synchronized Rockettes and
watch as the owl hops to a lower branch and then soars forth,
black against black, bird and night. Such sights inspired myths.
Maybe this is what silences the birders. They know their place.

Another of last season's owl admirers quickens her approach
as she spies the telescope aimed at the tree. "Is he back?" She
asks eagerly. Merrill smiles and nods. "Oh, my," she sighs. "That
changes everything."

And so it does. Emerson knew this when he wrote, "The
lover of nature is he whose inward and outward senses are still
truly adjusted to each other." Noting Constable's paintings and
Wordsworth's poetry, he observed that this nature lover "has
retained the spirit of infancy even into the era of manhood."

The remnants of that spirit of infancy are witnessed in children's drawings. For them it is perfectly natural to put a smiling
face on the sun or in a tree trunk, human emotions manifest in
nature because children see no separation between the two. They
are not just making pretty pictures, that will end up on refrigerator doors, but are revealing a truth we knew before reason
kicked imagination's shins and we hobbled away feeling foolish.

Oh no, not foolish at all, the Romanticists reassured us. The foolishness lies in the defenses of adulthood that protect us from vulnerability and separate us from an original oneness with the universe. This is no dream, this intimation of harmony, this sensed sublimity, they say; this is a reality we have known and forgotten. "Our birth is but a sleep and a forgetting," Wordsworth claimed in his "Intimations of Immortality."

> The Soul that rises with us, our life's Star,
> Hath had elsewhere its setting,
> And cometh from afar:
> Not in entire forgetfulness. . . .
> Heaven lies about us in our infancy!
> Shades of the prison-house begin to close
> Upon the growing Boy,
> But He beholds the light, and whence it flows,
> He sees it in his joy. . . .
> At length the Man perceives it die away,
> And fade into the light of common day.

A mist of that old awareness falls around us tonight. Something the owl left behind. Our excitement over the sighting results in expansiveness and loosens our tongues, allowing an uninhibited rush of chatter about love and beauty. The newcomer confides that he has just broken up with his girlfriend and wants someone to love in the new year. "Can you find me somebody?" Noreen happily describes how she alone saw the owl fly away last night. It was, she claims, her reward for having sat an hour on a hard, cold rock in the direction of the usual flight pattern.

Charles and Marie mount their bikes to rush off to the Shakespeare gardens in the hope of watching a saw-whet owl fly from his hemlock perch. "You're as beautiful as any owl," Charles tells a woman in the group. "But I've got to be off." Others make plans to meet tomorrow, same time, same place.

I notice a small feather on the ground beneath the tree and stretch my hand under the fence to collect it. Without thinking, I open my jacket and slip the fragile bit of fluff under my sweater and into my bra for safekeeping. I then forget about it until later that night when, as I undress for a bath, a dappled feather floats to my feet and rests between my toes. I look down, momentarily mystified. My husband, standing at the sink, notes the slow descent and my resulting blush. "Leda and the swan," he mutters, picking up his toothbrush.

I sputter as guiltily as a cheating wife. How to explain the owl feather? Why the need to explain? It's true that I've been covering my tracks, not mentioning where I've been each night, fearing that he might find me slightly mad at worst, obsessed at best. Perhaps the fear is my own that I may be slightly mad, that my daughter's accusation is correct, that I have gone bird crazy.

You hear of women like this, who give it all up for romance. Wasn't there something about the Duchess of York's mother leaving her young children and running off with an Argentine polo player? Then there's the character in Patrick McGrath's novel *Asylum* who deserts her family in favor of a mad murderer. And, of course, there's Anna Karenina, whose fate serves as a deterrent to women in pursuit of passion.

No, I'm not leaving home. But how odd that romance is so deeply personal, whatever its object, that although we are practically compelled to give it form in poetry, song, and painting, when speaking of it to one who isn't a partner to the experience we squirm, we blush, stammer, and surrender to being tongue-tied.

Romance *is* a sort of madness, I realize as I bend down to pick up the feather and drop it into my jewelry box. An essential madness if we are to be fully alive, but a bit unnerving all the same. One finds it in the most unlikely places.

4

AT THE PARK'S EDGE

Earlier that evening, before returning home with feather safely tucked against flesh, I leave the birders and step out onto Fifth Avenue and Seventy-ninth Street. Here I see what makes New York one of the most romantic cities on earth. There is a powerful seduction in its stubborn denial of limitations, its unspoken promise: You dream it, you can have it. The gray, dark days and early nights of December are upon us, but lights will burn long and bright to defy them. Street lamps, parlor lights, and the swerving headlights of cars and buses. Glass-skinned office buildings brighten the sky, that place once imagined by builders of Gothic cathedrals to be the gateway to heaven.

Walking through this part of the city is like walking through Success Canyon. The apartments that look out on Fifth and the park are inhabited by those whose accomplishments are extraordinary, either in terms of new heights of greed or creative genius. Those of us on the streets below can actually believe that such splendor is within our reach while we simultaneously sense our keen alienation from all that.

Is there anyone alive who doesn't feel like an outsider? For the romantic, such alienation is a catalyst for the romantic quest. Rather than spurning the object of fantasy and desire in order to relieve the pain of unrequited longing, rather than limiting his imagination within the confines of jealousy, the romantic fixes his gaze upon the object and for an imaginative moment knows and becomes it. He perceives a glimmer of a romantic truth that we are one. Through this act of perception eye (or "I") and object merge.

Naturally such an experience can travel into the realm of psychosis, where boundaries between self and other become confused, but the romantic rarely suffers such confusion. Aware of his own integrity, he is free to entertain the power of imagination. One as clear-sighted as Einstein proclaimed that our perception of ourselves as separate individuals is nothing but "optical delusion."

This city encourages that insight common to physicists and romantics that barriers are illusory and anything is possible. Pilgrims from all parts of the world arrive here for their share, responding to the compelling vision F. Scott Fitzgerald described in *Crack-Up*. "New York had all the iridescence of the beginning of the world."

But why, we might ask, why risk the beginning of the world, why not stay home where it's safe? Why enter so boldly against all odds? It's an all or nothing town, and many stay long after it becomes apparent that theirs is to be the latter fate.

In spite of the fact that Manhattan seems to run on cold and calculated pragmatism, on the ability to say No as though you mean it, and Yes with a seductiveness that cannot be refused, the romance of possibility is the energy that drives the place.

On Madison Avenue in the upper Seventies, the Mark and Carlyle hotels compete for the brightest and most elegant Christmas decorations. I stop in at the Mark bar, drawn by the false intimacy and secret-laden gloom of its small room, reminiscent of wood-paneled, dust-scented libraries. I am an outsider here, which is precisely why I come.

Vodka martini, straight up, two olives. Romantic because it takes me out of my time and place. It is, after all, my parents' drink. Something remembered vaguely in the half-light of childhood; what the glamorous grown-ups drank as we sat on the floor rubbing up against their silk-stockinged, gray-flanneled legs, eavesdropping on conversations that brought us images from another world.

When the waiter sets the long-stemmed, fragile crystal on the table and the olives capture and focus the transparency around them, I feel as though I'm playing dress-up. Stolen time between owl watching and dinner preparations. No one knows where I am. No one here knows me. I am alone, a bit lonely. I watch, I imagine. Very romantic.

Across from me, a middle-aged couple sit on a green velvet couch set into a darker green wall. Above them hang engravings of the drawing room at Buckingham House, the anteroom at Carlton House. Ah, yes, here's to dear old Britain, drink 'er down, drink 'er down.

The husband in the gray pinstripes looks down into his snifter of single-malt scotch, straight, no ice. She leans slightly toward him, pleading. A snippet of conversation: "What do you want from me . . . ?" He is silent out of habit, not choice, trained early to swallow words that rise from the heart and gather in the throat.

She'd driven in from New Canaan to meet him here. They've booked a room upstairs and a table down the street at Daniel. Although it was not spelled out, this is to be their evening to reach some sort of understanding, to rekindle sexual ardor that had cooled before either took notice of its waning. The kids are in college, he's made partner, and now that the time is theirs it weighs heavily. She takes a lace-edged handkerchief from her alligator bag and dabs at her eyes. A slight smudge of mascara blackens the linen. He stiffens and glances about the small room. Has anyone seen? There are only eight of us here, and I'm the sole spy.

She thinks there is hope in this city where anonymity releases inhibitions. No one knows them or cares should their arguments or lovemaking be overheard tonight. Like Nick Carraway crossing the Queensboro Bridge in his approach to Manhattan, she had sensed increasing freedom with each mile of distance put between herself and home. "Anything can happen now that we've slid over this bridge . . . anything at all."

At a table in the center of the room, two overweight men in suits custom made for a slimming effect chat with a pale young model who sits across from them, a black portfolio at her feet.

They tell her that with her grace and lovely features, and the hair, oh yes, they agree, the lovely hair, the future is hers. They drink shimmering red Cosmopolitans. Hers goes untouched. It is clear that when she gets up to say goodnight, thanking them for the drink, after they have handed her their cards and returned to their seats, their dreams will diverge. Hers will be of fashion shoots, while theirs will be of the imagined bliss of conquest.

In Manhattan, mundanity, that great enemy of romance, is a source of mockery. Here there are women who know how to tie scarves in knots a seasoned sailor would envy. Their hair rarely turns gray, and the natural added poundage that threatens after fifty finds few resting places. Two such specimens sit poised on the edges of their seats. Their long, thin legs gleam beneath pale stockings, and the pointed toes of their high heels graze evidence of the day's plunder, shopping bags from Armani, Bulgari, and Calvin Klein. Their hair is blond and shoulder length, and their eyes, thanks to plastic surgeon Dr. Dan Baker, are larger now than in their baby pictures. They listen to each other intently, leaning in to share whispered news of trysts, lingerie, and the foolishness of men.

I know that later, when I'm at home standing under the kitchen's fluorescent glare, scraping congealed chicken from dinner dishes, Bobby Short will begin to sing Cole Porter in the Café Carlyle one block south of the Mark. It is another of those Manhattan rooms that encourages romance, with its subtle nudge at nostalgia for a life more likely to have been dreamed than lived. There is just enough light to allow waiters to find their way to tables. When Bobby sings "You're the Top," men and women in the audience, not knowing Porter's raunchy, self-censored version, always lean closer to their partners, hoping that they might be thought of that way. They sip champagne and imagine themselves in another era. They've seen Fred Astaire movies and are delighted to be having a genuine art deco experience. "I love the north, south, east, and the west of you . . ." Bobby will hoarsely croon, and beneath tables hands will slide from knees to thighs.

They've seen the movies, read the books, they know of a

past in which ladies wore velvet that clung to their curves and gentlemen checked their hats at the door and delivered generous tips upon retrieving them. They've read of subtle perfumes that once laced the air, exotic signature scents created in Paris. They can almost believe they are a part of that former time as the music plays and street sounds are muffled.

Naturally, the romance dies by dawn as the characters ride subways and enter the flat light of corporate offices. And yet the possibility glimmers. Perhaps, between phone calls and meetings, one dreams a little of an evening of jazz, where the notes of stoned musicians float above smoke-filled rooms, of slow dancing high above the city in the Rainbow Room, of a shy first embrace on a bench overlooking the East River, of entwined limbs on clean linen, of an evening at home, phones turned off, doors bolted.

As night comes to a city surrounded by water, it's as though we inhabit a separate planet, as though Manhattan drifts away from the rest of the world. We loosen our hold on habit and inhibition and engage in behavior that is more sensual, in some cases more outrageous, and definitely more daringly romantic than when we are grounded by daylight and obligation.

We draw closer to one another out of primal fear of the dark. Lovers embrace, stargazers keep vigil, and birders lie in bed considering the habits of secretive owls. By our very thoughts we are connected to one another and to the creatures of our concerns.

5

A GENESIS LEGACY

When I enter the park in false spring, it's as though there were bodies everywhere. A large London Plane's trunk bears a raw gash, the sort of wound that causes one to avert the eyes. Yellow flesh ripped open above three feet of dark stump is all that remains of a sycamore tree. Shattered branches flung into careless clusters make clearer the meaning of the word "limb." The scene looks like the aftermath of the kind of disaster that elicits news reports, "Limbs were scattered everywhere."

What had begun as gray rain turned to sleet as the temperature dropped. It stings my eyelids and makes pelting sounds against the hardening ground. My dog lowers his head against the assault and marches dutifully on. I'm tempted to tell him, "You're the one who asked for this."

Trees adorned with ice glitter like Diana Ross in vintage performance gown.

But the trees fail to wear their finery lightly and bend and snap beneath the load.

Another dog walker approaches. "You know, it really isn't safe in here," she warns. Her golden retriever is oblivious and wags its tale at the prospect of a stranger's pat. "Safe for us or for the trees?" I ask. "You'd better get out. A few minutes ago a tree fell three feet from where my dog was standing."

She falls silent as we hear a loud retort. Gunfire? This is Manhattan in the nineties; it is entirely possible. An echo that isn't an echo is followed by a groan. In ancient Abyssinia this sound of a falling tree was thought to be God's curse.

Back home, I am surprised by my sense of heaviness. Silly, I think, this sadness over trees lost to ice storms. Nature, after all, is surgical in its sacrifices. Bob, always says so. "Nature is ugly and cruel, not romantic." We argue about it endlessly. When I tell him about the owl's midnight hunt, he replies, "You call that romance? I call that murder in Central Park."

Nonetheless, I am sad. After all, since the beginning of time we have been profoundly connected to trees, the *fons vitae* of the Garden, the *sacro bosco* of the Greeks. And yet we have disciplined ourselves to stay at a safe distance, fearing creation too fragile to hold the heaviness our hearts.

We are children of the Enlightenment, the Industrial Revolution, and secular humanism. We have inherited a hard-earned faith in infinite progress made possible by our obligation spelled out in Genesis to take dominion everywhere. But now I wonder. Now, as a fifty-year-old with skin as thin and heart as wobbly as any fifteen-year-old's, I begin to wonder if Genesis isn't one of the great, early romances rather than a mandate to take charge. If so, it serves the profound purpose of classic myths, reminding us of the kinship between ourselves, the earth, and all that dwell therein. It serves romance's grand purpose to persuade us that we are not alone.

The pages of my Bible crack slightly as I open it. They are so dry and unbent that I realize I may not have turned to this chapter since Sunday school. As I read, I am touched and amused by the gaiety, optimism, joy, sense of fun evident in this first book of the Bible. As God begins his task, he is like the Sorcerer's Apprentice working himself into a fever pitch of creative delight.

He starts with light, a fine idea, then divides it from darkness before moving on to firmament, dry land, and seas. "And God saw every thing that he had made, and behold, *it was* very good." There's an element of surprised delight in the textual repetition of God's observation that "it was good," as though he were standing over a stove, lowering a spoon into simmering sauce, raising it to nose and tongue, and savoring a new recipe. Wow! This is *good*!

Encouraged, the ideas come faster, ever more daring. Herbs

yielding seeds, fruit trees yielding fruit "after his kind," and, oh yes, don't forget the grass.

It's good! Then seasons and stars, light to rule both night and day. Great whales and cattle and creatures "after their kind," and "fowl that may fly above the earth in the open firmament of heaven." The generosity grows on itself. "God blessed them, saying, Be fruitful, and multiply, and fill the waters of the sea, and let fowl multiply in the earth to soar." The waters would teem with fish, the skies resound with birdsong. So good. So very, very good. What fun God was having. How in love with all that He had made. No love like it, said Baudelaire. None at all.

And so, as the story goes, He made "man in our image, after our likeness" as though longing for a partner in this dance. If God so loved His creation, and if man was made Godlike, then wouldn't it follow that it is within our truest and original nature to accept the waltz? To be caught up in an infinite and eternal romance with creation?

In the beginning "the earth was without form, and void; and darkness was upon the face of the deep." Ever since that beginning, we have yearned for form, color, and light. We plant trees and build cathedrals and seek to transcribe the music of the spheres into earthly études. We memorize our beloved's body. We paint creation's colors on canvas. We mourn trees lost to ice storms.

This frenzied drive to fill the void is captured in fifteenth-century Netherlandish painter Hieronymus Bosch's triptych *Garden of Earthly Delights,* hanging in Madrid's Prado, a masterpiece-laden, light-filled museum, perfect to me in every way but one. It has mounted the painting with its two panels open, and their painted exteriors facing the wall. Traditionally, these panels would have been kept closed, and opened during a mass or celebration. A human rendition of Let-There-Be-Light. Like a medieval morality play, the ancient struggle between darkness and light would have been dramatized in the act of opening and closing the triptych. Our time in history is missing such ritualistic acts of revelation.

I plaster myself up against the wall, first face-to then back-to, trying to peer behind the panels. A guard, speaking no English (another thing I love about this museum is that nobody seems to speak English), approaches sternly and motions me away. I fold my hands into a gesture of prayer and pleading. He smiles. I point to the panels and open and close my hands, showing him what I want. He shakes his head, No. I begin to get down on my knees. He shakes his head again. "Eeeez eem-possseeebull." The universal language.

I head out the doors and across the backyard of my hotel. And what a hotel it is: the Ritz of Madrid. "The Ritz of Madrid," a phrase that has been ringing in my head for years the way "Hail Mary, full of grace" must resound for the devout. Whenever those of us of limited means would sit around indulging our where-would-you-go-if-you-could-get-on-a-plane-and-go-anywhere-right-now fantasies, the list was always the same. "Africa! A safari!" "The Gritti Palace Hotel, Venice!" "The Bel-Air, Los Angeles!" "Tahiti! Tahiti! Tahiti!" "The Four Seasons, Milan!" And then occasionally there would be the clear, certain voice of my friend Joan Jakobson. A woman of unlimited means who's been every-where. We love her, nonetheless, and accept the authority of her statement when she says, "The Ritz in Madrid."

I've trusted her judgment about hotels ever since she described the Four Seasons of Milan in terms of a Carey Grant, Audrey Hepburn movie. "It's like that moment in *Charade* when Audrey says to Carey, 'You know what's wrong with you?' And he says, 'What?' And she says, 'Nothing.' That," says Joan, "is the Four Seasons in Milan."

So, in the middle of winter, when no one else would want to go there, the Ritz offers a special. Rebecca calls. "Mom, ever wanted to go to Madrid?" "I've never thought of it." "Well, lis-ten to this," and she rattles off the greatly reduced rates of hotel and airfare. "Gosh," say I, "it would be more expensive to stay home. We can't afford not to go." (That's what people always say about specials. It's a lie, but it satisfies our puritanical con-sciences, ever vigilant for even a hint of indulgence.)

We're on the next plane out and in the Prado within two hours of landing. We stand before paintings we've dreamed about and pined after. There it is! We reach for each other's hands. There's

Rogier Van der Weyden's *Descent from the Cross,* resonating with power and compassion. We both start to cry and blame jet lag. And here's Hans Memling's tender *Adoration of the Kings* with its bald-headed king kneeling before the infant Christ, whose tiny foot he presses to his hollow cheek. A simple, universal gesture that cuts away all powers, principalities, and preconceptions, and takes us immediately to the core of experience. I find I am standing with my hand to my cheek, remembering the soft flesh of every bare-foot baby I've ever kissed.

And then we repair to the Ritz. I love saying it, "Repair to the Ritz." Hot chocolate and sweet puffs of pastry are served in the golden light of the lobby. We feel blessed. We feel that we've just stepped from a Frederick Frieseke painting. We discuss how content we were when as we entered the hotel the handsome, straight-spined doormen bowed. How charmed by Luis of the very white teeth and years of dedicated concierge service (he has particularly warm memories of a young Frank Sinatra), who greeted us and asked if we would like him to arrange for a car and driver to drive us to Toledo, "You know, El Greco's *Toledo.*" I think of Joan. What's wrong with this hotel is nothing.

After naps and my aborted attempts to have the officials relent and close Bosch's panels, I approach Ana Rodríguez, a beautiful Ritz employee with bronze skin, generous brows, and a penchant for Hermès scarves. I've noticed that her body practically quivers with energy and enthusiasm as she tours the lobby, making certain that guests are well cared for. She seems like a good source. "Ana?" I introduce myself and tell of my plight. "I really need to see *The Garden of Earthly Delights* with the panels closed and then reopened in order to experience what that painting is really about."

As she thinks quietly, I begin to realize the extent of my impudence. How extraordinary to be separated from home, where I tend to accept No for an answer. I'm certain that I've never asked the Metropolitan Museum for special favors. It wouldn't have occurred to me. But here I feel completely within my rights to announce that there's something I am passionate about doing and there must be some way for it to be done.

"You want them to unhook the panels from the walls, close them, and then open them again?"

"That's right. Do you know anyone at the Prado?"

"Let me see what I can do." She quickly excuses herself, "Queen Elizabeth's cousin is checking in." She's spied the stately white-haired gentleman out of the corner of her eye and is at his side within seconds. He leans forward and kisses her hand.

Two days pass, in which I check in with Ana morning, noon, and night. Still no word back from the Prado. Our plane leaves tomorrow at noon.

Rebecca and I sit cosseted in the small, wood-paneled bar off the lobby, feeling melancholy over what we keep referring to as "our last glass of Rioja." Ana appears and announces, "My friend got back to me. If you go to the museum at nine tomorrow morning before you go to the airport, they'll do it for you."

"They'll close the panels?"

"Yes."

"Just like that?"

She gives the instructions. We are to go to the director's office and wait there for the curator of Northern Renaissance art, who will perform the ceremony for us.

"Thank you, thank you." Rebecca and I are bouncing up and down on our chairs like children in the backseat of a car that has just been steered off the highway and into the parking lot of a Dairy Queen.

"I hate the words 'no' and 'impossible,'" says Ana. "They are the ugliest words."

We go upstairs to pack so that we'll be ready and on the Prado's doorstep at nine sharp. We kiss the marble bathroom counters good-bye. We thank the bidet. We worship the view out over the garden of centuries-old trees. We say goodnight.

By nine-forty-five, we're still sitting outside the director's office. I begin to sweat. I keep looking at my watch. Rebecca slaps my wrist down. "Stop doing that, you're only making it worse." Chastened, I fold my hands in my lap. "Just breathe deeply," she adds, for good measure. She can be so bossy.

By ten, a young woman walking a pace behind a nine-month

pregnancy appears and motions for us to follow. She fetches a colleague from another office, and together they escort us into the gallery. The pregnant woman, the chief restorer of Northern Renaissance paintings, speaks to a guard, who grins and proceeds to disengage the alarms. "Now's your chance, Mom," Rebecca whispers.

Once all alarms are off, we take our places directly in front of the painting. Each woman moves to a panel. The restorer asks, "Estan listas?" I nod. They reach toward the wall, unhook the frames, and slowly close the painting. Is the gallery suddenly very quiet or does it just seem that way? I can hear the guard breathing. The painting's vibrant movement and color are shut behind a mask of blacks and grays.

I think of the force that draws people from all over the world to the site of a solar eclipse. Philip Carret, powerful, wealthy money manager, friend of the rich and the famous, was able to make his twentieth such trip three months before he died in 1998 at the age of 101. Any explanation would fall flat, said he. He found viewing an eclipse to be a "deeply religious and awe-inspiring experience . . . I don't think I can explain it to any rational person."

I can only imagine that it is a bit like my determination to view these outside panels. Earth's silent, dark beginnings.

I stand before them, aware that I am looking at the most profound interpretation of formlessness and void I may ever see. Tentative light begins to penetrate a fragile orb, the universe as delicate as a bubble floating in a gray sea. And darkness lay upon the waters and loneliness lies upon my heart.

The women stand as quietly as two pious altar boys. I am suddenly very homesick for the painting they've closed away. I ask them please to reopen the panels. They slowly pull them back and hold them for us. For one moment it is very, very good. Reds, yellows, greens, and blues rush to satisfy my sight, as though my eyes had been in a state of starvation for just these colors. The deep bright hues begin to take the shape of teeming life. Fish in the waters, birds in the sky, fruit and grass and cattle and man, who is delighted. And then the details swim into view and Paradise is ripped from consciousness. Yes, a heron stands on the shore, but a man is being devoured by a mussel, two birds fight over a dead frog, a duck-billed fish glares at a unicorn fish.

We are doomed for eternity to long for that evanescent Eden, that moment when color rushes in and satisfies a longing we didn't know we had. Before a mussel starts eating a man, before a surfeit of pleasure infects the world of the painting with regret.

A few years ago, I visited a comprehensive exhibition of Cézanne's life's work mounted by the Philadelphia Museum of Art. It was a moving display of the artist's long struggle with the discipline of form and line, his relentless reworking of similar scenes to find the truth within them and to make that truth visible. At the end of his life, he succeeded. One of his last paintings is of his garden, nonlinear and almost formless but for an exuberant rush of color. A vibrant, jubilant outpouring of creation. It was as if, at the end of his life, he finally understood that his entire career had been in pursuit of light as revealed in color, a truth hidden from view by demanding intellect and strictly trained eye. He was, at the end, given a glimpse of Paradise, and it was his backyard.

The true curse of the fall is neither pain nor toil, but eternal homesickness for a sensed Paradise. It is clear from this painting that Cézanne was heading home.

This same homesickness brings the birders and butterfly watchers into the park, brought Thoreau to his pond, Annie Dillard to her creek, inspired Virgil's dream of Arcadia, and Poussin's visual rendering. The romantic might claim that such responses are what was expected of us in the first place.

Absolutely, says Ellen Davis, Old Testament professor at Virginia Theological Seminary. The claim of Genesis that we were created in God's image implies just such an expectation. The word "image" is not accidental, she explains, but is a translation of *tselem*, Hebrew for a statue that was used in place of an absent king to serve as a reminder of his authority and guardianship. Therefore, having been created in His image, we are living reminders, active agents representing God's interests. We are expected to be partners in the ongoing dance of creation, exuberant agents rushing into darkness with light and form and color and songs of exaltation when it is good.

Sometimes the exaltation is a simple gesture. In his memoir, *Far Away and Long Ago*, W. H. Hudson describes "the head of an ancient and distinguished Argentine family" who, each night before retiring, visited the trees of his estate, laid his hand on their trunks, and whispered, "Goodnight."

At other times, exaltation takes the form of near-heroic deed. You should see David Fermoile saving the peepers, pickerel frogs, and spotted salamanders of Westchester County. On rainy nights, you can spot him on roads surrounding a wildlife preserve in the midst of Manhattan's affluent suburb. There he is, squatting on steaming pavement, scooping up slow salamanders and hastening their journeys to the other side before a fast-approaching car ends it all.

Each spring, reptiles emerging from their winter sleep in deep soil head for water to mate and lay eggs. If the only available water is across a road, so be it. They wait for rain. Once the pavement is wet and slick they can cross without the danger of their skins' drying out. But Mr. Fermoile knows of far greater dangers, and he is on the alert for the slightest patter against his window panes. With the first drops, he hastens into the night and acts as crossing guard for the clueless.

No easy task. The frogs, peepers, and salamanders have to make a round trip, and the road is well traveled by those with less urgent biological calls, those who floor the accelerator, listen to talk radio, sing along with Cher, or turn around to tell the kids in the backseat to pipe down. Watch out for peepers? Are you kidding? Poor Mr. Fermoile. No wonder the world's amphibian population has declined by 30 percent in the last thirty years.

This is not a man who discourages easily. He's living his romance. His love for these slippery creatures pulls him from a warm bed, away from made-for-TV movies in the middle of high suspense, and sometimes from dinner before he's taken the second bite of tuna casserole. He knows all this can wait, but the salamander won't.

The mid-nineteenth-century Barbizon school's photogra-

phers' and painters' compassionate connection to the Fontainebleau Forest also remind us of our Genesis legacy. This group,
loosely connected by shared anti-urban sentiments and a determination to liberate art from Classicism's formal composition
and mythical themes, composed the first generation of French
landscape painters to bring their full attention to nature. Finding their inspiration *en plein-air*, they left their studios, as Faust
left his study, to take their lessons from the play of light, the
movement of clouds, the postures of trees. They would create
the essential bridge for the Impressionists to cross out of Classicism into the light of day. "There is only one master here:
Corot," Monet would say of one of their members. "We are
nothing compared to him, nothing."

Descending from Poussin and Claude Lorrain, and looking
to their English near contemporary, Constable, who sketched in
oils from nature and spoke of his extensive studies of skies as, "a
good deal of skying," Corot and his fellow Fontainebleau
habitués imbued their art with a misty reverie for creation. Trees
took on the mystery and might of Gothic cathedrals, for which
forests were the mythical prototypes. We see this in Jean Baptiste
Camille Corot's deep green musings, B*lack Oaks at Bas-Brêau*
and photographer Eugene Cuvelier's stark, sharp-edged winter
branches striking through the veil of heaven, piercing the point
of astonishment where time and eternity intersect.

Imagine white-haired, stout Corot with pipe in mouth and
easel tucked under his arm. Imagine Théodore Rousseau at his
side and the young Cuvelier at whose wedding the two painters
recently served as witnesses tagging along, shouldering his tripod until the group was stopped in its tracks by something that
caught their fancy. Perhaps a rise of dry land where oaks rose
above rocks and reached for an indigo sky lightened by white
cumulous clouds. Imagine the reverent silence as tripod, camera, easel, palette, and paints were set up, the eyes never leaving
the subject that riveted them. Trees.

We can learn the great love stories of artists' lives by looking
at their body of work. Where their love is, their treasures are also.
A sense of hushed sacredness draws us to these rather than other,

perhaps equally masterful, examples of their *oeuvres*. Rembrandt's great romance was his mistress, Hendrickje, Jan Van Eyck's his Lord, and Barbizon artists' the trees of Fontainebleau Forest.

The trees so dazzled Rousseau that each leaf he painted glows with an other-worldly light, defying ominous clouds that block the sun. Like Plutarch before him, he was charmed by shadow and twilight, mesmerized by their dual capacity both to hide and reveal.

In 1854 as a protest against a planned clearing in the forest, Rousseau painted *The Edge of the Woods at Mont-Girard*. A mysterious luminosity of questionable source, similar to a nimbus in religious paintings, sets a tree trunk in shimmering glow. The protest and warning are clear. Cut this tree and you kill what is sacred among us.

In Corot's painting, this ephemeral light of dreams evokes a nagging nostalgia. Did we actually ever lie in green fields, gazing up at similar summer skies, or just wish we did? Did we intimately share such sylvan sanctuary or only dream it? We can't look at these paintings without feeling a pull into a past, remembered or imagined, in which we shared an intimacy with nature. They provide a fleeting return to our own internalized, vaguely recalled, and hoped-for Eden.

English painter and photographer Sir William Newton thought the power of the Barbizon school lay in the artists' ability to capture and represent nature's "atmospheric veil." Whatever it is, it has the power to draw us into an immutable knowledge shared across time with the ancient cave painters, the Druids, Celts, and Greeks, and each successive generation to our own. In spite of famine, flood, progress, we are so crucially bound to nature that we suffer bereavement we can't necessarily name when the connection is severed.

We are engaged in an ageless romance that binds us through the centuries to each person who has stood awed by the power of a hawk's precise dive or tree branches' upward stretch toward mystery. We, who stand in gathering darkness beneath spruce and oak, awaiting the black-outlined wings of an owl in flight, become part of this continuum.

On Eudora Welty's front lawn in Jackson, Mississippi, a formidable oak casts its shadow over cars passing on the quiet street, the house in front of which it stands, and a neighbor's driveway. Godzilla comes to Jackson. The tree is so mammoth that should it topple it would take Miss Welty's brick Tudor-style house with it. It is so large that it blocks the force of sunshine that would otherwise fill the Welty living room. No matter, the tree will remain exactly where it is, where her father found it when he bought the property upon which to build this house of his own design. "The builder told my parents to chop down that tree," she tells me during a visit. "But they told him, '*Never* chop down an oak tree.' They were country people. I guess that was something country people said."

Or was it an echo from Genesis or the Druids, who worshiped oaks, or from the ancient voices of the trees themselves? According to a story in Sir James George Frazer's *The Golden Bough*, "When an oak is being felled it gives a kind of shrieks or groans, that may be heard a mile off."

Thoreau fell "in love with a shrub oak," and was surprised by this "positive yearning." "What cousin of mine is the shrub oak?" he wondered. Besides shrieks and groans, does the oak emit a siren song heard by the romantic with ears tuned to possibility, or what the unromantic might call impossibility?

The Lithuanians revered oaks until the close of the fourteenth century, when conversion to Christianity brought an end to the intense relationship between human and habitat. No more animism, no more spirits in trees, no more gods in sacred groves.

Our own connection to trees is stubborn if subdued. Thomas Hardy was told that the reason the trees in his yard failed to thrive was because he looked at them before breakfast. He took this to heart. Those of us who live in families and face the mornings together shouldn't find such a theory far-fetched. Though it is appalling that according to old German law the punishment for peeling bark from a standing tree was to nail the offender's navel to the tree prior to driving him, as described by Sir James, "round and round the tree till all his guts were wound about its trunk." I'm not altogether certain that members of the Central Park Conservancy might not, for a fleeting moment, consider the punishment mete and just.

An eye for an eye. A belly button for bark.

In that park in this century bark peeling is a lesser offense. Maria Hernandez has outlined for me the odds of a tree growing in Central Park. Never mind those who might look at them before breakfast, there are others who carve declarations of love into their trunks, swing on their branches, and snap off their flowering sprigs. Such perfect centerpieces. Then there is the extensive foot traffic over their soil, pollution from Fifth Avenue's cars and buses, summer's drought and winter's freeze. That they are here at all is amazing. Nature's determination astonishes.

Trees survive because they choose to, says gardener Marino Ciccion, an azure-eyed Northern Italian who works at Twombleys Nursery in Monroe, Connecticut. "In thousands of years trees will have eyes if that's what's required for survival." Clearing up any possible confusion he quickly adds, "Not eyes like ours. Tree eyes."

We stand among pots of trees and shrubs, boxes of borders, trays of perennials. Rain soaks us as he explains that it is precisely this drive to survive that inspires his love for trees. "They want to survive as we do, even though they don't have feelings as we know them." But that, he assures me in softly accented tones, does not mean they don't have feelings.

"They almost cajole in order to survive. For instance, apple and cherry trees make fruit so sweet that humans and birds can't resist. This spreads their seeds far and wide." He smiles. "Nature is like science fiction. We don't have to go to outer space. The bewildering is right here."

He's never read Thoreau, who, more than one hundred years ago, said pretty much the same thing. "Nature is a wizard. The Concord nights are stranger than the Arabian nights." We keep singing the same song over and over. Through all of human history, the love songs are a variation on the same theme: This is beautiful, this is mysterious, I don't understand, but for this moment I feel at home and homeless, in and out of time, alone but not apart.

Marino loves the pear when it blossoms. The deep green of plum. He reaches up and strokes the weeping cherry. "This one I don't love as much. Because of its name. I prefer to call it 'cascading cherry.'" He grows sad as he pats the thin trunk. "There is so much sweetness," he says, sighing, "so much sweetness you can't possess."

And that, of course, is the whole point. So much sweetness we can't possess. Possession may be nine-tenths of the law, but it kills nine-tenths of romance.

He may long to possess the sweetness, may grow sad-eyed with yearning, but Marino is cheered by his certainty that we two soaked human beings, standing in rising mud and sneezing from sweet, wet pollen, are related to trees. "In spite of our differences, our unique characteristics, we are somehow connected." And that, he says, "relieves my mind and heart."

On the Island of Skye, according to *Darker Superstitions of Scotland,* published in Edinburgh in 1834, there was "'a fair wood, which none presumes to cut . . .'" lest they be "visited afterwards by 'some signal inconvenience.'"

We are visited daily by such "signal inconvenience"—smog-smudged air, toxic water, vanishing species. Cut the tree, sever the sacred connection, and we are visited by the signal inconvenience of being spiritually stranded strangers upon the earth.

In our struggle to reconnect to an ancient and intense Genesis legacy, we create a romance. Birders in the park, who dream of bonding with hawks and owls, even though they know those birds will never sacrifice wilderness for human love, Nabokov with his butterfly net in pursuit of indigo flight, catalogers, painters, photographers, planters and pruners of trees, we are all driven to dispel the inevitable loneliness of disconnection.

"I write," says W. S. Merwin in a poem to a whale, "as though you could understand / And I could say it."

There is a man I meet many mornings as I walk a path along the East River. He shares a wooden bench with pigeons, bags of stale bread, bagels, and birdseed. He grows awkward at my approach. As I guide my dog around the fresh pools of bird droppings, he glances nervously up from his bags, then looks deeper into them to avoid a potential greeting. Sometimes as many as three pigeons perch on an outstretched arm.

Where does it get him, this romance with pigeons? He looks abandoned, lost. I presume that he doesn't confuse the birds' eating instinct with love. Or does he? He comes here every day, hoping for this moment and more. Probably for the same reason that the Central Park birders keep vigil from first to last light at hawk-fledging time and during spring migration.

Yet, for all our attempts to press against it, we can get just so close to nature and then something snaps.

In A.D. 109, Pliny the Younger wrote a letter describing a "friendship" between a dolphin and a boy it had saved from drowning off the Tunisian coast. For weeks following the rescue, the two would reunite at the water's edge, where the boy would climb onto the dolphin's back to be carried seaward and later returned to shore. Then as now such an event was bound to attract attention, and a second-century equivalent of busloads of arriving tourists so strained the resources of their destination that civil strife erupted. The villagers determined that the only way to save their homes was to kill the attraction.

Pliny does not write of the boy's heartbreak, but I can imagine it. When I was a child, you would have thought I was on a mission from God given the focus and determination of my rescue efforts on behalf of bald baby robins fallen from their nests. I would carry them home, their gray skin smooth and fluttering in the callused palm of my hand. There I would deliver them to the sickroom set up for my ministrations. Matchboxes lined with tissues. An eye dropper. A can and shovel for collecting worms. A Sisters of Mercy infirmary. The birds always died. I was always surprised and woebegone.

There is no question that engaging in a romance with nature can break your heart. Count on it. Many of us were attracted to a series of recent news reports of gray wolves released into Yellowstone National Park to repopulate the northern Rocky Mountains. We were devastated when we learned that one of them, a ninety-two-pound female, was shot to death. We'd become more attached than we knew.

In romantic love, we yearn to merge with qualities we perceive in the other and find lacking in ourselves. When such romancing occurs in our perception of nature, we are not diminishing its facts, but holding them up as a mirror to an idealized version of ourselves, an act that allows us to believe that we too can be noble, authentic, purposeful, and present. Just like a wolf. Anthropomorphizing may be disdained by science, but it is romantic imagination's tool for illuminating Einstein's theory that our perception of ourselves as separate beings is an optical delusion.

Jack London illustrates this contention in *Call of the Wild*, when Buck, a domesticated dog, returns to wilderness and his true nature. By blurring the boundaries between human, wolf, and dog, the author dramatizes our interconnection.

> There is an ecstasy that marks the summit of life, and beyond which life cannot rise. And such is the paradox of living, this ecstasy comes when one is most alive, and it comes as a complete forgetfulness that one is alive. This ecstasy, this forgetfulness of living, comes to the artist, caught up and out of himself in a sheet of flame: and it came to Buck, leading the pack, sounding the old wolf cry, straining after the food that was alive and that fled swiftly before him through the moonlight. He was sounding the deeps of his nature, and of the parts of his nature that were deeper than he, going back into the womb of Time. He was mastered by the sheer surging of life, the tidal wave of being, the perfect joy of each separate muscle, joint and sinew in that it was everything that was not death. . . .

Romance is energized by the prospect of this perfect joy, this exaltation of everything that is not death. For a fleeting moment, it relieves us of forethoughts of grief.

Bison, horses, and deer appear to gallop toward us out of thirty-thousand-year-old cave paintings. The myth of Achilles holds us spellbound with its description of the young hero raised by a centaur, part man, part beast, and nourished on the marrow of wild animals so that he would grow to become like them in swiftness, cunning, and strength.

Such primal desire to merge with mystery and might lives on. We call it a hunger for beauty and find nourishment in the marrow of art, music, nature, poetry.

How lonely we are. How relentlessly we yearn, like W. S. Merwin, for a common language, the ability to speak as though the other could understand.

It can happen. At least Cliff says so. Cliff, savvy street kid, law school friend. Brilliant and clear-headed, he'd never met a fact he didn't like and was well suited to his future profession. We, his classmates, trusted his integrity, his quick grasp of legal issues, reasoning, and holdings. We were full of admiration, though not surprise, when he was chosen above all the rest to clerk for Supreme Court Justice William Brennan.

So naturally we snapped to serious attention the day our study group sat together in an unair-conditioned classroom cramming for the July bar exam and Cliff looked up from the criminal-law text to ask, "Did I ever tell you about the dog I had that talked?"

Well, no, as a matter of fact, no he hadn't. We pushed our notes on hearsay evidence aside, unwrapped our tunafish, peanut-butter, and salami sandwiches and awaited the telling.

"When I was a student at the University of California in the early seventies, I lived in a commune in Berkeley. We had this really great dog. He'd walk me to class in the morning and he'd always be there to meet me when I was leaving the campus in the afternoon."

"What about when your schedule changed?"

"Ssshhh."

"Well, one night eight of us were having dinner, sitting around this big table in the living room. The front door was open and the dog sort of sauntered in from the porch. As he walked toward the kitchen, he passed us and said, 'Hi, guys.'"

"How much weed were you smoking?"

"What did you do?"

"We ran out to the street."

"Why?"

"We were scared."

I have credited the era's free-flowing drugs, but, just between us, I've also fervently hoped that the dog really did talk. I hope that he really did wander in casually, greet the guys, continue into the kitchen to drink water out of his bowl, and then go about his doggie ways.

It's high romance, and I want it to be true.

There's another story, not firsthand but well documented, of an Akita, one of the fierce and loyal breed of Japanese dogs, that accompanied his master to the train station every morning. Once he'd seen him safely aboard, he'd walk home and return nine hours later to meet the evening train. After his master died, he continued the routine until his own death, whereupon the citizens of the Japanese town in which the two had lived erected a statue of the dog outside the train station.

And who can blame them? What is love if not such patient vigilance? Such single-mindedness undeterred by reason?

Showing up in its name is all that we can do. Isn't this what we desire in our human lovers? Who would not be moved to erect a statue in honor of hearts so different beating as one? It helps explain why the story was compelling enough to inspire a public television documentary about Akitas.

Hollywood has built a golden city promulgating such dreams. *Old Yeller*, *Bambi*, *The Yearling*, *The Bear*, *The Lion King*, and *Babe*, celluloid animals endowed with loyalty, steadfastness, and forbearance and free of identity crisis and second-guessing, the very characteristics we long for in ourselves. Our embarrassed sobs over the death of a cinematic beast have less to do with the animal than our recognition of how vulnerable and frail such qualities are, how unlikely to survive in a defensive world.

I think back to that gray wolf, sleek and low to the ground, as it once ran through the forests of Yellowstone. I think of her mating, perfunctory and to the point. I think of her nursing her pups. There's a purity to it all. A magnificence. Life sharpened and simplified.

We struggle for this in our own lives. "I want," writes poet

Jane Cooper, "a radiance of attention . . . a kind of awe attending the spaces between us." That kind of attention is only possible once we surgically simplify our existence, ridding it of the excesses of noise and seductive distraction. Few are willing to chip experience away to the bone, but some actually try. They attempt the simplicity into which awe can be born by following a Zen path. "Before enlightenment chop wood, carry water. After enlightenment chop wood, carry water." Perhaps they seek a Christian life: "Come to me as little children." And there is a group that has modeled itself after nineteenth-century British Luddites, who protested industrialization. Leaving computers, faxes, and phones behind, they've formed a community in Midwestern farmland, where they live lives of undistracted deliberation.

And for what? To chop wood and carry water? Yes, because before, after, and while chopping and carrying there is the possibility of enlightenment, a radiance of attention. After they'd hunted, carved spears from antlers, renewed seams in clothing and tents, the painters of the Lascaux caves in France lowered themselves deep within the earth to record and exalt their experience in hues of ochre and black.

In his book *Lascaux, or the Birth of Art*, Georges Bataille notes the "irrepressible festive exuberance" and "generous kindliness" evidenced in the paintings. In his opinion, these ancient expressions of beauty fulfill art's purpose to make known the wonder of ordinary experience, "a desire implicit in the human being's very essence."

You would think, upon reviewing the evidence, that such desire is imprinted on our DNA. Note, for instance, the artist's reverent affection for a deer he engraved over 24,000 years ago on the interior wall of Les Combarelles cave in the Dordogne Valley. It's there in the grace of posture—taut muscles straining forward, a majestic sweep of antlers rising upward, small hooves touching the earth lightly, a delicate stretch of tongue toward water. All revealed through a radiance of attention.

Joseph Campbell observed that ancient hunters looked to animals to learn how to live. Judging from cave paintings, they also looked to the animals and learned about love. Rembrandt's paintings of Hendrickje Stoffels are no more tender. In fact, there is a striking similarity between the deer at the edge of water and Hendrickje's delicate testing of its depths in *A Woman Bathing in a Stream*.

The observing artist and we who observe their art share a yearning to connect to the elusive, to be present when and where time and eternity intersect. The anonymous artist painting in half-light with ochre, oxide, and carbon ground to powder between stones and mixed with animal fat, bone marrow, or blood. The less-anonymous Rembrandt painting with pigment and oil in his studio. Both driven to connect with the "other," to capture it in a net of longing, to possess it as art. We are moved by the love born into their silent, patient watching and waiting, and the art born into the space between object and desire.

Love is peculiar. Why deer? Why trees? Why amphibians? Why birds? Why reptiles, butterflies, reef fish? Why dogs, wolves, exotic cats?

Passion's path is a mystery, and there are bees crawling on Dr. P. Kirk Visscher's nose. They're on his cheeks and neck. They're making their nervous way to the chest hair curling out of his open shirt. He smiles. In every other respect this entomologist appears to be an ordinary man. He is, however, a man obsessed. Bees. He wants to know everything there is to know about them. He embarked on this quest when he was six years old, and so far, this is what he knows:

1. The best way to relieve bee-sting is to pull out the stinger.

2. "Undertaker bees" specialize in removing dead bees from hives. Worker bees do in fact, and on occasion, lay eggs in colonies with a queen. These unfertilized eggs can develop into drones if they escape the other workers' intention to sniff them out and devour them.

3. When swarming, a phenomenon that occurs when a hive becomes over-crowded, as many as 20,000 bees all fly in the same direction to a new site.

Dr. Visscher knows all this and more, and yet he says he is left with a burning question, "I wonder what it is to be a bee." Me, too. I wonder what it is to be a bee, an owl, a hawk, my dog, my daughter, my husband.

I once attended a grand-rounds presentation featuring psychiatrist and psychoanalyst Dr. Charles Fisher at Mount Sinai Hospital in Manhattan. This gentle, unassuming man, engaged in pioneer studies of dreams and REM sleep, held his audience in thrall as he brought them up to date on his latest discoveries. At the end of an hour, the lights came up, the slides were returned to their boxes, the graphs and charts rolled and fastened with rubber bands, and Fisher, preeminent researcher and practitioner, remained standing silently behind the podium. At last he spoke. Staring out at his audience he sighed, "So now we know she dreams." He shrugged ruefully and added, "But does she dream of me?"

In the end, when all the facts are in, this is what we want to know.

"Play hard to get," my father used to tell me. "Always keep a man guessing" was the advice of a former generation of women to their daughters. Nature is the queen of hard-to-get. Chances are Dr. Visscher will never know what it is to be a bee, but the quest will get him out of bed in the morning, will drive him to show up, to watch and wonder, to focus a radiance of attention.

Chances are pretty good that nature doesn't dream of us, doesn't respond to our seductions. It will refuse all invitations to sit down at a table specially set with candles, flowers, our best china and silver. It won't unfold its soul over the course of an evening and a bottle of chilled Chardonnay. The most we can expect is the unfolding of our own souls as we keep vigil, remaining available for revelation, for the slow, sweet disclosure of secrets. If we're distracted by judgment and doubt, the moment will occur without us.

I have a friend whose six-year-old son, Anderson, pined for a boa constrictor. When his understandably reluctant mother relented in the spirit of Christmas, the overjoyed recipient of such large-heartedness hugged the gift as the giver prayed that the favor would not be returned. Had he thought of the name Jake in that instant or had he dreamed of it when this peculiar desire was born? All that my friend reports is that Anderson held the snake in his small, thin arms and whispered, "Oh, Jake, is this all a dream?"

Yes. It's all a dream, but one that we insist upon. We give our hearts away and await the feathered, furry, or slippery response.

6

SOME SPOOKY ACTION
AT A DISTANCE

————•———

Early Spring, Central Park

In late February, the dog and I entered a silent, empty park. Other dog walkers had settled for a quick dash to the corner to avoid intermittent downpours. Nannies, mothers, and toddlers stayed home. They had a point. We would make quick work of this. I pulled my collar up against the wind as we walked beneath bare branches slicked black by rain. Near the model-boat pond, I saw two figures in familiar birding posture, arms raised at the elbows, heads leaning slightly back at the neck. They lowered their binoculars as I drew near enough to inquire what they'd seen today. "Well," said one rather shyly, "the red-tailed hawks mated at 2:10 P.M. We looked at our watches."

For the past three years, the regulars have been watching this pair of red-tails who've made Manhattan their home. Something wild and powerful has come to live among them. They're captivated by the birds' beauty, by their ability to terrify the pigeon population and to spot a rat six blocks away. Qualities New Yorkers would like for themselves.

"Where were they when they mated?" I wanted to know.

"On a window ledge at Seventy-third and Fifth." Classy. How lucky the occupants were if they were at home to witness it. "Oh, yes," my informant responded quietly and seriously. "Not only are they rich, they're rich in hawks."

Rich in hawks, but do they know it? If they are romantics,

of course they do. If not, they will be concerned about the bird droppings on their windowsills. "How in the world did you happen to see this?" I asked.

"We looked up."

Yes, but at the right moment and in the right place. Inspired.

When I reported the news to my daughter that evening, when I told her how marvelous it was that the hawks had mated in such a beautiful place. "I mean, it's like having an afternoon tryst in one of the Carlyle Hotel's tower suites." She humored me, "Right, Mom. I'm sure that's why they did it there. They liked the view."

Two months ago, in a darkening winter afternoon, my husband and I had met one of the birders and asked if she'd seen the hawks over the winter. "Look up," she said, cocking her head in the direction of branches overhead. There was the male looming directly above us. His white breast was set off by the shock of red blood dripping from talons curled around a beheaded pigeon.

"How did you know *where* to look?"

"I noticed a commotion among the pigeons, and as I walked along I just kept my eyes open. Then, when I came to this tree, I saw pigeon feathers floating down." No big deal. Just follow the bread crumbs. Connect the dots.

The romantic has to believe the bread crumbs were left as a trail, that the dots will make a whole. That's crazy. We all know the universe is random. Yes and no, says Episcopal priest James Annan. We may know this, yet faith requires a belief in purpose, in design over chaos, love over rejection. Faith doesn't require answers but a trust that if we dare reach out a hand another one, unforeseen, will receive it. That we will be made whole. The ultimate romance. Exactly as Michelangelo painted it in the center of the Sistine Chapel ceiling. God's hand stretching toward Adam's. The birders may be less lofty, but the yearning is similar. If they reach into the apparent void, maybe nature will respond.

And who's to say it won't? Quantum physicists tell us that even atoms do certain things only when being watched. Recently, Dr. Nicolas Gisin of the University of Geneva was able to demonstrate the theory that "entangled" particles, those sharing common origins and properties, remain in instantaneous "touch" with each other over great distances of separation. Einstein referred to this as "spooky action at a distance" and doubted it. This new generation of physicists speak of the spookiness as the "magic" of "quantum weirdness."

Weird that Gisin was able to separate two photons of light by seven miles and then observe them respond simultaneously to stimulus applied just to one of them. No matter, Gisin explains. This will happen even if the particles are separated "by the entire universe." Two photons that beat as one.

"A man and a woman / Are one. / A man and a woman and a blackbird / Are one," wrote Wallace Stevens. Poets and mystics have always known the news that science now brings us.

What made Nobel physicist Richard Feynman tick, writes colleague Arthur Zajonc, was his determination to follow "the path of beauty." Inspired by the mystery he found there, he "stalked the phenomena of physics with an ancient and honorable instrument, the confidence that perfection lay at the root of existence."

Mystery, it seems, grows proportionally with knowledge. The romantic may not be equipped with Gisin's training, but he is born with Feynman's "honorable instrument." He intuits an innate connection between himself and the universe, a spooky connection at any distance.

In mid-March, the hawks lay eggs and Merrill returns to his accustomed post. Behind him, the regular hawk addicts assemble on the bench they've warmed for three seasons. They peer through their binoculars, wait for hawk action, and take turns going to a nearby coffee shop for refills of hot chocolate. Merrill stands next to a telescope rigged with a camera aimed at the nest the hawks built directly over Mary Tyler Moore's apartment and next door to Woody Allen's. Location. Location. Location. It prompts one of the group to disparage these high-end birds. "Star fuckers," he mumbles into his coffee mug.

The day is gray with winds that sent us back inside for the scarves and gloves we'd left behind. Merrill shivers against the gusts. His face is red from the cold and his natural reticence loosened by news he's eager to share.

"So, what's up?" I ask, pausing with the dog for a brief moment because conversation with Merrill is always brief. Not for him the run-on sentence, the free association. But this is not to be brief. What he'd seen had banished his shyness.

He tells me, "A few hours ago the male flew to the nest with a pigeon and delivered it to the female. He sat on the eggs while she flew off with the prey to a tree on Seventy-second Street and the park drive. She really likes that tree because from there she has a perfect view of the nest." Then, with a smile he adds, "And from there she can keep an eye on him."

He tells me that when the female flew from the nest, the birders followed her to this "favorite" tree. Dragging the telescope along, they ran up the hill to Seventy-second Street and found the hawk on a low branch, her beak buried deep in red-fleshed pigeon. From this vantage point, they were able to see a number-inscribed band on her leg.

"We immediately called the number in to the Department of Fish and Wildlife, then they referred us to the Bird Banding Laboratory in Laurel, Maryland. Well, it turns out . . ." Pausing, he takes out a red bandanna, blows his nose, and continues: "Well, it turns out she's the mate this male had when they first built a nest here in 1992. Those eggs never hatched, she was injured and disappeared."

According to Merrill, whose story is beginning to take on the dimensions of *A Love Affair to Remember*, when this female was driven into the side of an apartment building by an angry flock of crows, the impact broke her wing. A birder who witnessed the attack picked the hawk up from the sidewalk, wrapped it in her coat, and drove it to Millington, New Jersey, where Dr. Leonard Soucy, Jr., presides over the Raptor Trust, providing care for the feathered fearful and broken. "He set the wing and took care of her. He was quite certain she would never fly again, but after six months she showed signs of wanting to fly, so he let her go."

Merrill is not used to storytelling, to the slow, rich accumulation of fact and surmise, for twists and turns away from and back to the plot. He rushes ahead with the news, "Meanwhile, the male took another mate, the one we saw last year." The one found dead this winter on a New Jersey highway, supposedly hit by a car. Merrill insinuates that this is unlikely. "I think that maybe she was shot." Regardless of the circumstances, her surviving mate wasted little time in finding a replacement.

Recently, my friend Helen, mourning the death of her best friend, told me that she regularly called her friend's husband to commiserate. "So yesterday, six months after she died, he answers the phone and says, 'I've found someone.' Found someone? Barbara, it's only six months! God!" she said. "Women mourn. Men replace."

And so it was with the hawk. What the birders hadn't known until today was that he'd replaced with his original mate.

How did they find each other again? I can't help wondering how he was affected when she broke her wing and disappeared. Is there such a thing as emotional bonding among birds?

I've not found the answer to this. We know that red-tailed hawks, ravens, swans, mourning doves, albatrosses, and wild geese probably pair for life, but what drives that pairing? Zoologist Marcy Cottreu Houle writes of a pair of peregrine falcons that built a nest into the edge of a high cliff where they warmed their eggs against the assault of Rocky Mountain winds. Soon after the chicks hatched, the female disappeared. As the days passed and she failed to return, the male grew increasingly agitated, repeatedly peering into the nest as though he might have missed her the first time he looked. Forced to feed the chicks alone, he hunted, returned with prey, and again methodically searched the nest. At the end of the day, he would settle into the downy warmth of his chicks' company within the intricate assembly of twigs. There he would wait, occasionally startling the silence with a shrieking call. After three days of this, he stood on the edge of his aerie and emitted "a cry like the screeching moan of a wounded animal.... The sadness ... was unmistakable." He remained motionless in the nest for the rest of the day.

Houle claims that cry ended any doubt she may have harbored "that an animal can suffer emotions that we humans think belong to our species alone."

In her book *Lads Before the Wind*, Marine biologist Karen Pryor writes that following the death of its mate, Kiko, a dolphin, stopped eating and commenced swimming with its eyes shut tight. Round and round in circles it went, blinded to circumstance. Pryor concluded that "he did not want to look on a world that did not contain Kiko."

O.K., maybe in New York we're different. But just last night, months after this chapter had neared completion and I was convinced of hawk love, I ran into the birders stationed near the boat pond, looking up to the building next to the nest. "Didn't you know?" This is how one knows the regulars, that question never has to be asked of them. No, I know nothing. "The female died last week. Poisoned when she ate a tainted pigeon."

"Some lunatic who's trying to kill off the pigeons in the park is lacing birdseed with poison."

Noreen sits weeping on the bench. "I'm still grieving, and they're all excited about the new female."

"New female?"

"That's what they're looking at. They've already given her a name." She removes a ball of wet tissues from her pocket and holds them to her red eyes.

"How'd he find a new mate so fast? Take out a personal ad in *New York* magazine?"

"I don't know, but he's showing her all the places. He's even taken her to the nest." This brings on a fresh rush of tears.

A reporter from the *Post* approaches, "I was at the pigeon protest and wrote a story about that, now I want a story on the new female. What can you tell me?"

Don't believe what you hear. We may be jaded, we may pretend to ignore our celebrities, but bring a reporter into any group of New Yorkers, and there's a fight to be the quoted one.

I reluctantly pick up a pair of binoculars and look at the new mate. She's mottled black rather than bearing the vibrant red hues of her predecessor. Just between us girls, I think she's ugly.

Love stories from the wild. I spare Rebecca this one.

Sometimes these stories claim that love jumps species. Like some terrifying, flesh-devouring virus from the rain forest. In his book *When Elephants Weep*, Jeffrey Moussaieff reports that when a particular whooping crane raised by a man was ready to mate, she rejected all other cranes and was, instead, attracted to "Caucasian men of average height with dark hair."

Following the death of a particular gentleman who needed the assistance of crutches in order to walk, an otter he had raised was adopted by another family. They spent the succeeding years in hot pursuit of an animal that consistently ran away to the doorsteps of men with crutches. Why, you might ask, didn't the family simply start walking with crutches?

Do they have to be true? Not in order to serve the truth. These stories and Merrill's tale of long-lost love returned, serve a purpose similar to myths. They create a sense of kinship in Merrill's case between birds and birders. They ease the loneliness of our alienation. Here is something the hawks and we hold in common, the pursuit of happy endings.

7

A GOD SANDWICH

In May, as my husband, dog, and I come upon the hawk watchers sitting on their regular bench behind two telescopes, they turn in our direction and give a thumbs-up sign of triumph. They have seen the male return to the nest with a pigeon. "And, after giving it to the female," says Charles with excitement, "instead of flying off with it to her favorite tree, she tore it into little pieces!" We look blank but Charles is patient with beginners. "Tore it up in little pieces and leaned into the nest! She was feeding her young! They've hatched!"

Nerves have been a bit frayed around here. Two years ago when the eggs failed to hatch, days went by and the birders grew quieter and sadder. The atmosphere became increasingly funereal as possible causes were discussed. Could it have been rat poison in the park? They were taking no chances and persuaded the bureaucratic Parks Department to refrain from all use of poisons during mating season. The rats thrived and two hearty chicks hatched, but the group continues to be wary.

"Phew," sighs a birder arriving in time to hear the end of Charles's report. "I worried about it all last night." Up until now, there had been no sign that the eggs had hatched and the estimated incubation time had passed. Yesterday, the female began to exhibit what appeared to us to be bizarre behavior as she frantically bobbed up and down on the nest. I thought of the Rocky Mountain peregrine falcon and shared my concern with Marie Winn. Could those erratic movements be some sort of death ritual? She confessed that she too had been contemplating the possibility.

"Nonsense," said my husband, "She's simply feeding the babies." Nonetheless, as Marie and I parted, I on my way to church, we shrugged sadly and murmured the usual well-here's-hopings. "I'll pray for them," I joked. Today when I return home from the park there is a message from Marie, who was unaware that I'd already heard the news. Her voice is ecstatic, "Whatever you did in church worked!"

This sense of shared triumph makes the group particularly buoyant as they huddle around the telescopes, waiting for their turns, hoping to spot a small downy head, an open beak reaching for food. An intense drama has arisen around an event unfolding as unself-consciously as the cherry blossoms and sticky green buds of linden and maple. Life against all odds.

Early June is fledging time, and Merrill takes his two-week vacation in order to stand vigil from dawn to dusk, to be present at the moment that decides the fate of the new generation. The tentative walk to the edge of the nest, the testing of open space, and then the leap of faith and fate. Borne on wings or overcome by gravity.

Marie gets up early enough to ride her bike over from the West Side and is here by 5:30 A.M. Charles, a late sleeper, forgoes habit and luxury and arrives soon after.

And here is gentle Jane Koryn, who appeared last season as the birders' angel. She lives below Woody Allen, one building north of the nest, and had been observing the early-morning gatherings from her apartment window. One day at 6 A.M., she arrived carrying croissants and brioches wrapped in French Provincial napkins and piled into a wicker basket. Coffee and tea, lemon, sugar, cream. Since then, the group has counted on her kindness.

And the others, who include a retired ninety-year-old German nurse and her niece, both single, no strings attached. They migrate with the birds to all corners of the earth. There are two magazine photo editors, a shy young man who speaks little English and knows birds by their songs, an executive from an ad agency, a retired World War II sniper, who has the sharpest, most restless eyes in the bunch. We rely on him for full reports of everything that crosses the distant sky or perches in nearby bushes too thick for normal eyes to penetrate. And then there is Sister Somebody or Other. I can never remember the second part of her name because each time we're introduced I automatically start singing to myself, "Oh, listen, Sister, I love my mister man, and I can't tell you why." Furthermore, I'm completely distracted by the black lashes she's painted on the skin under her eyes. And then there's the question of isn't she hot under that long, thick black wig she's adjusted to her head? And how come nobody ever comments on the fact that sometimes she seems to be wearing false vampire teeth? It appears to be birding etiquette not to discuss idiosyncrasies. Just another "uncommon to locally fairly common" visitor. So Sister shows up, is welcomed, and busies herself with reams of paper and information she shares with passersby who haven't heard the hawk news. She and mysterious others show up at hawk time and disappear again. It's all considered perfectly normal.

Frederick Law Olmsted would be pleased. Unlike earlier admirers of arcadias, from Virgil to the Valois and Bourbon kings for whom Edenic parks were lordly possessions, he believed that parks were an exercise in democracy, nature unbound by social hierarchies. This group meets his ideal with their easy camaraderie, their common desire to connect with hawks.

Their determination to know everything there is to know about the bird forces them from sleep, causes them to leave work early, tell little lies ("Got to go to an aunt's funeral"), to play hooky. They are driven to show up in all weather, sacrifice vacation time, neglect ringing phones and mounting bills, because there are passions that overwhelm routine and the competing desires for warmth, shelter, and comfort.

I remember lines forming outside Carnegie Hall twelve hours before tickets went on sale for pianist Vladimir Horowitz's historic return to the concert stage. One recent summer when *The Tempest* was to be performed in Central Park, Shakespeare lovers spent the night there in order to be first in line when the box office opened in the morning. In the deep, cold winter, art lovers stood for five hours in ten blustery degrees hoping to gain admittance to a Vermeer exhibit at Washington's National Gallery. Once inside, they shook snow off coats, pulled mittens off hands, and blew on them until sensation returned. They released their hair from woolen caps and stamped up and down to bring circulation back to numbed feet. The air grew misty with their breath as they grinned triumphantly and shared tales of their ordeal.

"I've been out there since 5 A.M."

"I actually lost the feeling in my fingers."

"The end of my nose started turning white. You know, like frostbite."

There was happy agreement that they were glad to pay the price of discomfort for the joy awaiting them.

What is the joy? The fervent hope and often wavering belief that there are important messages that come to us through nature, music, poetry, and art. A vision that those bringing the message will share it with us if we bare our souls to their inspiration.

Greek philosopher Gorgias understood the full life-changing power of those moments in which message is sent and received, knew that "through sight the soul receives an impression even in its inner features."

We know so much more than we think we do. So what if we don't know that the Latin root of inspire is *spirare*, to breathe, or that in fourteenth century Middle English the word *inspiren* meant to breathe upon or into? Without knowing any of this, we know absolutely that to be moved, to be inspired is to feel touched and entered by a gentle breeze. "I am not thinking, madame. I am moved."

Consider visual images of inspiration in Medieval and Renaissance annunciation paintings; the angel Gabriel surprising the Virgin at her prayers, bringing her the news that will change the course of history. She turns her head slightly in response to the presence in her room and a shower of gold is exhaled from the angel's mouth, and in some cases, from the mouth of God in the upper left-hand corner of the canvas. Golden breath. Mary, thus breathed upon, becomes through inspiration the bearer of a God incarnate.

We are equally vulnerable targets, we who stand and wait and watch. Things might not turn out as planned. We might be amazed. Keats urges us to let it happen, but it takes a lot of nerve, and I doubt he would blame us should we avert our eyes. Anyone who's seen those paintings, really seen them, would understand the observer who hurries on, who keeps her appointment with destiny as carefully outlined in her Filofax.

And yet. The romantic knows that the opposite of "inspire" is "expire," knows that to shield oneself from inspiration is to be less alive. I often think of a Mark Helprin story in which the narrator's aging father calls out against inevitability, "More life! More life!" Standing and sleeping in line for a concert, play, or art exhibition, squatting in cold rain with binoculars trained on tree branches is the romantic's echo to that refrain. More life!

There is an urgency to the task. Birders fear a terrible loss should they fall asleep at their posts.

Last season, when the first hawk chicks fledged and birders dispersed for the night, one said, "Maybe they'll remember how much we loved them and come back next year." She was new to bird-watching. The veterans tolerated her sentiment.

Even a veteran, excited to find one of the fledglings perched rather shakily on a branch to which it had first flown but seeming too frightened to fly again, called out reassuringly, "Remember me? I'm your Aunt Martha. I know you can do it."

Aunt Martha who had been watching through her binoculars for six weeks. Aunt Martha who didn't sleep that night, so worried was she about the bird.

During that first fledging, when telescopes were set up on the edge of the model-boat pond and the birders were sharing news and bagels, another regular confessed that he too hadn't been able to sleep. He'd left the park only after it had become too dark to watch a fledgling cling to the edge of Woody Allen's terrace, its first perch after leaving the nest that afternoon. "I worried about it all night. I was scared that it might lose its grip and fall to Fifth Avenue. Every time the wind blew, I held my breath and sort of clutched the edge of my bed." "So did we," came the chorus from those who weren't new to risk, who wear badges on their hats from birding expeditions to the Poles, Patagonia, and the Pacific, who are founders of birding clubs and members of the Audubon Society.

Naturally there was an assumption that worry served as a guardian. That concern sent through the night would find its way to a small hawk and support it against high winds and fear of the dark. Maybe it worked. By morning the bird had success-fully flown to the next building.

Yet we are sternly reprimanded for "caring" so much lest we blind ourselves to the "facts" and "reality" of nature. Anthropo-morphizing, we are warned, clouds our vision.

And it can. Diane Fossey's articles published in *National Geographic* downplayed infanticide among gorillas. When she first discovered the practice she hastened to excuse and then to cover it up. Marianna Torgovnick notes in an article in *Yale Review* that "Fossey had begun with an idealized image of goril-las living in gentle, primitive harmony—Eden translated to the animal world."

Similarly, while Jane Goodall was engaged in chimpanzee research in Gombe she locked her own infant son inside a wire cage for protection after discovering "positive proof that chimps would kill and eat young baboons or human infants." Goodall did not release this grim reality to the public. It certainly wasn't there in her reports; that made many of us little girls want to run away to Africa to live with the chimps.

Both scientists, having fallen in love with their subjects, found reality disruptive of the "romance" they had come to cherish, a romance they were willing to sustain at truth's peril. Their scientific observation had suddenly become, according to Torgovnick, "a disruptive element in the narrative of idyllic ani-mal life that the primatologist wants to tell and the public, at least at first, wants to hear."

I'm that public. A tape from the television show *Nova* has been sitting on my bookshelf, the seal of its cellophane packing still unbroken after six months. "Did you see the show about gang rape by dolphins?" my stepson asked. When I cringed and let him know that I'd missed it, he suggested that I'd better have a look. I have complete faith in his judgment. I ordered the tape immediately, and here it sits.

Why would I want to know that these mammals, Kiko of

the tender heart, Pliny's dolphin of the noble rescue, are a bit too much like us? Do I really want to know if they share our weakness for gang mentality? Spare me the brutality of nature that goes beyond the need to procure food. I want the happy story of harmony in the forest primeval, peace beneath the stormy seas. But Torgovnick is a scientist and won't spare me the details.

She has a point. The fact is that to be in harmony with nature requires an awareness of the dark side. The truth of nature, resonating with the truth of ourselves, is what makes harmony possible. Otherwise we engage in sentimental denial. Yet anthropomorphizing is a romantic exercise that serves a vital purpose. It allows us to recognize ourselves in the other and to forge a connection that may be crucial to our well-being.

Eudora Welty once said of storytelling, "You need to tell the lies of fiction to get to the truth of human nature." Perhaps anthropomorphizing is a fiction that reveals the truth of ancient kinship.

Moussaieff writes about a Tanzanian game warden who fatally shot three female elephants and severely wounded a half-grown male. He was just doing his job, controlling the elephant population. What was not part of the job was killing mothers with calves. He had failed to see the two babies hidden behind the females' great bulk. When he realized his mistake, he attempted to frighten the babies away into deeper jungle, where he hoped the herd would adopt them. The babies refused to budge. Instead, they stubbornly leaned against the wounded male until they were able to support him sufficiently to lead him to safety.

Not a children's book, not an animal movie, whose producers know that the money is where the tears are. Not some fiction that makes us weep until we go home and hug our dog and feel better. If it is a fact, as Moussaieff suggests, that animals are capable of compassion and courage, what a dangerous world for us. Our hearts may not be built for the strain.

Not long ago, a three-year-old boy fell eighteen feet into the primate exhibit at Chicago's Brookfield Zoo, where, to the amazement of terrified witnesses, Binti Jua, an eight-year-old western lowland gorilla scooped up the child and carried him to safety. Frans B. M. de Waal, a scientist at Emory University's Yerkes Primate Center and author of *Good Natured: The Origins of Right and Wrong in Human and Other Animals*, saw this as evidence of compassion. He claims that to deny that animals possess qualities we deem exclusively "human" distorts our ability to make scientifically valid observations.

Granted, Binti Jua was raised by humans, who rewarded her for parental behavior, but "no one had ever taught her how to react to an unconscious boy invading her space." Dolphins in the wild are similarly "untrained" in rescue missions. It's not as though they're Coast Guard Academy graduates.

As further evidence to bolster his claim, De Waal cites a heroic dolphin deed in July 1995 in the Red Sea's Gulf of Aqaba. A swimmer attacked by sharks was suddenly surrounded by a school of dolphins slapping the water with their tails and flippers, successfully keeping the attacking sharks at bay.

Both examples, he asserts, go "a long way toward showing that compassion is a natural tendency in animals."

He's in the business of scientific observation, not sentimental wish fulfillment. Even Darwin knew that nature is more complicated than "a gladiator show . . . a grim arena where the strong eliminate the weak without second thought."

None of this surprises a romantic, who knows that avenues to truth are varied, who knows that even though our century reveres science and stakes its claims on empirical proof, proof and truth are not necessarily the same.

The truth, as I am coming to perceive or relearn as I travel widely in Central Park, is to be found in the passionate connection children have to their environment. Wordsworth knew this. I suppose we all did.

There was a meadow I played in as a child. Dappled with buttercups and bluets, it was there that I headed when the school bus dropped me off at the end of a long dirt road. Once there, I would fall spread-eagled to the ground to be cushioned by cool grass and covered by sky. A God sandwich, I called that moment when my body was spread thin between two slices of creation.

I had forgotten this until a recent rainy day when I was floating on my back in a tropical sea. Water from above filled my eyes and mouth as water below bolstered me. For an instant I was bound by Paradise.

I am learning that one of the great gifts of romance is its reminder of our rightful place in this God sandwich, snug between earth and firmament, awash in a lumpy, overflowing spread of creatures that creep, fly, and swim and those who are moved on occasion to proclaim, "This is good!"

Part II

ARCHITECTURE

8

A LOVE AFFAIR
WITH THE AIR

An architect makes love to the air. He believes that he can shape and thereby lay claim to it. He is at play in the fields of the Lord.

Let there be light and form and jubilant song fixed in brick, stone, timber, and mortar.

He is a naturalist who, pressing his nose against nature, caressing its land and sky, dreams of merger. Fingers of twelfth-century Gothic spires probe the clouds as though to release the power of heaven. The twentieth-century cantilevered, horizontal thrust of Frank Lloyd Wright's structures probe nature's mysteries, dividing air as a bird's wing slices it in flight, or a tree branch scrapes it in leafless winter.

The romantic architect takes on the mantle of divinity as he attempts to reveal what he senses to be divine. For him, as for Emerson and Wordsworth, divinity does not necessarily flow from a Godhead but is an eternally present, beneficent grace waiting to be found. He acts upon this belief against all odds. He puts his trust in the power of inspiration to pursue Paradise.

It is no accident that Pythagoras, sixth-century lover of form and secret worshiper of numbers, believed that the music of the spheres could be replicated by numbers, and that Italian Renaissance architect Palladio would use those formulas to create "harmonic" spaces aesthetically pleasing to the eye. Energy into matter. Matter into energy. And energy never dies. The great romance, albeit quantum physics. Music of the spheres transformed to geometric shapes, which bring music to mind.

Many years ago, I saw a *New York Times* photograph of Fallingwater, the 1935 house-on-a-waterfall Frank Lloyd Wright designed for Edgar and Lillian Kaufmann in rural southwestern Pennsylvania. I cut that picture out and carried it in my wallet for a long time, the way a guy might take his sweetheart's picture off to war or prison. A house in the woods, as discreetly part of its surroundings as bird song. A house not only built on a brook but inspired by and incorporating it. Every child's dream of home. A place among treetops built above a waterfall. A place for a wild child. A haven to keep her safe while she dreams of being one with nature. A grown-up's tree house. A twentieth-century Dove Cottage. Rousseau's cabin.

In the photograph, man's intrusion into nature appeared more sexual union than careless invasion. An act born of earthly love.

Frank Lloyd Wright first turned a sharp eye on the American landscape when he was mesmerized, as a small boy, by the way trees, boulders, plains gave shape to empty space. He longed to mimic that power. I wanted to see for myself if he had succeeded. If so, then I suspected that Fallingwater was more than brilliant design, that it was great romance.

9

TURN LEFT AT NORMALVILLE

—·—

This is country built on coal and dreams abandoned long ago. Perhaps, if it were May rather than November, the word "sad" wouldn't keeping coming to mind as I drive southwest from the Pittsburgh airport toward the West Virginia border. In spring, forgiving dogwood and exuberant foliage would steal attention from the bleakness of gray rock protruding from barren land, of two- and three-room tarpaper shacks abandoned in favor of rust-stained trailers propped on cinder blocks out back. Green pastures would nourish bony cows now seeking shelter beneath the few remaining eaves of skeletal barns.

The snow swirls around my car as I drive through California, Pennsylvania, about ten miles south of Houston, Pennsylvania, places where it's hard to imagine the sun ever shines. Gray rivers beneath gray skies, gray smokestacks no longer warmed by fires below.

Company towns, or coal-patch towns, as they're called around here. Owners came long enough to see that a mine would be profitable, erected makeshift housing for employees, and returned to their own cities. Most of the structures are built on river banks deep within shadow-oppressed hollows. Each town has a church, Baptist or Methodist, an occasional Assembly of God, but no one's left to rustle in the pews. No more restless, red-eared Sunday mornings in stiff, clean clothes, no more coughing against the silence, no more "Rock of Ages" sung out against hopelessness.

But for an occasional wisp of wood smoke rising from a chimney, I would take these for ghost towns, these tiny outposts with their lofty, anywhere-but-here names.

Sometimes you can tell when the inhabitants just gave up trying to make things right with a pretty name. There are Brave, Bumblebee, Jollytown, Lover, Fairchance, Fairhope, Good Intent, and Daisytown. And then there are Grindstone, Crucible, Saltlick, Cokesburg, Tire Hill, Newcomer, and Normalville.

In two hours of driving along two-lane roads, I've passed three centers of commerce, Dull's Market, Roko's All Sports Café, and the Stepping Stone Christian Book Store. A dented red pickup truck is parked in front of Dull's, Roko's has a fire going but no customers, and Stepping Stone is shut tight, waiting for a miracle. The slow amble of an old man is the only human movement in this place, so still that neither bird nor leaf disturbs the air. He walks along the side of the road, his chin and mouth hidden within a frayed wool collar, his gait giving the impression that there's nowhere to go.

I keep wondering if Frank Lloyd Wright noticed. This was the route he probably took on his first and many later journeys to the site upon which Pittsburgh department-store magnate Edgar Kaufmann commissioned him to design a family weekend retreat. How could something as romantic as Fallingwater, the resulting house, have been dreamed in this place that mocks dreams? And how could seventy thousand pilgrims a year make the same trek without leaving a trace? Traveling through this land that seems to have swallowed its settlers' hearts and souls, I feel as though I'm on the brink of a black hole in space.

Maybe in spring, I think. Maybe in spring it would be different. But Wright's visits were not limited to "pretty" seasons.

Through Ohiophyle and then, within five miles of my destination, I enter parkland, part of more than three thousand acres assembled by the Kaufmanns and their foundation, and given along with Fallingwater as a conservation in the care of the Western Pennsylvania Conservancy in 1963. Here the scene grows pastoral. No more buildings, no imagined fumes of long-cold coal. To my right are pine forests and to the left a tumultuous, wide brook rushing from a pounding waterfall. The road follows the water's lead, until a turnoff with a small wooden sign announces Fallingwater and indicates that buses are to park here.

Today there are no buses, no tourists, no pilgrims, no tours. The house is being restored and is closed for the season. I've been given permission to visit after having requested time alone with the house. "I want to get a sense of what it's about," I had said when making my reservation over the phone, thinking that in one visit such a thing would be possible. Such an over-estimation of power is part optimism, part pride as a safeguard against fear of questions without answers.

Four minutes past the turn-off I wonder if I've missed a driveway possibly obscured by the deep forest of second-growth trees rising high on either side of the narrow road. Now I'm certain that I'm lost. The dirt road dips into brief clearings then climbs back to pine and hemlock. I'm looking for a dramatic approach in which Fallingwater will await me like a Venetian doge seated at the top of the Palazzo's grand staircase. Like Chartres rising above fields of corn, visible for miles so that the pilgrim has something on which to fix her sights.

I drive by flat, concrete roofs that seem to tumble seriatim down the bank toward a stream. I could hit them with one toss of a stone, but feel as far away as a hawk circling overhead. I pause, wonder, and decide that the lack of drama and visual trumpet blare disqualify this as my destination. I continue on into deeper wilderness. Patches of ice skimming deep ruts crack beneath my tires, and a dense canopy of pines darkens the day. A gardener's truck approaches with rakes and shovels rattling in back. There's not enough room for two to pass, so I pull into frozen bracken, roll down my window and call out for directions. "You just drove past it," he shouts, not coming to a full stop and driving on.

I circle back, dip down a drive to my right. The pebbly roadway narrows to an aisle lined by looming rock ledges that almost scrape the sides of the car. I'm here. The series of roofs I'd seen from a hawk's view rise above and spill below these ledges. Far from presenting a ceremonial entrance, Fallingwater plays hide-and-seek. I could have missed it. The view contracts rather than widens. After receding enough to allow sun to penetrate this site, nature closes in. The porte-cochère, a reinforced concrete trellis through which an oak tree grows, creates a tunnel-like approach, with walls of native cliff on one side and the echoing stonework of the house on the other. I slow the car, fearful of removing its paint.

When my sister, brother, and I were children on family road trips, we were always excited by mountains that periodically gave way to tunnels along the Pennsylvania Turnpike. As we approached their wide-mouthed entrances, we beset our parents with questions. Was there always a hole in the mountain or did somebody have to dig it? How did they do that? What holds it up? Will it fall down? Our questions always ceased as we entered the dark caverns, suddenly hearing the sound of each other's breathing and the car's tires against pavement. I think Wright was similarly affected and re-created that experience in this approach to Fallingwater. We aren't meant to barge right in without a thought. We are meant to be full of eager questions, then to grow quiet enough to hear our breath, expectant enough to be a bit fearful and totally alert.

As I face the entrance door, I turn my back to banks of rhododendron and mountain-laurel bushes hovering above ivy and moss-covered rocks awash with spring water caught by cold air and fashioned into ice fangs grazing the driveway. It makes me laugh. Welcome to Fallingwater is not a trumpet blare but tinkling spring water frozen into silence. Dramatic photographs led me to imagine that I would be stunned by the crashing sounds of the falls, the rush of Bear Run. Instead, I am whispered into a welcome.

Clinton Piper, a young curatorial assistant who has agreed to meet me, opens a narrow, low door fashioned of clear glass recessed in stonework. Rather than finding myself in a great hall, I stand cosseted in a snug, rock-sided entryway beneath a six-foot-four ceiling. This offers me a moment to get my bearings. A respite from wilderness, a rest for my eyes. I'm reminded of the ritual of Eucharist when one kneels in silence and the priest invites participants to enter the ancient riddle, to empty ourselves so that we may be filled. Is it humanly possible to be that empty? To be that vigilant, that patient? As I stand here I begin to sense that Wright may be about to demonstrate just how this is done. In carefully delineated spaces on a modest human scale, one opening into another, the whole never visible from any part, he reminds us that we cannot predict our path, cannot see the universe in its entirety, can only wait for it to unfold. There is no "Presto!" and the flourish of a cape followed by revelation. The most we can do is meet each slow unfolding as though it were a magic trick. Because it is.

Clinton points the way to the living room, visible from where we stand. Cantilevered layers of stone form the back walls and the supporting beam to the right of sliding glass doors, which open onto a corner balcony above the waterfall. Along the entire southeastern exposure leading to and extending at a right angle from the doors, are windows framed in steel painted in Wright's signature Cherokee red, a color mixed to match the iron oxide of boulders. These windows stretch like crystal wings above cantilevered walnut benches upholstered in sandstone hues and anchoring the room as though to reassure that no pilot's voice will shortly announce takeoff.

At first, my attention is caught by the constant movement of tree branches scratching at the windows like eager hands. And then I am mesmerized by the way the clear glass plays with shadow and light as a cat will tease a sunbeam, as the stained glass at Chartres made me feel as though I were seeing light for the first time.

Of course, it wasn't the first time. The actual first time was a shock that occurred one May afternoon when our third-grade teacher held up a prism, told us that's what it was, walked to the window of our dusty, chalk-scented schoolroom, and adjusted the small glass object until it fragmented the invisible into rays of iridescent, dancing colors. I wondered back then what made her think she had the right. What made her think we were ready for such a thing? Once she had revealed that she held that power in her hand, I was never quite comfortable with her again.

But now I'm older, light deprived, and ready for this triumphant show. Wright is like a gleeful Prometheus who has gotten away with it and celebrates his catch by urging others to grab hold. He boldly sites the house so that neither the sun's fiery rising, nor setting, nor any rays in between can escape its claim. A greedy, joyous design.

"Let the modern now work with light," Wright wrote in 1931, "light diffused, light reflected, light refracted—light for its own sake." Especially for its own sake.

The Egyptian god Ra claims, "I am the one who openeth his eyes, and there is light."

Ha! says Einstein, "All the fifty years of conscious brooding have brought me no closer to the answer to the question, 'What are light quanta?' Of course today every rascal thinks he knows the answer, but he is deluding himself."

And a light came into the world.

And as Goethe lay dying his last words were, "More light. More light." I've always taken this for an announcement rather than a demand.

For Wright it seems to have been a mantra. The thick woods surrounding the site make shadows more prevalent than sunlight. And so it is the sudden presence of light that creates the drama in the approach to the house. The visitor emerges from the gloom of leafy overhang to view concrete roofs and terraces bathed in sun. The effect is so strikingly similar to that of Northern Renaissance paintings in which a golden nimbus glows above a sanctified subject that it gives the place a sense of being blessed. Here, in this embracing light, it seems inevitable that man would come to live a contemplative life. That here he would learn something about himself and the space he occupied and what they had to do with each other. Years later Edgar Kaufmann, Jr., would note that this was the place where his family experienced nature "as the habitat that has formed us."

This would have pleased the architect, whose design is based on the belief that nature imposes itself upon, changes, and possibly redeems us as surely as we impose ourselves upon it. First, Wright seems to tell us, we have to know our place. To that end, he sets us on the sun's path from the moment we enter the house from the east and follow the flow of interior spaces westward. Such an intimate dance with the universe has moved men vast distances in their souls and in fact.

And they followed a great star that was in the east. Oh, we are very wise men, indeed.

Sunbeams bounce off the living room's sandstone floor, a surface surprisingly dry to my touch, considering that it looks like a saturated, glacial brook bed. "Johnson's Liquid Wax, every Monday," Clinton explains. Its massive, irregularly shaped stones were quarried on the property then cut and polished, not for the man-over-nature perfection of marble, but to pay homage, to remind us of the power of water, ice, and ages. To remind us of the ground upon which we stand. To humble us.

The pale gray, cantilevered stones of exterior and interior walls were similarly quarried and stacked to resemble not only the ledges along the banks of the immediate site, but those that line the two-hour approach to the house. They fit into the region's natural scheme of things and speak of its history, more than 600 million years of struggle and surrender between retreating sea and earthly forces, of horizontal plains buckling into parallel folds of stone. Here those foreboding protuberances are domesticated, but not dominated. I have the sense that if the waterfall would just be quiet for a moment, and if I could achieve just the right amount of watchful silence, I might hear these stones sing their ancient stories, might awaken to the fact that the earth moves under my feet and nothing is ever quite certain, not even time and space. Rock of ages in a quantum universe.

I turn my back to the living-room windows and what begins to feel like an assault of sun and nature's nagging, as persistent as any two-year-old's. My retreat leads to the stony gray corner of the room where the hearth waits. How odd that this is the verb one thinks of, but it is what a hearth appears to do. Wait for a fire. Wait for our presence. An expectant womb of stone. There are no screens to discourage the sense of being inevitably drawn to it as to a campfire.

A massive boulder splits and spreads like lava from beneath the hearth into the room. "We can see the base of that rock if you want to come with me to the basement," Clinton offers. Assenting, I run my hand along its cold surface as we make our steep descent to where the boulder rises through the cellar floor. It seems to have insisted on its right to be here and Wright complied, sensing when to shape nature and when to allow it to shape him. The boulder became the anchor from which the main spaces swing as lightly as a boat in harbor. The living room to the south, swooping out over the falls, the kitchen snug in the west, stairs and passageways along the north, entrance to the east. "On this rock will I build my church."

For all of Fallingwater's stark simplicity, in spite of its coy teasing and persistent wooing of nature, for all its lack of grandeur, it reminds me of Gothic cathedrals. The stone reminds me, the silence reminds me, and above all, the pervasive sense that this design was born of a knowledge I can only intuit. This was the house of Wright's old age and could only have been divined after life had been lived in the full panoply of suffering and joy that brings one to the cool, clear certainty that we are here for but the blink of an eye. Wise elders tell me that all that matters before the slow inevitable closing of the eye is to search for truth and beauty, and if they are found, to share the sight.

After years of retreat and lack of work, having reached the age of sixty-eight, Wright knew something I want to know. I feel if I stay here long enough I might begin to understand. Such a quest for knowledge is a sensuous beckoning, different from a drive to know the names of fifty states and their capitals, or batting averages, or the recipe for perfect pie crust. I suspect it's more like the desire experienced by some as they age to learn ancient Greek. Journalist I. F. Stone began his studies at sixty-eight. Oliver Wendell Holmes returned to them at the end of his life. Writer Paul Beeching came to the language in his late fifties. As he and his teacher translated lines from *Anabasis*, describing the defeated Greeks' joy at reaching their long-sought escape, these two twentieth-century, sedentary, middle-aged men alone in a small classroom, "Unable to contain ourselves, began shouting, 'The sea! The sea! Thalatta! Thalatta!'" He knew in that instant why he had been drawn to this perplexing undertaking, the study of two-thousand-year-old sentences. "I knew then what I was doing. I knew that unconsciously I had always longed for this sort of firsthand knowledge of the beautiful, and I was now aware that time was growing short."

This has nothing to do with reason or intellect or competition or being "cultured," it has to do with tapping into the river of time and human yearning. Beeching tells us that the Greeks sang of life and death, "especially death" and he recalls Miss Tew, a retired classics teacher from his past. He imagines her today, sitting in the sun of her New Orleans balcony, reading the *Iliad*. As she reads, her lips move, "a sure sign that she is getting very old and she is still singing."

Fallingwater is Frank Lloyd Wright singing. It is no accident that one thinks of music in this house. It is not just the distant, constant sound of the falls, although that serves as a reminder that all the senses must be awake in order to "see." Rather, the design itself seems musical, as though melody has been shaped by reinforced concrete. I keep imagining Bach's *B Minor Suite*, his cantatas and fugues, his partitas reminiscent of rain splashing from tree leaf to rocky banks and river, gathering force in the falls and then surrendering to the seaward journey.

What is dramatically different about occupying rather than looking at pictures of the house is that the photographs are of still, silent spaces which, when visited, are found to be vibrating with energy. It is like the difference between staring at musical notation on a page if you don't read music and being at a concert. As the music itself begins to surround, envelop, and then penetrate us, the experience becomes visual as well as auditory. Music creates shadows and light in the same way an artist does through chiaroscuro. The spaces of Fallingwater are alive with the "sounds" of shadow, light and history.

The design echoes the Pythagorean belief that the mysterious "harmony" of numbers creates what is beautiful to the eye and soul. That when architecture incorporates celestial music in specific geometric shapes the spaces "sing."

Perhaps this is why we feel such a palpable presence in ancient buildings long unoccupied. The Pantheon and Parthenon built on Pythagorean, harmonic proportions are powerfully seductive. We feel as though our eyes will allow us to merge with the mystery we encounter there.

And they return us to nature, which was here in the first place. The spiral of seeds within a sunflower, the numbers of petals on flowers, the distance between leaves growing on a branch all similarly satisfy the Pythagorean mathematical for- mula for the golden section, the means to truth and beauty.

We don't need to know all this as we stand in any space that awakens our senses. If we hear music as we stare at proportion and design, it is not because we understand mathematics or physics or Pythagoras, but because we naturally sense what has always been here and was later explained in theorem and equation.

I ask Clinton if he ever hears music as he stands in these spaces, or gazes at the exterior from the many vantage points on the property, upward from the falls, or downward from the bank above the guest quarters. "No, but a professor of architecture at Victoria University of Wellington in New Zealand recently visited and said that being here is like listening to Beethoven's *Pathétique*."

"Absolutely not!" my oboist friend Bill Frosch demurs when I return home with the news. "Fallingwater is much too restrained for Beethoven. Bach is what that house is all about. Specifically his *23rd Cantata*." He asks, "Have you ever noticed how that piece unfolds without a clue as to what will follow, how its strange changes of key startle, how you know that everything fits together, but the whole is somehow evasive? How it is full of surprise and flight and yet, at the end, returns to the rock solid base?" Well, no, actually, I haven't, but it sure sounds like Fallingwater to me.

It makes sense, considering Wright's early exposure to music, thanks to his father's keen ear and lively interest. He once told a group of architecture students, "Poets are the ones you want to consort with if you're architects. . . . And music, Beethoven, all the real originals, Bach, too." As a child in his prairie home, he would fall asleep with the sound of music in his ears as his father played downstairs, late into the night. "My father taught me to see a sym- phony as an edifice of sound and I never listen to a symphony

now that I don't see a building." Like music, he told them, architecture is "the rhythm and expression of the human soul and the
spirit." Like any masterpiece, an edifice is "a warm outpouring of
the heart of man, [of] human delight in life . . . we glimpse the infinite. That glimpse . . . is what makes art sacred."

I'm relieved. Even though I understand that in order to
"know" a work of art, we must suspend disbelief and allow our
uncensored responses free reign, my conviction wavers owing to
an immediate distrust of precisely that nonverbal, visceral
response. I feel safer with the scholarly, with something somebody
really smart has said or written before. As a result, I am in awe of
the courage of the English Romanticists—Blake, Coleridge,
Wordsworth, Shelley, and Keats—who held steadfastly to their
belief in the integrity of the individual's response to experience
and the crucial role of imagination and intuition in revealing its
camouflaged truths. How brave of them to trust that. To commit
their lives to it. To keep singing it until the end. After all, they were
singing in a time infatuated with Locke and Newton, and the
concept of the individual as a mere passive observer of an exter-
nal, mechanistic world.

These Romanticists gave us their notion of things. No formulas, no theorems, no proofs. They simply gave us a language
for the heart. They said our lives depended on it. Even though
their religious persuasions varied from Catholicism to Panthe-
ism, in their creative lives they seem to have adhered to
Thomas's warning in the Gnostic Gospels. "If you bring forth
what is within you, what you bring forth will save you. If you
do not bring forth what is within you, what you do not bring
forth will destroy you." Nothing more. Nothing less.

Naturally, they were often dismissed as overwrought. Today
we tend to distrust their lack of "edge." Yet lately I'm wondering just what we've gained through this affection for the edge?
What insight? Of course it protects us from being unsettled by
experience born of vulnerability. My father used to say,
"Nobody likes a smart aleck." Shows you what he didn't know.
In my town, in my time, just about everybody loves a smart
aleck. They're the ones invited to the parties.

For all their belief in the power of the self, the Romanticists were selfless compared to us smart alecks. Their selves were in service to a higher power, the divine gift of imagination capable of unlocking the secrets of the universe.

I wish I had the courage to live like that, to trust my instincts instead of looking over my shoulder to see what sages of old have to say on the subject. It serves me right, I think, when I check in with them upon my return home and discover that Goethe, who absolutely trusted the power of instinct, noted, "I call architecture frozen music." I feel as though he's shaking his finger at my wavering faith in the validity of immediate, sensorial experience. "The senses do not deceive," he scolds, "but the judgment deceives."

Goethe was optimistically certain that our senses, dulled by institutional learning, could be awakened and sharpened by use. Like the Romanticists who emulated him, he believed in using the self as a sounding board to discern the hidden harmonies within a basically beautiful world. Such availability, he believed, would awaken in us new organs of perception. The act of looking would create seeing and seeing in turn would deepen our ability to look. Thoreau and Emerson were to carry on in this tradition. So does Tom Fiore.

Before departing for Pennsylvania, I'd walked to Central Park with dog and binoculars. Nothing. Just the usual pigeon, starling, and sparrow. I headed for the boat house and the "Bird Book" to see if keener eyes and ears had detected what I had missed. Oh, yes, indeed, there was a complete page of single-spaced, handwritten notations. The ballpoint pen had left such deep depressions in the white-lined paper that it was as though the words had been written in Braille. Tom's observations are always noted with this focused, physical intensity.

"Hermit Thrush . . . Wood Duck . . . American Coot, 2 adult Mute Swans, pair of Buffleheads, 12 Northern Shovelers, 8 Ruddy Ducks . . . great Blue Heron and Ringnecked pheasant . . . Tufted Titmice, White-breasted Nuthatches . . . Dark-eyed Juncos . . . Pied-billed Grebe . . . Yellow-bellied Sapsucker, Hairy Woodpecker . . . Mockingbird." No wonder he presses his pen into the page so hard. He's writing for the blind.

He generously tells us the specifics of where to look, echoing Goethe's certainty that we simply have to open our senses in order to see. Here's how. If you want to spot the evasive long-eared owl, Tom advises, "try standing on the flat boulder and looking into the branches, about three feet *left* of the trunk. You should manage to see it." Yeh, right.

I'm happy he has faith in our senses; sometimes I fear that I've been educated out of mine. If we listen like Pythagoras, if we watch like Galileo, will we really gain the ears to hear and the eyes to see? I want to believe it. Tom Fiore makes me think it might be so.

Wright asks us to bring that faith to the slow, unpredictable unfolding of Fallingwater. Mix it all up, he seems to say. Listen with your eyes, look with your ears. Like all true romantics, he urges us to forfeit our preconceptions, our habits of perception. He dares us to be present in the space, to wait to see what it has to say to us.

He asks no more of us than he did of himself when standing on this site waiting for nature to speak. And it did. The very stones sang for him. Their song, he said, was "a story and a longing to me." The stream's song would stay in his ears long after he returned home to Taliesin and his drafting board, and it was that song, along with the wind in the trees, the longing of stone, the heartache sung by the wood thrush, that would become manifest in his design. He wrote Kaufmann after that first visit that "a domicile has taken vague shape in my mind to the music of the stream."

It is therefore not surprising that at Fallingwater the wonder and awe inspired by the structure are a result of nonstructure. We are moved because there is nothing to hold on to. We dare to be moved because we are anchored in stone. Wright's gift for creating space that both secures and launches us made me imagine I had a hawk's view upon my approach and continue to feel as though I'm soaring even within the house. That gift makes the spaces sing.

The power of shaped emptiness is dramatized by structures without visible means of support; cantilevered balconies that propel themselves into open air, cantilevered shelving, desks, couches,

ottomans, and night tables that jut out into the interiors. As dramatically as flying buttresses in the twelfth century, they mock our
traditional concepts of support and bolstering, gravity and possibility

"Oh, yeh?" Wright seems to challenge us. "You think you
know how gravity works? Well, watch this." With which he
turns floors into bird wings testing the air. "You think you
know where you begin and nature ends? Well, take a look at
this!" He welcomes boulders to the hearth, invites a tree into
the porte-cochère, makes us walk on water.

In "Thirteen Ways of Looking at a Blackbird," poet Wallace
Stevens muses, "I do not know which to prefer, / The beauty of
inflections / Or the beauty of innuendoes, / The blackbird
whistling / Or just after."

Fallingwater is inflection and innuendo, structure and suggestion, spaces singing because strictly shaped by instruments of concrete and steel, as Pythagoras shaped celestial sound with precisely
proportioned strings. Yes, an edifice is an "outpouring," a "song,"
but it rises in answer to mathematical expectations.

Late sixteenth-, early seventeenth-century astronomer and
philosopher Johannes Kepler believed that the planets "sang" as
they orbited the sun.

Eastern mystics have proclaimed that there is a vibration
that fills the air, a beautiful harmony underlying the apparent
chaos of existence. We can feel it, they tell us, we can hear it if
we'd just sit still, just be quiet.

And the Romanticists, in spite of their compulsion for creative expression, sent the same message. Just stop talking, stop
making such a racket and you'll discover that these spaces aren't
as empty as they appear. They have a life of their own. See and
hear what they have to say and then sing your song, tell your
story, design your dwelling. Make the planets sing. Shape the
void with a poem, a cantata, a seductive shape. Bring back the
news, they urged us. Tell us what you discovered on your watch.

It could be argued that there's nothing to be discovered.
Nothing "real" that can't be touched, smelled, seen, that won't
answer to laboratory testing or intellect. It could be surmised that

we indulge pretty fantasies of hidden harmony to serve our propensity for order. Our reason is not programmed for comfort within chaos. Our reason is like our mother's surprise arrival in a messy dormitory room or our mother-in-law coming upon last night's dirty dinner dishes in the sink. Reason scurries around to set things straight.

And yet mystery will have its way with us. Sometimes it breaks into the most rational and scientific of minds. Once when my husband and I were together in Venice, he repeatedly turned to me and asked, "Do you hear it?" "What?" "That music." "What music?"

We'd be chugging up the Grand Canal on a crowded *vaporetto*, walking home, single file, down a narrow alley after dinner, or sitting at breakfast, when he would suddenly listen with intensity and be mystified by my response, No, I did not hear it.

Not even at two in the morning, the time of least distraction, when he wakened me to ask, "*Now* do you hear it?" We lay silently in the dark, and all that I could hear was the call of a seabird and the creak of gondolas shifting at their moorings. I turned on the light. There were tears running down his face. "It's so beautiful," he said.

I had to wait a few years before my own experience with the merger of space, time, and sound. I had traveled alone on assignment to the Rhine country of southwestern Germany. It was cold and very quiet that late afternoon in November when I checked into an otherwise deserted former hunting lodge in dense pine forests high above the river. I accepted the concierge's suggestion that I warm myself with tea, cakes, and sweet wine. Once I was settled into thick down cushions before a baronial fireplace and experiencing that particular contentment that comes from shutting out the cold, filling the stomach, and sitting before a fire, the waiter asked if I liked music. "Yes. Very much." "Well, then, you should know that the nuns sing at vespers at the Abbey of St. Hildegarde of Bingen." He explained that a half hour's walk through the vineyards would bring me there just in time.

I bundled up against the still, dry cold of the dark evening and found my way to a serpentine path across the vineyard's frozen ground. Just as I began to fear that I might get lost, a full moon rose above a distant spire. This was the rebuilt abbey of nuns devoted to the work of Hildegarde, twelfth-century mystic, composer, naturalist, poet, early environmentalist, feminist, and founder of two monastic orders. Although she's never been canonized, she is known around here as Saint, and why not? She's also referred to as the Sibyl of the Rhine, owing to a talent for prophesy that brought political as well as religious pilgrims to her door. The original abbey across the river burned to the ground and the order reestablished itself in the midst of this isolated vineyard so high above of the Rhine that lit tugboats working through the night look like fireflies over water.

When I reached the stone church surrounded by thick walls resembling those of a medieval castle, it seemed so deserted that I supposed there must have been a mistake. The only sound came from the wind's movement against the frozen resistance of barren vines. The first two doors that I tried to open were bolted shut. I circled around to the side of the church and saw steps leading to another door. This one gave to my weight and opened onto space made dramatic by vaulted ceilings that urged eye and spirit upward. The pews were wooden and empty. Dim light came from candles on an altar decorated with pine and holly boughs from the surrounding woods. As I entered, I again wondered if there had been some mistake, something missed in translation, but it seemed to matter less and less as the stillness slowly became a comforting presence rather than the mere absence of sound.

A nun's black habit rustled as she walked up the aisle and sat opposite me. Her shallow breathing and the dull, thin retort of rosary bead against bead, the occasional snap of candle flame caught by a breeze stealing in through chinks in stone were the only sounds.

She rose from her knees and approached me with an open book. One side in Latin, the other in German. We smiled at each other as I accepted the gift as though any of it would do me the least bit of good.

Then the music came. For the first time I understood the expression "otherworldly." I had never understood how sound could evoke such a response. If it were, in fact, "otherworldly," how would we know? And yet that was what I seemed to be hearing. I'm still uncertain why it brought to mind Pythagoras's music of the spheres, which is not available to our ordinary range of hearing.

Perhaps it was like Justice Potter Stewart's consideration of whether pornography was protected by the First Amendment. As he joined the court's struggle to define pornography he sputtered with exasperation, "I know it when I see it."

I knew celestial music when I heard it, although I couldn't define it. The mellow, sad tones of an ancient wind instrument hovering over a dark plain. Haunting, lonely cadences making loneliness keen and sharp like footsteps against the cobblestones of an empty Italian square at midnight. A reminder that the spaces we yearn to fill are as untouchable as infinity.

Soon harmonies embraced, bolstered, flew above, and danced alongside the original lone sound. The music became a melding, a combination of what it was and the echo of itself. It began to occur to me that what I was hearing was the a cappella choir of Hildegarde's nuns cloistered behind a screen.

If we, their audience of two, had not been there, would they have sung? Of course. They didn't even know we were there. Their song was inspired and received by something beyond my power to comprehend.

Kepler believed that the art of singing polyphonically was man's discovery of music that imitated God, a means of reproducing "the everlastingness of all created time in some short part of an hour."

My presence was incidental, like that of a wanderer in a summer pasture where a meadowlark begins to sing. Even the Kaufmanns' presence at Fallingwater was incidental, although they commissioned, owned, and inhabited it.

Frank Lloyd Wright had no choice but to sing, so inspired was he by the site's clear run of brook, constant tumble of falls, stubborn rise of ancient boulders, a sky shaped by branches, sharply delineated in winter, festooned in summer. Nature's intrinsic harmony sang through him and became manifest. Like Bach, what choice did he have?

And like Bach he invites us to follow and we do, though we don't have a clue where we'll end up. We follow because the beauty of this moment makes us trust the next. The bass notes—walls, ceilings, floors—secure us for the flight of arpeggios. We stake our lives on this slow unfolding, room by room, note by note.

The Ryoan-Ji Zen garden in Kyoto refuses to be seen with a sweep of an eye. A visitor can only meditate on each of its intricate spaces. One at a time. To this end, the use of cameras is discouraged, lest you fool yourself into thinking you can capture its entirety. Lest you lose your focus through your desire for memento.

Like that garden, like Bach's music, Fallingwater asks for nothing and everything in return, our full attention. To keep us on our toes, the attention is required to shift constantly. A dance between our conscious observation and the artist's preconscious inspiration.

Wright uses the hallways of Fallingwater to this end. Unlike those unremarkable, blank spaces in many homes, passageways here take on the excitement of anticipatory approach like that inspired by cathedral aisles and pilgrims' paths. Stark, narrow, stone-lined, and darker than their adjoining rooms, these hallways awaken an ancient, amorphous fear and thrill, that enduring impulse to move ahead even if what awaits is unseen, uncharted, and holds only a promise of light. These passages allow us to get our bearings, like the inlaid stone labyrinth on the floor just within the doors of Chartres cathedral. When the medieval pilgrim finally reached his destination, he was required to walk the labyrinth to its center, where he was to pray before the cathedral would "receive" him. A meditation to quiet the chatter of the mind, the overwhelming excitement of arrival, the lust of the eye. In its hallways, Fallingwater closes around us, gives us respite from and prepares us for awe. The brief absence of light deepens our awareness of an ancient dependency.

Wright domesticates the very elements that have inspired and terrified man since the beginning of time. By containing, framing, and making them safe, he allows us to observe their power in quiet wonder. Earth, fire, air, water. The floors look like water; we never stop hearing the sound of water. The floors are made of the earth's floor. Standing on them, we become part of all time.

Fallingwater invites us in shyly, makes us comfortable without fuss or frills, and then delivers us to some place we had no intention of going. We realize a great romantic ideal by becoming part of an endless chain of being. Fallingwater succeeds in clearing our eyes of Einstein's "optical delusion" that we are separate and distinct from nature and each other, past and future.

Maybe when people speak of being kidnapped by aliens, this is all they're describing, the experience of going along, minding their own business, expecting this day to be like any other, and suddenly being caught off guard so that habitual perception gives way to something wonderful and strange. How to explain it? We hate that we can't. Not being in control of our destiny is abhorrent. Better an out-of-body experience, an alien visitation.

I had expected this very earthly visit to be a form of respect due one of America's great architectural landmarks. I wanted to study how the uniquely American, dual dream of existing in forest primeval and the full flush of industrial progress could be made visible in one dwelling. To see for myself the insistently horizontal lines probing the unknown of here and now rather than Gothic, vertical thrusts toward the unknown of heaven.

If we have a national religion, it is a belief that the promised land is here at hand, or at the very farthest just over the horizon and certainly within the borders. It's here for the taking, and Fallingwater is its cathedral, a structure embodying our faith in the power of not being fenced in, of being free of the confines of class, birth, tradition; steadfast but capable of great change at the last moment.

Fallingwater turns out to be a structural response to questions raised by Wallace Stevens in his poem "Sunday Morning," a hymnal echo of Emerson.

What is divinity if it can come
Only in silent shadows and in dreams?

Shall she not find in comforts of the sun,
In pungent fruit and bright, green wings, or else
In any balm or beauty of the earth,
Things to be cherished like the thought of heaven?

The poet's own answer becomes the definitive statement of the essentially American "religion":

Divinity must live within herself:
Passions of rain, or moods in falling snow;
Grievings in loneliness, or unsubdued
Elations when the forest blooms; gusty
Emotions on wet roads on autumn nights . . .

What I had found in Central Park, the meadows of child-hood, the waters of a tropical sea, a painting in the Prado, these elations, and gusty emotions I now find in Fallingwater.

That is why I've come. Perhaps you have been to Oak Park, Illinois, or the Wright homes and studios at Taliesin East and Tal-iesin West. Perhaps you've visited his Prairie houses and Holly-wood houses, and now you come to see what Wright designed in old age. Perhaps you're like the man I met at the Vermeer exhibi-tion in Washington, D.C., who stood shakily supported by his walker and wept as he told me, "I've spent my entire adult life traveling the world looking at Vermeers and now I've seen them all." He reminded me of the old lady in Truman Capote's story "A Christmas Memory," who tells her young companion as they watch their kites take to a cold, blue sky, "As for me, I could leave the world with today in my eyes."

Perhaps you come to Fallingwater because you're a culture collector, and there's nothing wrong with that. But I think that chances are pretty good that, like me, you come looking for the beauty of inflection and are baffled to find instead the beauty of innuendo.

The structure, poised for flight like a great blue heron at water's edge, releases our imaginations to soar beyond its walls. Fallingwater urges us to consider infinity. It catches us up in a poetry of space that points beyond itself as the poetry of words points to what is beyond the power of words.

This is the great romance of the house. Wright's structure is merely a kick start to our imaginations his way of showing us what he had seen, and doubtless only seen in fleeting flashes of insight and light. It presents us with the paradox of romance, allowing us to sense what we do not know, to see what will remain unseen, seducing us and eluding our grasp. We also know that by the mere fact of being here we have been changed.

Romantic structure demands this and only this, that we surrender to the possibility of merger and transformation. Wright, an enthusiastic pianist, said that he did not so much play the piano as allow it to play him. He expects the same of us, to allow ourselves to be played by the inflection and innuendo of his design. Our reward is the reward of the romantic moment in which surrender carries us beyond the limits of ourselves.

Such a journey doesn't necessarily require a trip to this site or other historic monuments. And it certainly doesn't require advanced studies or critic's credentials. We lose our sense of physical boundaries when making love. We travel beyond what we assumed were the limits of our intellects when reading Shakespeare's sonnets. We forfeit the loneliness of passive observation when we stand before a painting long enough to become participants in the artist's vision. The romantic moment offers us as close an encounter with infinity as we are apt to have in this life. And it comes so quickly and dissipates so swiftly that we are not certain it has happened at all. "Do you hear the music?" my husband asked and no, I did not. By the time I listened, all I heard was the sound of water splashing against the walls of fifteenth-century palazzi.

This is what the Romanticists urged us to see, to hear, the idea of the thing as well as the thing itself. What Emerson saw in the face of nature, what Wallace Stevens heard in the silence after a blackbird sang, what the mystic experiences when kneeling in prayer or sitting in meditation, what the quantum physicist knows but is hard pressed to tell in language we can understand, these are mysteries stuttering toward expression. The world is emblematic. The romantic moment is our opportunity to see beyond the emblem to the infinite idea, to what Keats called Truth and Beauty. It requires contemplation, coming to rest within ourselves, daring to put down our armor and open to experience without knowing what to expect. Romance will always deliver us to a place beyond our expectations. Guaranteed.

My husband looked at Venice and heard music. Clinton and I move into the kitchen of Fallingwater, and I hear Bach in a simple, small, silent room furnished foremost with sunlight. The old wood-burning Aga stove purchased by Edgar Kaufmann, Jr., duplicates the one used for cooking when this was home rather than museum. The original refrigerator is small, the sink simple porcelain. Outside the southern wall of windows trees open and close their embrace of sky. Clinton moves to the corner where the window is free of horizontal framing in order to open our view to the outside and to dramatize the sense that nature is pushing against the panes. He opens a section and the sound of the falls rushes in. He smiles at my response to this sudden additional presence. "That's why every room has a window like this," he explains.

Did the cooks wear sunglasses? I want to know. Did they ever complain that cooking in nature was not as comfortable as back home in the Pittsburgh kitchen? Here there are no barriers to the light, no escaping it. It warms and blinds. We squint against it and retreat to darker stairs, ascending to three bedrooms on the second floor and one on the third. None are much larger than monastic cells. The master bedroom, the largest of the upstairs rooms, is 14 feet 11 inches by 17 feet, its terrace 255 square feet. The room's stark simplicity prohibits any distraction from the show going on just beyond the walls. Here too light is the honored, invited guest, the sun by day, lit hearth by night.

A framed section of the score for Bach's *English Suite* hangs on the wall above the hearth. Did the Kaufmanns also hear music here? Is that why they hung this gift from Paul Koch as the focal point of the room?

We step outside onto a cantilevered terrace just beyond the bed. The sun warms us against the brisk wind that causes oak, maple, and beech trees to sway. All is silent but for the call of a jay and the constant flow of water, gently from springs, a barely perceptible soprano above the bass notes of Bear Run falling from rocky heights to cold, rushing depths.

"How many bathrooms you got here?" I ask Clinton as I imagine twenty-five tourists overcome by this constant bladder stimulation. "The birds love it here," he says in response. Clinton is a shy lad.

What's not to love? Running water, promised perches, havens among branches. Thinking of "my" hawks back home, I ask if there are Fallingwater hawks. "Oh, yes, in the spring and summer they're plentiful. As are scarlet tanagers, indigo buntings. Right now we mostly have chickadees and cardinals, juncoes and titmice. I don't know, there are bird books in the house; we could look it up."

But we forget about birds as we walk into Edgar Kaufmann's sitting room. As in the other rooms there is the fireplace that looks as though it has been carved into the stone wall of a cave, a sort of sight gag to open the mind to the entire history of a species drawn to contained fire for warmth, love, and stories. A cantilevered terrace opens onto sunlight and the music of the falls. A chickadee sings in the woods.

Books on design, art, city planning, and nature line shelves and lie on tree-stump tables made from chestnut trees, "killed when a blight took most of those on the property." The Kaufmanns were early and adamant environmentalists. Had they wanted to chop down a live tree the hand of Frank Lloyd Wright would have stayed their own.

Even long distance his high and at times fierce moral stand loomed over them. Once, in a scolding letter, he told Edgar Kaufmann that he didn't even deserve the house. "To hell with the whole thing," was his response upon learning that, at the behest of Kaufmann's Pittsburgh engineers, additional steel beams, twice the weight of reinforcing rods specified by Wright, had been installed, "for safety," beneath the main floor. It would turn out, years later that this "support" added hazardous weight to the cantilevering.

I ask Clinton if that nervous act of defiance could be responsible for the fact that the house now groans and gives beneath its mass, requiring workmen like those who have just arrived with tarps, fans, and tools to hoist the living room's great floor stones and add yet additional support. "Nobody knows," he says. "But the house was overbuilt." There are problems in Paradise. "The flat roofs leak on rainy days, on snowy days, and on sunny days when the snow melts." Though Wright was certain that the parapets strengthened the horizontal concrete slabs, it begins to appear that they weigh on them.

Clinton steers us from personal praise or blame and he is right. This house moves beyond personality quirks and the ubiquitous human need to be right, to be boss, to take dominion everywhere. For all its unpredictable twists and turns, this house sets things straight. It reminds us where we stand in the scheme of things, on a bridge between man and nature, visible and invisible, mass and energy, knowledge and mystery, isolation and union, discord and harmony. The bridge we must cross from Bear Run wilderness to the house, the bridge of terraces over the falls, the covered bridge connecting main house to hillside and staff quarters, all these remind us.

Clinton and I enter an enclosed passageway that will lead us from the second floor of the main house to the hillside site of guest and servant quarters. Although we remain inside, a cliff protrudes into our path and its crevices shine with the runoff of melting snow. The moss garden that I had noticed as I entered the house continues its greeny growth inside these walls. We follow it to an opening onto a path that in turn opens to the hill. Above us is a canopy of concrete that dips and folds like water running down a brook bed. If we could freeze-frame the water of Bear Run as it surges over the falls, this is what it would look like. Below the eight-foot canopy a small ceramic jar rests as though to catch the "water" as well as to draw the eye to the play of light around a spherical surface in contrast to the flat planes.

At the top of the path a thirty-foot pool follows the brow of the hill and is sunk below sandstone terraces resembling the floors of the house. Cantilevered steps descend into dark water, reflecting maple, sycamore, mountain laurel, and white sky. With a wild, chaotic flow of stems, wisteria appears to grow directly from the beams and frames of the trellised entrance, Wright's reminder that we do not take dominion everywhere. We can honor nature, we can welcome, revere, and mimic it. But in the end it will transform us. Wisteria will have its way.

As I stand inside the guest quarters, a smaller version of the main house, and look down at the winding steps that have brought me here, I know that every sensual pleasure, whether warmth, the sight of still water, or distant sound of falls and rustling of frosted mountain laurel, are all a deliberate effect of Wright's design.

He knew how to effect a creative partnership with materials, geometric shapes, sound, and light. This was more than scientific and mathematical engineering. This was a love affair. The materials, he said, "are all by nature, friendly and beautiful." And he used them to reflect a deeply romantic view of the universe, a belief that it will comfort as well as confront, that order and harmony exist within the apparent chaos. That we may safely dwell in a world that wants to be beautiful.

Historian and author Elaine Pagels tells me of a night driving through the Colorado mountains with her late husband, physicist Heinz Pagels. "Suddenly it was as though I were seeing all the pine trees in a new light. I asked Heinz, 'Do you suppose those trees and the stars are in some sort of musical, mathematical harmony?'" She adds, "It was a moment of astonishment and I have no idea where the perception came from, but Heinz surprised me. He said, 'Of course. That's what physics is all about.'"

Pythagoras, Kepler, quantum physicists, Wright, cathedral builders all have shared that moment of astonishment and staked their lives on it.

Romance dares us to do the same with its insistent reminder that we exist in a state of perpetual merging within one large quantum soup. It is the means by which we very ordinary mortals cross the limitations of space and time without benefit of Hubble telescope or atom smashers or a genius for numbers. It is how we, without the gifts of Bach and Beethoven and the English Romantic poets and Homer and the Barbizon school of artists and Olmsted and Thoreau, transport ourselves across the boundaries that habitual perception have taught us are impenetrable. It is how we come home.

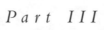

Part III

THE WORLD IS A
GREAT BIG TOY

10

WE'LL TURN MANHATTAN
INTO AN ISLE OF JOY

A month into my return from Fallingwater, I want to leave again. Although I assert that romance is in our own backyards, they can begin to look awfully backyardy after a while. We know where the puddles collect after rain. We know the bare spots where the grass won't grow. We know the same old crow that calls from the same old pine too early in the morning. Where's the romance in all this familiarity? A bit like a spouse. Loved, but, oh, it's you again.

There's a reason the Romantic poets found inspiration in leaving home. Byron to Venice and Greece, Shelley to Lake Como. The restrained Henry James's imagination took flight when he was on the other side of the Atlantic. Daisy Miller could only exist in Rome. Goethe writes that the first act of nineteenth-century Germans crossing the Italian border was to get drunk.

There is a release of inhibition once we leave home. A sharpening of the senses, a readiness for adventure and discovery.

Did Thoreau insist that all that was right here between our door and gate because he couldn't afford the fare beyond? Didn't want to leave Mom? Suffered travel phobias?

His challenge looms again and I adjust the focus of the witnessing eye on the here and now of my life.

Knowing of my restlessness, a friend who believes romance lies anywhere but here invites me to Tahiti. I am tempted, very,

very tempted, but I have a date with Jacques Torres, executive pastry chef of Le Cirque 2000. Jacques of sugar-spun fantasies, Jacques of the miniature chocolate stove, Jacques of the palate's delight. Jacques who smells like freshly scraped vanilla beans.

In late March, when the air matched the color of the pavement, I ventured into the whimsical warmth of the restaurant. Le Cirque of the snootiness.

I wanted to see how owner Sirio Maccioni had maintained the circus theme of his former restaurant when he moved it from the Mayfair Hotel on Sixty-fifth and Park Avenue to the Villard mansion on Madison and Fiftieth Street. The Villard mansion where the Landmarks Preservation Commission is boss and sees that Nothing Is Altered. The Villard mansion with its interiors by Stanford White, celebrating America's Gilded Age when an eighteen-year-old Bavarian named Hidgard could come to America without money or passable English, change his name to Villard because he liked the French sound of it, head out West, make his fortune in railroads, return to Manhattan, hire McKim, Mead & White to design a mansion in the style of a cinquecento palazzo and move in by the age of thirty.

How to take august space decorated with Landmark-sanctified paintings and with ceilings gilded like the dome of heaven and make it so droll that a little lame balloon man whistling far and wee might wander in to sell pink cotton candy on the end of a stick. A place where a diner would wave him over and request that he "Come back when I've finished my foie gras and Beaume de Venise."

How to create an arena for haute cuisine and for patrons resembling the eighteenth-century German court of Clemens August the Elector, who occasionally invited the public to the palace for the honor of standing on a second-story gallery to observe the nobility dining below.

How to create whimsy within the weightiness of Corinthian columns, La Farge lunette paintings, Della Robbia reliefs, and marble, marble everywhere?

How to alert the newcomer entering this space that the

experience awaiting her is not about satisfying hunger? This is celebration. This is food as vehicle for transcendence.

How to create an atmosphere that will awaken her senses to this possibility the moment she leans against the great bronze doors? Sirio would think about all this very seriously, because Sirio knows that the art of dining is like the art of sex. Foreplay begins long before contact.

When I pushed against that door, it barely gave to my weight. Message received. Only the powerful may enter here.

It was clear that in a few days, when this new version of Le Cirque officially opened, I would no longer be welcome across the threshold in blue jeans and sneakers.

I would not have been surprised had a trumpet heralded my ascent of the ceremonial stairs lined with vegetable-laden platters and rustic baskets big enough to hold a pair of three-month-old twins. Eggplants, artichokes, ugli fruit, oranges, peppers, onions, pineapples filled and tumbled out of them. I felt like Persephone returning from the Underworld, like a pilgrim climbing to a sacred temple, offerings to the gods marking my way.

"Are bird-watchers born or made?" my friend Paul asked as we strolled through the park yesterday, passing many of my old pals with binoculars swinging from their necks. Are sensualists born or made? Those who thrill to the sounds of a symphony, the sight of color on canvas, the scent of lilacs in June, the taste of chocolate on the tongue? Wordsworth and Emerson would probably tell us born and then unmade. That the child's intense engagement with the world is educated out of us, but not irrevocably banished. Romance is the way we reclaim it. The romantic believes that she can. She has expectations of wonder and hesitates to blink lest she miss the potential awe of happenstance.

As I climbed those marble stairs outlined in mosaic tiles, I considered Proust and that crumb of madeleine. Keats and the nightingale. William Carlos Williams and a red wheelbarrow in the rain. Dvorak and the song of the redstart. I thought of Wallace Stevens's jar in Tennessee and began to entertain the possibilities of High Romance in Haute Cuisine. Stevens wrote:

I placed a jar in Tennessee,
And round it was, upon a hill.
It made the slovenly wilderness
Surround that hill.

The wilderness rose up to it,
And sprawled around, no longer wild.
The jar was round upon the ground
And tall and of a port in air.

It took dominion everywhere.
The jar was gray and bare.
It did not give of bird or bush,
Like nothing else in Tennessee.

It occurred to me that imagination is the jar in Tennessee. What extraordinary power that gives us. That jar travels. We can take it anywhere. To the park, to the beach, to exotic ports, to bed. Place it anywhere and romance will rise up to it and sprawl around. The jar is the imagination Blake claimed was no less than divine because it allows us to see beyond seeing, to hear beyond evident sound, to taste more than the flavors that light on our tongues, to know beyond knowing, to order the world through our senses, to contain wonder in a form we can understand.

In the form of a chocolate stove, for instance. A four-inch chocolate stove served on a plate decorated with kitchen tiles of fruit sauce. A dark chocolate stove with white chocolate burners holding two thimble-size dark chocolate pots with white chocolate handles.

Jacques Torres happened to walk by that day as I strolled unchecked, amused and taking notes. After introductions, I asked about his plans as pastry chef for thrilling the customers. He grinned. "Why don't you sit down here in the bar for a moment and I'll bring you something." Off with the frayed-cuff parka, off with the green gloves decorated with reindeer and one thumb peering through its own hole. Down into a green, velvet-backed banquette, up against blue velvet pillows tossed like the circus balls appliquéed on them. Snug behind a circus-ball table centered by an underlit blue star in Mr. Villard's former music room complete with choir loft.

Glancing up, I began to see that the restaurant's designer, Adam Tihany, had been inspired rather than daunted by the preponderance of Landmark-sacred Pre-Raphaelite splendor he was forbidden to change. Above the burnished bar he had hung a circus high wire from which a brushed-steel clock rode across the room. A child's humorous mimicking of adult behavior. The designer's response to the 1886 do-not-touch, gleaming bronze zodiac clock designed by Stanford White and Augustus Saint-Gaudens and carved into the mansion's marble stairwell.

It was clear that the children had been invited to this party and the grown-up who took himself too seriously would be shown no mercy. For each touch of Gilded Age formality there was a responding architectural giggle. A plastic torch in full plastic flame shining on a scene of nudes in classical relief, velvet chairs resembling those to be found in throne rooms were one-armed and had multicolored clown-suit buttons parading down their pop-art-colored backs. The children were here holding their hands over their mouths to contain the mirth escaping between their fingers.

Jacques returned and grinned at my amazement as he set the chocolate stove on the table in front of me. "This," he explained, "is how the waiters will serve it." With a delicate flourish of thumb and forefinger borne upward by a stiff, extended pinkie, he lifted each pot, which he gently rested at the side of the plate before lifting the stove by its white chocolate chimney to reveal three parchment-thin layers of hazelnut cake filled with alternating coffee butter cream and ganache and finished with a glittering chocolate glaze. "*Callebaut* from Belgium." Of course. He poured the pots' contents, raspberry and passion fruit sauce, onto compliant pastry.

On later visits I would know to stay the waiter's hand and lift the pots myself, emptying their contents directly into my uplifted mouth. Mainlining heaven is how I think of it. Like taking communion and hoping for the best. When Rebecca is my dining companion, she wishes I wouldn't do this. So what. The best part is when I stick my tongue in afterward. The tip just fits and licks up the last pungent drops of fruit essence.

Jacques wouldn't disapprove. He's a sensualist, as all great chefs must be.

Once when on assignment in Versailles (yes, sometimes it's easier to be a romantic than at others) I ordered something that sounded not at all appealing but so terribly French I couldn't resist. "Warmed oysters and foie gras served on the half shell," I told the waiter.

I was dining alone in the dining room of the Trianon Palace Hotel, located, thanks to a revolution, on the Sun King's 250 acres. The rain threw itself heedlessly against the window, and Marie Antoinette's woolly lambs that had grazed outside by day now sought shelter at her farm down the road.

I settled into the romance of perfect solitude. In my twenties, this would have been lonely torture. In my forties it had become a blessing for which I was deeply grateful.

The room graced its diners with soft-hued walls and chandelier glow. At nearby tables, women with whom I'd been sharing the hotel's Givenchy Spa, the subject of my article, sat smoking unfiltered cigarettes, eating foie gras, drinking red wine, and being radiant in the way people are when partaking of the high luxury of dining as art rather than strict necessity. Only a heretic would have spoken of fat, cholesterol, nicotine. Only a well-meaning, health-conscious, decidedly unromantic, deadly serious American.

A glass of champagne was poured. A covered plate arrived, its silver dome lifted to present oysters shimmering in reflected candlelight. "Thank you," I murmured, catching a subtle scent of briny sea meeting deeper undertones. "Merci," as I dove beneath the surf of memory and tasted the salt of childhood summers.

The oysters perched lightly on a small slab of fresh foie gras. The man in the tuxedo backed away, leaving me to the privacy required by such an encounter.

I picked up the small fork he had left by my plate, delicate but hefty enough to take the job seriously, and delivered an entire oyster and its bed of foie gras to my tongue. There was a moan. I looked around. The French ladies still floated in the bubble of their merriment, still smoked, still drank. A serious middle-aged couple looked past each other to find something outside their silence. A white-haired gentleman dining alone stared contentedly into the middle distance as he awaited the next course. I slowly realized, first with horror, then amazement, then delight, that the moan had come from me.

The me of stoical upbringing on New England's rigid shores. My unguarded palate had allowed the art of a French chef to break through centuries of training and genetic mutation to release a primal howl of sensual delight. Well, not a howl exactly, but to those of us of a Jamesian bent any public display of spontaneity is followed by discomfort. Who heard? Who saw?

I wanted to bow down before the chef who had dreamed of such a dish. But this was France and I a foreigner.

I did not moan when I ate my first Jacques Torres dessert. But, in the words of Mel Brooks's two-thousand-year-old man describing the first-ever sexual encounter, I was thrilled and delighted.

A friend had described Jacques as "So handsome he looks like a movie star."

Later I called and let her know we had met. "Movie star?" I asked.

"Yes! Isn't he gorgeous?"

"How many times have you eaten his desserts?"

"Four, five. Well, sometimes he gives me four at once."

"How tall do you think he is?"

"Six feet."

"My dear. You have fallen in love with *les pâtisseries* and therefore in love with their creator. A well-known syndrome. The opposite of kill-the-messenger. He's five feet seven tops and he's very nice, but no, he is not a movie star."

"You think?"

"I think."

A romantic quest grants you entry into a world of beauty and pleasure. Whenever I get a whiff of something that might offer up the elusive romantic experience, I follow the scent. So, within a week, I called almost-movie-star-handsome Jacques, and asked if I might come and watch him cook.

"But, of course."

"I'll try to stay out of the way. I'll just stand in a corner and take notes."

"Better yet, put on a white coat and cook with us. Then you'll be completely out of the way."

I admit I'm scared. At first ecstatic and then, when I wake up this morning, scared. "What if he asks me to make a soufflé and it falls?" I ask my husband.

"I doubt that he's going to ask you to make soufflés this early in the morning," he responds, carefully guiding his razor across one soapy cheek.   ·

"O.K., O.K. You're probably right. But I'm still scared." I start to get dressed then return to the bathroom. "You know the soufflés I'm talking about, right? The soufflés we ate in the old Le Cirque? Remember how we felt as though if we didn't clamp our teeth shut after each bite it would float into the air like a cloud? Remember..."

He gets that won't-she-ever-stop-talking look in his eye, that why-does-she-do-this-to-me-before-coffee tightness around his mouth. His restraint contracts the muscles of his jaw. He rinses his face, dries it, takes a deep breath and repeats, "It's too early in the day to make soufflés."

"O.K., O.K." I depart before he can suggest, "But it's not too early to make pancakes."

I walk the thirty-nine blocks to Madison Avenue and Fiftieth Street in an attempt to exhaust my nervous energy. Entering the Villard courtyard is as intimidating as it's meant to be. Your heart was meant to beat a little faster as you entered here in the 1800s beneath the brass lantern hanging from the elaborate wrought-iron arch looming above the gate. You were meant to understand, as you left the then less than savory avenue at your back, that you were being received into an affirmation that In-America-Your-Dreams-Can-Come-True. A sort of social identification with the aggressor.

The young Henry Villard wanted this design to incorporate

the foreboding pomp and circumstance of Europe's noble homes from which he had been excluded. Now he would receive the invited after they had completed the requisite passage through wrought-iron gates, climbed five granite steps outside, seven marble steps within, crossed an ornate, mosaic-tile threshold reflecting the matching, vaulted ceiling, and waited before the ornately carved eleven-foot-tall marble fireplace with the Three Graces carved into its mantel. A girl could begin to have second thoughts.

I begin to pity the out-of-town tourist with money and enthusiasm who enters here and slowly begins to feel like less than she is. The suit that she thought was perfect a moment ago, two blocks back, seems suddenly too bright, the stockings, so carefully chosen, too pale, the purse too beige. Or so she thinks as she attempts to stand tall before the disinterested glance of the restaurant's general manager, the guardian of the gates, the straight-spined, not a slouch to his frame, film noir star handsome Benito Sevarin, whose beautiful blue eyes are bereft of warm welcome. A nod, a walk to a table, one a bit too close to other diners. No words exchanged.

Of course it's all a game. Benito is more similar to the young Henry Villard née Hidgard than not, as is his boss, the Tuscan orphan. As are large numbers of those who enter here. Let's pretend. Let's play doge for a Day. Elector for an evening. That is the folly of the place. I am headed for its heart.

Past the young woman who stands behind a desk lit at each corner by a red, yellow, green, or orange torch. She is answering the phone by 9 A.M. and stares at the red and green circus tent above her head as she responds again and again, "No, I'm sorry, we have nothing for two months." The other phone is ringing before she's said good-bye. Through the marble-walled bar and the carved wood-paneled dining room with its clown-suit chairs. Some of their backs have been lowered since my first visit because comedian Joan Rivers complained that her friends couldn't wear hats in chairs that tall. Give them bread, circuses, and hats.

The energy of the kitchen rushes at me. The sound of pots colliding, ladles falling, dishwashers buzzing, glass shattering, fans humming. A man polishes silver bowls, a woman chops vegetables. Thump, thump, thumpity, thump. It's as though everyone is getting ready for a grand party. A wedding. An opening night. The air of expectation and excitement. It's hard to believe they do this every day.

The vegetable chopper looks behind me, smiles, bows slightly, and says, "Good morning, Chef Sottha." The maestro has arrived, the executive chef in his *toque blanche*, who excites the palates of the privileged with such inspirations as roast quail risotto served with a broken quail egg on top, curried seafood spaghetti, roast cod with Szechuan spices and beans. The creator of seductive music for the tongue is a delicate, slim man with serene demeanor and shy smile. A Cambodian who at first turned this job down. "I'm not ready," he told the insistent Sirio. Not being American, he believed in slow, painstaking training before going public with his talents. He continued to hone his skills elsewhere until Sirio could stand it no longer and told him he'd design the kitchen of his dreams if he would please just come and be his chef. So here he is in his palace. A man far from home, who seems very much at home right here beneath a stainless-steel ceiling reflected in stainless-steel counters, in front of two blue enamel Bonnet stoves. Stockpots hold a gleam like that of Northern Renaissance paintings, in which they symbolize the miracle in the ordinary, the light that had come into the world. Here they make me feel as though I'm on sacred ground in this kitchen overseen by a gentle man who describes the process I'm watching and hearing as "the orchestra warming up."

I suddenly think of a poetic young man for whom I once cooked. The race was on between AIDS and me for his pound of flesh, and I was losing. One day, a day he and I both knew was getting close to the last, I served up a buttery polenta. Ordinary. Simple. Not particularly interesting. Or so I thought until he took the first bite, closed his eyes, and grinned. "Oh, Barbara," he sighed, "This is a symphony."

I think of him whenever the taste of food reminds me that flavor can transport, it carries with it beauty and music and poetry. And I think of him now as Sottha Khunn warms up his musicians before they perform their symphony.

I move toward the back of the kitchen, to the spacious section reserved for the complex pastry hierarchy Jacques Torres and his assistants. Past the room reserved for chocolate making, I follow the caramel scent of burning bananas. Jacques is nowhere to be seen, but his crew is hard at work led by a short, wiry man with a dark complexion, serious air, black sideburns and mustache, who tosses the fruit back and forth in a cast-iron skillet. The complex aromas of bitter burned sugar and sunny tropics lead me straight to his station. "May I ask what you're making?"

"Ah," says he, his face relaxing from concentration to merriment, "the bananas for Banana Moon Cakes."

I know this particular confection from Jacques's cookbook, in which he describes its inspirational birth in a mountain village in France. "When the moon is out, it shines so brightly that it feels as if you could touch it if you only stood on the roof. I was inspired to create this dessert by the summer moon of that small village."

"And now," says the dark, handsome banana stirring stranger, as he reaches for a bottle of rum, "we add this." A burst of flame. Sizzle, splatter. Scents of sugar in its many guises.

A taller, darker man enters. Could I please move to a less-traveled part of the kitchen?

"She's not in my way, Terrence," says Banana Moon Cake Man.

"Whatever you say, Chef Cisco." Cisco, short for Señor Francisco Gugierrez, short for Moon Cake Man, short for Merlin, concocter of love potions, short for Jacques' assistant, grins. "They call me many things around here: 'Pancho,' 'Paco,' 'Pancho Paco,' 'Jésus' . . . " His laugh is musical, starting at low *g*, rising to middle *g,* and ending in a giggle at high *c.* A song of enthusiasm sung by a man blessed by that Platonic invasion of a god. The god of delight. The god of delicious. His good humor is infectious and surprising, considering that he's been on his feet working the alchemy since 5 A.M.

Following introductions, I explain my presence. "Jacques Torres invited me to come and cook with him."

"He hasn't come in yet," Terrence, assistant to Francisco responds," but too bad you didn't come even earlier, like at six-thirty this morning when Cisco was making his crême brulées."

World-famous crême brulées served in the former Le Cirque. World-famous crême brulées that have delighted millions of custard-coated tongues.

"How long have you been cooking professionally, Terrence?"

"Seventeen years."

"And you still get so excited about crême brulée?"

"Cisco's are magic. That's the part of pastry making that people forget. Pastry is made from very simple things, the most basic things, butter, eggs, flour, vanilla, and the rest is magic. Pure magic."

He calls over my shoulder, "Hey, Cisco, can I make a crême brulée for the little lady here?"

"Sure."

Terrence disappears into another part of the pastry kitchen, compartmentalized according to various tasks. Service. Pastry making. Chocolate tantalizing.

Another young man in a white coat walks up to the stove where Francisco stands and puts his arm around him. "I've missed you, man. We all missed you." They embrace. "I missed you, too."

I ask Francisco where he's been. "Each year I go home to Mexico for two weeks. To a tiny little village where the only sound is the sound of the river."

"Do you cook while you're there?"

"Are you kidding? My wife never lets me in the kitchen. She says, 'This is not Le Cirque.' She says I make a mess."

"Chef Cisco, shall I melt the chocolate for the soufflé?"

What an odd and endearing courtliness presides over this kitchen. Your Highness, Your Honor, Chef. Alongside the bonhomie and camaraderie is respect for the one who holds the magic in his hands.

Yes, the young woman with orange hair, matching penciled brows, and many earrings should go right ahead. I consider my husband's early-morning reassurance and nervously inquire, "*Now*, you make soufflés? *Now*?"

"Just the initial steps."

And here comes Jacques of the chocolate stoves apologizing

for being late. And here comes my crême brulée. To which do I bow first? Terrence settles it. "Don't eat it yet. It's still very hot."

The sugar crackles, hardening to a crust. Ice skimming a winter pond.

Jacques's blue eyes crinkle, becoming part of a smile that seems to start at the side of his neck. His dark blond hair is short and boyishly unstyled. His air is that of one engaged in the work he is born to do. Like Francisco. Like Michelangelo on the scaffolding of the Sistine Chapel. Like Gershwin hearing the first strains of *Rhapsody in Blue*. Frank Lloyd Wright standing on the shores of Bear Run. Balboa spying the Pacific. Like a midwife embracing new baby and mother in one fell swoop. This is a particular joy, this joy generated by deep gratitude for the work at hand. Joy combined with reverie and peace rather than boisterous jubilation. These are people called into communion with something bigger than themselves, an experience that the rest of us hunger for and sometimes achieve in the fleeting romantic interlude.

The rubber soles of Jacques's black shoes squish against the terra-cotta tiles. The creases along the laces are permanent archives for flour and finely ground nuts of past cakes, tarts, tuiles. He wears khakis, a white coat, and the healthy look of a man equally comfortable in ski goggles, motorcycle helmet, or scuba gear. The easy grace of one at home in his own skin.

"Ah, eat your crême brulée," he advises. I wonder if there is a natural correlative between the number of musical inflections the French can put into the name of a dessert and the sublimity of its flavor. "Share with me. I couldn't possibly eat all this." I extend the white porcelain dish to him, but he shakes his head and moves off to ready himself for work.

Tap, tap, my spoon cracks against the hardened sugar, then shatters it and falls through to soft, flowing custard studded with vanilla-bean seeds. My tongue suddenly awakens to a tapestry of textures, hot and cold temperatures and flavors of vanilla, heavy cream, and burnt sugar. Flavor follows flavor like the aftershocks of an earthquake. I close my eyes, as unthinking a gesture as it is when you want the full experience of a kiss. Soft on the tongue, hard sugar against the teeth.

"So?"

I open my eyes to see tall Terrence peering down at me. It takes a moment to speak.

"Oh, my."

"See what I told you. The simple things in life are always the best. Cream, eggs, vanilla, sugar. And then the magic."

Later when relating all this to Rebecca, she says, "Just like Chartres. Stones, mortar and magic."

"You're right. Just like Fallingwater. Steel, concrete, water, magic."

"You want to make this with me sometime?" Francisco asks, pointing to my empty dish. "I usually start very early in the morning, but you want to come, I'll wait for you."

Terrence assures me it's worth rising early to watch Francisco at this task he loves. "It's such an honor working with this gentleman," he says of Francisco, and adds, "It's art we're creating here. The only difference is we don't have galleries to hang it in." I think of the paintings that live on in my mind long after I've left the galleries, the museums. The art that truly moves us also moves with us. No walls required.

Francisco is still talking about the art of crème brulée. "If anything goes wrong with my crème brulée, I'm sick for week." His face takes on the expression of one in mourning.

"Do you have any idea how happy your desserts make people?" I want to know. "Do you ever go out there into the dining room and notice how all conversation stops and all you see are smiles and all you hear are yummmmmmms?"

"Oh, no. I'm much too shy." But around pastries and creams he's not shy. He's full of gusto. "This is where I'm happy." He wipes his hands on a towel and moves back to the stove to heat a vat of oil. "Would you like to help me make bombolini?" He asks the question with the eager inflection of a child saying, "Hey! I've got an idea!" So much enthusiasm you would think that these were the first rather than the six thousandth he's probably made.

"Would I ever!"

It seems that I'm not the only one cheered by these pastry-cream-filled puffs of fried leavened sweet dough. Sirio loves them so much he sent Jacques on a bombolini mission to Italy to learn how to make them.

Francisco checks that the dough of yeast, flour, eggs, and butter has reached just the right consistency. If too sticky or not sticky enough it will resist his attempts to shape it into perfectly rounded puffs. "They *must* be perfect. Rich people don't eat with their mouths, they eat with their eyes."

The dough has already risen in a bowl for two hours, and then on baking sheets for an additional two. It's been cut into circles, has defied gravity and practically levitated. Even before frying, the dough gives off a sweet scent enticing enough to tempt me to snatch off a piece and pop it in my mouth before it hits the oil. But I'm new here. I'm on good behavior.

Francisco checks the temperature. If the oil is too hot the outside of the bombolini will burn before the inside cooks. If too cool, they will absorb the oil and sink with greasy weight. And we wouldn't want that to happen. We wouldn't want Francisco to be sick for a week.

When the oil is just right, something Francisco seems to divine from the aroma, from the amount of sweat collecting on his brow, from some secret communication between the man and his art. When he's read all the signs, he carefully lowers the doughy balls one at a time into the deep pan. "Only seven at a time, otherwise it doesn't work." Magic or science? A bit of both. "Too many bombolini at once," Jacques explains as he observes the proceedings over our shoulder, "and the temperature of the oil drops and the bombolini won't fry evenly." But of course.

After three to five minutes Francisco begins to lift them from the oil, and I begin to wonder when I get my white coat and my job. Finally I'm invited in. "Now, we cover them with sugar," announced with the enthusiasm of a father telling his child, "Now we go to the beach and make sand castles! Hooray!"

I'm allowed to follow his example. Hold the bombolino like a bambino about to be lowered into a shallow bath. (Bombolino? Bombolina? Who knows? It doesn't matter, you always eat more than one.) Roll, pat, lift gently, admire. "Now," he grins, and I expect a white dove to fly from his apron pocket, or a rabbit to pounce from his sleeve. "Now, watch this!" He fills a muslin pastry bag until it overflows with egg-rich pastry cream. Stab. A sudden push of its quarter-inch tip into the bombolini's pudgy centers. Squeeze. Squirt. The pastries swell with this sudden impregnation. Francisco knows exactly when enough is enough and removes the tip.

Splat. Suddenly the cream gushes out over the pastry and onto the counter. Francisco laughs and parades around the kitchen proudly displaying the result of his overeager squeeze. He offers the creamy mess to a junior cook, who accepts with pleasure and returns grinning and spitting out the metal tip, which had also blown into the pastry.

Jacques motions me away from his disciples and into the inner sanctum. He stands like god of the fruit between trays of mangos, melons, blackberries, strawberries, raspberries. What's that maple leaf doing there? I point to the edge of the counter. And those pussy-willow branches?

"Oh, they're from Central Park. Kris, my girlfriend, and I go there to watch birds, but each time I go I see something I could turn into a pastry design."

"Are you always thinking about pastry?"

"But of course." That inimitable French shrug. "I look at a tree and I think, 'Chocolate leaf.' Kris gets scared because I'll suddenly see something in the house and bring it in to make a mold or something. I see desserts everywhere."

Jacques tastes life in his mind's tongue.

"This weekend when Kris and I were in a coffee shop I was watching two American kids drink hot chocolate, and I noticed that the best part for them, the part that made them the happiest, was the marshmallow on top. So I've been thinking about marshmallows all week. What can I do with marshmallows to make people that happy?"

"And the pussy willows?"

"I don't know yet."

Chances are pretty good we'll be seeing sugar spun into twigs and branches that look just like that. Jacques watched glass blow-

ers as a child and began to imagine the art being transferred to the
kitchen. He'd fallen in love with cooking when he was fourteen
and made "Roquefort-cheese sauce on tournedos. Then for
dessert, two slices of canned pineapple, some kirsch and whipped
cream. I was in heaven."

At fifteen, he went to the pastry chef of his small town in
the South of France and asked if he could work Sundays and in
the summer. A deal was made, his life took shape.

"I loved it so much. At sixteen I apprenticed for two years
with another pastry chef and I studied with a glass blower."

His enthusiasm for the art extends to that created in Murano.
He collects ornate Venetian glasses into which he scoops freshly
made gelato. After the rich people who "eat with their eyes" have
finished every last bite, the glasses are washed by hand. "The con-
tainer," he explains, "is as important as what's in it." Like the frame
of a painting. Like the landscape of a home. Like the sky around
the moon.

Does he ever get bored? Does he ever wake up in the morning and think, "I can't make one more chocolate clown hat?" Or,
"Please God, not another chocolate oozing fountain." Or, "Never
again a chocolate caldron filled with spun sugar and piña colada
Bavarian. "

"But that was my thank-you present to Kris for taking me
to Virgin Gorda and introducing me to piña coladas. Each time
I make it I'm reminded of that wonderful trip."

Doesn't he ever tire of molding passion-fruit puree, apricot
mousse, and crème brulée into the shape of a 1930s French
lady's hat, then filling a spray can (filched from Kris's tool chest)
with white chocolate for the finishing touch? Doesn't he sometimes think that he doesn't want to meet the architectural rigors
required to make Manhattan, layers of almond paste cake filled
with cream and stacked to resemble the Chrysler building?

He doesn't understand the questions. I try to explain bore-
dom. I try to explain mundanity. I say everybody has trouble
facing the morning sometimes. He looks blank. I try French.

"Not make another Manhattan? Of course I'll always make
Manhattans. I love this place. Making that dessert is my way of

capturing the city's spirit. The chocolate-grid streets, the gold-leaf display of wealth, the mango-sauce cabs, the rising tower . . ." It's as though I'd asked Bach if he didn't grow weary of the music in his head.

"You've got to do what you love with your life. You've got to have the guts to do what you think is right. . . ." That shrug again. Enough said. The words are in the sauce.

11

LET'S FACE THE MUSIC
AND DANCE

My brother-in-law, Dan, throws himself a fiftieth-birthday bash at the Rainbow Room in Rockefeller Center. We're invited.

He's asked Andrea Marcovicci to come and sing. Flies her in from L.A., all expenses paid. Andrea Marcovicci who can turn a torch song into a bonfire and make your toes curl away from its sizzle, flies in from L.A., takes a cab to Rockefeller Center, rides the express, art deco elevator to the sixty-fifth floor, takes off her coat and chic cloche hat, walks to the microphone, and sings directly to Dan. Sings to Dan, then dances with him, sighing and humming "Our Love Is Here to Stay." A Fred and Ginger moment. Well, at least a Ginger moment.

We all fall for it and keep falling and falling and falling. We who sit on the sidelines in our party dresses and party shoes and black tuxedoes, we who mind our manners the best we can, remembering to talk to both the person on our left and the one on our right, we who sit at the candlelit, white-linen-draped, round tables eager for a bite of the lobster tail the waiter has set before us, can't take our eyes off the dancers.

Andrea motions for my sister Becky to come and dance with Dan and for the hundred assembled to join in the song. Somehow it doesn't feel awkward, like some enforced sing-along. Somehow it doesn't feel like my grandmother's favorite Lawrence Welk show. ("Oh, Barbie, you remind me of the oldest Lennon sister," referring to the icky-sticky sweet, teen and pre-teen sister singing group, the rage of 1950s grandmothers. Translation: Barbie, grow up to be as demure and talented as Janet Not-a-Mean-Bone-in-Her-Body Lennon and you might just have a fighting chance in this world.)

We don't hesitate. We fling our romantic dreams onto the dance floor with reckless abandon, we send them soaring to swoop and sway with Becky and Dan. Diminutive Becky in her high, high heels and scoop-back black satin dress. Substantial Dan in his element. We smile, some shed tears, we think we sound lovely as we sing, we think the couple's beautiful. We want to be like that. In love. In sync. Survivors. Their love is here to stay.

We fall for it and keep falling. We fall for it every time. After the dance one of Dan's oldest friends, a guy who's been around, a guy who's tried his hand at marriage once or twice or three times, puts his arms around the birthday boy and weeps a bit as he says, "I'm so happy for you and Becky." Dan, a manly man, moves quickly from the path of this emotional flow. From words bleeding from a heart broken by jettisoned hope. "I really *mean* it," he calls after Dan's departing tuxedoed figure.

At the time, it seemed important to say. Knowing all he knows about the pains and turmoil of marriage, about how love can rub you raw and cause you to run from it, he is happy for his friend. He is happy to see that it can work, which is to say that in the end, in intervals, in the blink of an evening, the silky filaments of romance can weave hope back together, can bind what is broken. Can culminate in a dance and a vow.

That's as good as it gets, and Dan's friend who has not been as lucky knows this. We need the Fred and Ginger moments to remind us. Our marital bonds depend on the momentary fiction that speaks to the greater truth. That the struggle to stay the course is worth the price and what we get in return isn't happily ever after, but if we're lucky, a dance in the Rainbow Room with its Christmas-light backdrop of Manhattan's bridges and sky-scrapers against a blue-black sky cradling a crescent moon. That Andrea Marcovicci will be singing directly to us is too much to ask. But not too much for Dan the Romance Man.

When Andrea sings, "Long ago and far away, / I dreamed a

dream one day, /And now that dream is here beside me," we all imagine the love of our lives singing it to us. "There's a purity, a hopefulness to those songs," Andrea tells me when she comes to sit down for dinner. That's why she sings the songs of Jerome Kern, Oscar Hammerstein, the Gershwins. Why she loves them. "They resurrect romantic idealism, they allow for the perfection of romantic love and the hope that each of us can have it. They leave no room for cynicism. Even with songs like 'They're singing songs of love, but not for me . . .' we aren't being told we'll *never have* it. They may not be singing songs of love for me today, but maybe they will tomorrow."

We are drawn to the songs because, she explains, "They are conversational, and the conversation is beautiful. Words in romance are so important but few of us can talk that language. The songs do it for us. Imagine," Andrea says, beaming, "imagine being able to say to your beloved or have your beloved say to you, 'You are the promised kiss of springtime that makes the lonely winter seem long . . .' Boy, Hammerstein must have gone home happy that day.

"Or think about 'Long Ago and Far Away,'" she says, speaking the lyrics, "'Long ago and far away, I dreamed a dream one day, and now that dream is here beside me.' The song doesn't say, he's here beside me and he owes alimony or he doesn't make as much money as I'd like, or he doesn't like my mother. What it does say is 'I had a dream and now that dream has come true and love has made me more than I was before.'"

And that is the meaning of Dan's and Becky's dance. Each is more than they were because they love each other and love demands great change and growth and learning. Love results in suffering and suffering results in wisdom. The dance, the torch song, the celebratory events are like the church liturgy, rituals practiced, words spoken to awaken an awareness that what we're talking about is beyond everyday words. So face the music and dance.

When Dan's friend spoke of his happiness for Dan and Becky, he was acknowledging the price of love. The price asked, the price paid. A princely sum. He was saying he knew all this and was thus rejoicing in the miracle of their having paid and paid and paid in order, for a moment, to twirl around the dance floor, gathering our dreams of love to their center. Like Sufis in the whirl of their dance, like religious pilgrims walking Chartres's labyrinth. They dance the mystery that is beyond words. I had a dream and I am better for it. Neither the Sufis nor the religious pilgrims become saints through the dance. The dance does not mean that Becky and Dan will not feel the dark encroachment of Monday morning, when the alarm awakens them to the work at hand, worrying about children, meeting book-contract deadlines, facing again a recent grievous family loss: It doesn't mean that each won't say words to the other in the following week that will annoy or hurt.

Each week the Catholic and Episcopalian live the everydayness of jealousy, greed, misunderstanding, ignorance, stubbornness, and self-righteousness, then, perhaps weekly, each participates in the ancient act of confession. "We have erred and strayed from thy ways like lost sheep. . . . We have left undone those things which we ought to have done, and we have done those things which we ought not to have done." That said, we rise from our knees, dust off the dirt left by the person preceding us, who'd used the prayer stool as a footstool. We head from the gloom of great stone walls into the light of day, and we think for a moment, "Hey, I can do this, I can live a 'Godly and righteous life.'" Fresh start. New beginning. Similarly the romantic ritual makes us believe we can make fresh starts. Prayer, after all, right up there with song, is high romance. We bring to it our yearning that struggles for words. We bring our chagrin over follies, our admission of weakness. We do all this, in spite of evidence to the contrary, out of the fervent hope that we will merge with something larger, better than ourselves. That we will be made complete, this day and evermore, amen.

Andrea's songs and Becky's and Dan's dance make such completion seem entirely possible. We all had a dream long ago and far away. "The brain," according to neurophysiologist, Rodolfo Llinas, "is a dreaming machine." He's seen it on his very own magnetoencephalograph machine. Yes, indeed. Perhaps, he ventures, we even dream *in utero*. Perhaps we dream before that. Perhaps we are dreamed into being as the aborigines believe creation was sung into being. Let there be light to the tune of the seventies theme song, "Age of Aquarius": "Let the sun shine, let the sun shine, let the sun shine in."

It isn't all that farfetched to imagine that love dreamed us into being, that we were dreaming of love when we came into being, that we spend our lives chasing that dream. Chasing forward rather than realizing it was back there, back then. An endless circle. The labyrinth in Chartres, the Tibetan Buddhist mandala depicting the circle of the spiritual universe, the Hindu wedding ritual in which the couple, bound together by a silk scarf, walk seven times in a circle as a reminder that the action of one spouse will now affect the other, Plato's original round man, "Terrible was their might and strength, and the thoughts of their hearts were great . . . the gods could not suffer their insolence to go unrestrained." The power of the circle that knows no beginning, no ending, no start, no finish.

Becky and Dan dancing round and round and round, beneath the chandeliers, against the sky, sets us to dreaming the romantic dream. We stubbornly set our sights on it. "See," we say, if a bit defensively, "see, here's the proof in the dance."

As we prepare to leave the party, my husband heads for the coatroom. "No, it's not that way, it's this way," say I, heading off in the opposite direction, I who have no sense of direction, but a relentless certainty that I am right. We argue about it. We reach an impasse. He, of the perfect sense of direction—put him down in any jungle, set him adrift in the middle of the Pacific, and he'll find his way home—turns out to be correct. I sulk. How come he always gets to be right? I don't like him. Mr. Know-It-All. Mr. Thinks-He-Knows-Everything. Show-off.

When we marry we marry each other and the five-year-old versions of each other. There are always four of us in this bed. Sometimes it's enough to make you gasp for air.

And yet "to feel in the night the nearness of you." By the time we've gotten home, by the time we've climbed into bed and turned off the lights and twisted and turned and tossed pillows about like dogs circling and circling and circling before lying down, by the time the dust and the duvet settle, by the time we've groaned about getting to bed so late, by the time we drift into sleep, our arms and legs entwine. They are dreamed into entwining. We are dreamed back into love.

Which is exactly why we keep going back to those old songs. Out of our lives into the illusion, the yearning for a time resembling Hesiod's golden age, when "men lived like gods without sorrow of heart remote and free from toil and grief." In this, our post torch song, post doo-wopp age beset with "stick-it-to-me" lyrics, Gershwin, Kern, and Hammerstein remind us that the closest we'll come to Paradise on this earth is "to feel in the night the nearness of you."

My daughter thinks that my husband and I have an unadventursesome, certainly far from romantic life. "Where were you last night," she asks. "I called but there wasn't any answer. And you forgot to turn on the answering machine."

"We were out for dinner. We went to the bar at Quatorze."

"Oh, *that's* really original," says she.

What would have impressed her as romantic would have been if I'd responded, "Well, your dad surprised me. Yesterday morning he brought me breakfast in bed (naturally) and underneath a silver vase holding a single white rose were two round-trip tickets to Paris. On the *Concorde*. Departing in two hours. He'd done all the packing for me and everything in that suitcase was new. After all, we were coming back this morning; all I needed was a tooth-brush, nightgown, and something to wear out to the dinner he had arranged for Alain Ducasse to prepare especially for us. So that's where we were when you called."

Now *that* she would have considered romantic. That would have spoken of marriage as I imagine she dreams it, seven years into hers, thirty-one into mine. That would have allowed her to dream, as we all do, as Becky and Dan dance, that in spite of all the wear and tear, despite the familiarity, the fights, sickness, grief, despite the constant battering of eroding forces, this marriage was a flourishing garden of Paradise, blessed by the gods, a golden time.

But, no. Bob and I had been sitting at the bar at Quatorze, a small French bistro a few blocks from home, feeling blessed by familiarity. Basking in mundanity. A Finlandia martini with three olives, thank you. French fries on the way. Chocolate bread pudding for dessert. The blessing of words spoken to just the person you want to speak them to, the blessing of that quickening when, turning from the bar to each other, the knees touch, those familiar, terribly bony knees, and a wave of love passes through me as it once did when I'd feel infant Rebecca's down-covered head in the crook of my arm.

Odd. A couple of years ago I might have missed this moment, having had my sights set on Paris, or, O.K., I'll say it, maybe a diamond, something out of my life that would bring me back into it. There was a loneliness then that set me on this quest for the meaning of romance. I thought it was loneliness. Now, I think I may have been dozing.

The moment at the bar wasn't planned, wasn't orchestrated, wasn't out of the ordinary, since we go there when we grow weary of cooking and dishwashing. Somehow in spite of Rebecca's rolling eyes, it was decidedly romantic. There's something to be said for being ready, a lot to be said for serendipity, which ghosts by so quietly you could miss your chance, could sleep right through it.

The Romantic poets headed from home to find the exotic on foreign shores. The exotic that would arouse a quickening similar to that caused by a brush of knee against familiar bony knee. Travel opened their eyes to serendipity. They'd traveled far, they weren't about to sleep through experience. I have also found that some of the most romantic moments of my life have occurred far from home, simply because I was not operating in the almost perpetual slumber that exists in our ordinary lives.

There was a night in Venice, some twenty years ago, when Bob, Rebecca, and I headed for late dinner in a restaurant across from La Fenice opera house. "No room, no problem," said the owner/chef, smiling. With which he walked to the back of his crowded establishment, met us at the door with a round table, guided us out into the darkened square, set the table down, swooped chairs from the air and waiters from inside rooms. White tablecloth and napkins, three wine glasses, three water glasses, six plates. Three chairs scraping against stone as we settled in.

I don't remember what we ate, just that we ate in darkness and stillness that rubbed up against us like a cat. We ate and stared at the silent façade of the closed-for-the-season opera house.

There was a sultry day once on Lake Como when the air was mauve, the trees dripping green, and we could barely speak against the heat. We were seated at lunch beneath a large shading oak. A glass pitcher of local red wine was brought to the table. A loaf of bread.

A morning in Mississippi, waking alone to the aromas of coffee and fresh biscuits in an inn I just happened to find in a little town the river had left behind.

A July 4th weekend when most of Manhattan had headed for beaches and I stood in a nearly vacant gallery of the Metropolitan Museum. Stood in the silence, gazed at Petrus Christus's painting *Virgin and Child in a Chamber,* and felt my grown daughter take my hand.

Each of these moments was unplanned and might have passed uneventfully. Yet now, years later, like Wordsworth contemplating past emotion in present tranquillity, I wonder what it was that causes me, when recalling these times, to see them within the golden nimbus of romance? What made the events so romantic at the time? Definitely the silence. Silence that kept distraction at bay. We noticed the awakening of our senses since we weren't chattering and listening to each other. The solitude of my solitary journey down Mississippi's Natchez Trace. Solitude that brings with it enforced silence. Being part of history in Venice, a place where so many have lived and died and loved before us that my husband commented, "Being there puts it all in perspective. Being there makes it O.K. to die." Being out of time and part of nature on a lake north of Milan that inspired Shelley. Sitting beneath a tree that must have been there when he was, being pressed to earth by the heaviness of summer air, lightened by the cool depths of local wine.

Awake, awake, awake. The poets watch wide-eyed, they dare not blink. The composers open their ears, straining to hear the music of the spheres. The chefs flick their tongues like divining rods. The lovers dare their hearts to break. Wake up, wake up. Wake up to the dream of union, reach back in yearning to the golden time, the Garden of Eden, when a man and a woman were one, a man, a woman, and a blackbird were one.

And so we marry in spite of all the odds against such a union. We fall for this seemingly insane dream of man and woman as one. Opposites commingling on some demilitarized zone. Fat him, slim her. Gregarious her, shy him. Bold him, timid her. She who loves the opera, he who is tone deaf. We're such suckers for the dream that all it takes to keep it alive is a spin around the dance floor, a touch of knees, entwining limbs in sleep. The brief interludes before we go back to scrapping for space, vying for power, before we return to concerns about what should we have for dinner, how much did you say that dress cost, why are you such a slob, this refrigerator is a mess, turn down the music, I don't like that friend of yours, you coddle the children, why don't you discipline the dog, I'm not your maid, get off the phone and pay attention to me, I don't want to go camping, how could you have said/done that last night at that dinner party, stop breathing through your mouth, I'm leaving, I can't take it any longer.

Last year as my husband and I entered Saint James Church, he spotted Mark Anschutz, our rector, standing in the narthex at the head of the line of altar boys and girls, banner bearers, cross carriers, and choir members, waiting for the organ's cue to march down the aisle. "Why don't you go to the pew? I'll be with you in a minute," Bob suggested, and went to speak to Mark. When he rejoined me and the organ started playing, "Now thank we all our God . . ." and the congregation breathed a sigh of relief that this was a familiar hymn in a manageable range, when the choir began its processional, singing mightily in our ears as it passed, Bob whispered, "I asked Mark to marry us again after the service." Just like that.

We were going to renew our vows. No fanfare. No cake. No witnesses. After the prayers, after more hymns, after kneeling, standing and sitting, Bible lessons from New and Old Testament, after a sermon about who remembers what, after the choir retreated to "Oh God, our help in ages past, our hope for years to come . . ." and the congregation followed, feeling a bit righteous and eager for cookies and coffee in an adjoining room, after the children flew forth to daylight as though shot through rubber bands, Mark motioned us to the front of the emptied church. "Let's go to the high altar for this occasion," he said with his particular infectious enthusiasm.

I was stunned by what awaited me. Shocked by vows I had repeated heedlessly, youthfully thirty years before. Had I known, had I really understood what I was saying, had I understood the steadfastness required by these promises, I would have turned on my heel. And I wouldn't have been the least bit embarrassed if the guests had sat with opened mouths, wondering, "Do we still get cake and champagne? Will she send back the presents?"

This time, undistracted by the loveliness of a you-only-get-to-wear-it-once dress, the tears of my husband, the thoughts of sex, this time sobered by hits and near misses of heartache, I listened with fascination and deep admiration for the perspicacity of whoever dreamed up these vows, which bring all romance killers to the fore, and then dare us to look them in the eye, to stare them down and proclaim, "I do." "I will."

Anybody with her wits about her would wear a crash helmet instead of a veil as the words are said over her head, ". . . marriage is not to be entered into unadvisedly or lightly . . . for richer for poorer, in sickness and in health, to love and to cherish. . . ." Sickness, poverty. The big threats. And yet we stand there with straight faces and awed hearts promising not only to be steadfast in adversity but to be loving. Not only to be loving, but to be faithful.

Who wouldn't prefer to be unfaithful when infidelity promises romance, the new, the unexpected, maybe even a plane ticket to Paris when things turn sour at home? It is within the nature of the beast we call marriage that things always turn sour at home. Things fall apart, the original dreams will not hold. Love changes, but "in change is true," writes poet Wendell Berry in "The Dance":

I would have each couple turn,
join and unjoin, be lost
in the greater turning
of other couples, woven
in the circle of a dance,
the song of long time flowing

over them, so they may return,
turn again in to themselves
out of desire greater than their own,
belonging to all, to each,
to the dance, and to the song
that moves them through the night.

The romantic interlude, be it the dance, dinner out, the moment of serendipity that prompts one to reach for the other's hand, each acts out our ancient yearning to be drawn from isolation into union.

We who watch Becky and Dan dance, we who hang our hopes on Andrea's words, sung with the wryness of one who has loved and lost and lost and lost and loved again, we don't look back. We follow the folly with open eyes and hearts. We grab hold in spite of all the odds against such tenaciousness. We'll hold on just as long as we can.

12

AND NOW A FEW WORDS ON ROMANCE FROM THE FOLKS WHO BROUGHT YOU *MISSION: IMPOSSIBLE* AND *GODZILLA*

Rebecca informs me that this is the end of the twentieth century and people want to know what celebrities think. "Enough about Thoreau." She tells me I should talk to movie stars about romance.

O.K., I agree, find me a movie star. "Better than that," says she, "how about you come with me to Venice?" I must have hesitated a beat because she adds, "That'd be Italy not California."

Her magazine is sending her to cover a major celebrity event. "Lots of grist for your mill, Ma," says she. Sure. Why not? Who would say, no?

So here we are, darling, long-lashed Tom Cruise and I, standing beneath the Tiepolo ceiling and hand-blown Venetian glass chandeliers of fourteenth-century Palazzo Pisani della Moretta. He's sweet and short. His manners are perfect. He looks me right in the eye and repeats my name so that I know we have connected on a Deep, Meaningful level. I ask for his thoughts on the subject of romance. "Romance? Ask my wife. She knows a lot more about that than I do."

I thank him, but do not kiss, although he presents a soft cheek. I cross the room, wobbly in stiletto heels unaccustomed to marble. Long, tall, currently curly, currently blond Nicole Kidman stands surrounded by admirers, whom she bathes in lipsticked warmth. I introduce myself; the men paying court are annoyed by the intrusion. I announce my mission: "Your husband said you know about romance." "He did?" She laughs. The guys laugh. I wait. End of conversation.

I ask Harrison Ford. "A light rain helps," says he. I like that.

Thank you, Rebecca. I have come to Venice for celebrity quotes and find romance in the silence all around me.

There are few places on earth that make me feel more as though I'm in that old-time God Sandwich than Venice, which holds me lightly between sea and sky.

I drift between time and eternity, between corporeal self and just beyond. I blend with the air. When I hear a strain of music coming from a music store, choral voices from a church, I am drawn there as though possessing neither weight nor will.

Even the architecture seems weightless, seems to defy gravity. The doges' pink and white marble palace floats on a fanciful foundation. A lacy arcade, which would create mere adornment atop a normal building in a normal city, purports to support this grand marble mass. But then everything is turned upside down in this city made of mud. Sixth-century mud dug from the lagoon and tossed higher and higher, held in place by wood pilings. A mad attempt to create living spaces where no barbarian would tread. Who would, you ask? Who would dream of such a thing, let alone live there? Why not just join the barbarians? Ah, but these are the things that dreams are made on and there have always been suckers for dreams. Prospero's island afloat in the firmament. A cloud not quite sky-borne. A wisp in time.

"Time, like an ever-rolling stream, / Bears all its sons away; / They fly forgotten, as a dream / Dies at the opening day." On a good Sunday, the hymn choosers at Saint James forgo their challenge that we should try Something New, expand our horizons and vocal cords beyond the old-time favorites. Beyond the favorites of our grandfathers and their grandfathers before them. On those good Sundays we're spared discord and novelty as the organ strikes up the old familiar strains of Isaac Watts's eighteenth-century St. Anne. "Time, like an ever-rolling stream . . ." We make a joyful noise, all ye nations. We swing we sway. We're rocking and rollin' here. "Bears all her sons away." We love this hymn. You'd never know we're singing about our complete lack of significance. But then Isaac Watts and Venice make the prophet Isaiah's contention acceptable: All flesh is grass, / And all its loveliness is like the / flower of the field. / The grass withers, the flower / fades. . . .

Here below the sky, afloat on the sea, in a never-never landscape of dreams inhabited for a few breaths by centuries of mortals who looked upon it all with the same awe, the same wonder, we enter history's flow. Time like an ever-rolling stream, not time the stagnant pool, not time the dammed reservoir, but time as sourceless as the ancient Nile. It bears us away, it doesn't drown us. It supports, cradles, enfolds us. We are Moses in the bulrushes. If we're lucky, no pharaoh's daughter will pluck us from the cool springs.

The morning after my fruitless interviews, Rebecca and I rise late. To recover from a surfeit of celebrities, we head for lunch on the Lido, a strip of sand bordered by beach cabanas. A spit of land favored by gamblers and moviemakers and those traveling with children who prefer pools to palazzi. I imagine Byron swimming here from his rooms on the Grand Canal. A long, long swim. For us, a lazy twenty-minute boat ride in the hotel's varnished mahogany launch.

We dine on octopus served under large oaks next to a pool dug into the shady lawn of Thomas Mann's favored Hôtel des Bains. As we wait for espresso and fruit, I wander onto the great marble verandah for a view of the flat sea edged with striped canvas cabanas as bright-colored as children's marbles. Inside the lobby, a cool, dark retreat from the sea's reflected glare, I ask if I might see the dining room where Mann took his meals. To my surprise, I'm ushered right in.

The draperies are drawn. Dust motes swim across a hair-thin shaft of light. There is a slight sour scent of past meals mingling with perfume and memories of the ladies who lingered here. I am not alone. I see Mann sitting in the gloom. I see the family walk in with their son, Tadzio in his striped sailor suit with red breast knot. Tadzio, whom Mann, or Aschenbach or Mann's inspiration will envelop, love, and contain in art. The beautiful boy. The promise, innocence, beauty that is too frail for this world.

Back at the pool, a Hollywood hopeful in cowboy boots and string bikini prances for no good reason. Dark tresses curl their way down her back. Large sunglasses shade her eyes. Long legs, slightly rounded belly, very rounded breasts. Italian trying to look American. She's heard that important producers are in town. Maybe, oh, just maybe she'll be discovered.

Cherries in a cut-glass bowl of ice water. Apricots and peaches on a plate. Wallace Stevens's, "Death is the mother of beauty . . . / She causes boys to pile new plums and pears / On disregarded plate." We lean back in our chairs and stare at a disinterested sky shaped by a canopy of green above our heads. An afternoon breeze begins to rise from the warm sea. Birds sing more quietly. There are longer intervals of silence. A child splashes in the pool. His mother's eyes grow heavy.

I am one of a long procession of pilgrims who have come to these Lagoon islands to give their bounty to the living and the dead, to experience romance as both yearning and the forms to which it gives rise. Pilgrimages, romantic or religious, don't come with guarantees, and some arrive to disappointment. Montaigne found Venice, "Other than . . . imagined and not quite wonderful." I wonder if he didn't find the strange melancholy and sensual quality of the air vaguely irritating. For D. H. Lawrence it was "An abhorrent, green, slippery city." Boys who wished they were girls came, men who wanted to be women, nuns who preferred to party. Poets, dreamers, liars, the fanciful, and fearful forever drawn to these islands where anything is possible, to islands dreamed rather than formed, where reality and illusion blend in the quantum soup of romance.

Henry James came and was stirred beyond his profound intellect. Wagner, Proust, Goethe, Nietzsche sought inspiration. The painters came. Sargent, Monet, Hassam, Whistler, Prendergast. They knew that here the veil between self and art, senses and physical surroundings was very thin. You can see it in their work. A blur between light and form. Cézanne's garden. The mystery of light coming into the world. Color. Color. Color.

The molecules dance in Venice, and you can see them. How else to explain the shimmer in the air, the sense that the mirth and tragedy of ages past are dancing and dirging, are playing out their ancient pageantry in the spaces around us.

"This place is so beautiful I want to marry it," exudes Dean Devlin, writer and coproducer of *Independence Day* and *Godzilla*. "I dress up for Venice," says Rebecca's colleague Jessica Shaw, when asked about the flowing chiffon gowns she wears each evening as we sit on the Gritti Palace Hotel terrace for our habitual nightcap. We sit and watch Venice settle into itself when it is no longer called upon to bolster the happy hysteria of tourists packed into gondolas six abreast, snapping photographs of the stripe-shirted tenor, whose voice practically stirs up white caps on the Grand Canal's murky surface.

When no longer called upon to fulfill expectations of those who have entered dreaming, the islands seem to breathe a deep sigh. We sigh with them and stare at the moon over Santa Maria della Salute. Beauty and Truth and Experience begin their stealthy, nocturnal peregrinations. We are being stalked.

Hollywood's producers call it a day and unload their cell phones like pistols at the door. They hang their Armani suits outside their rooms for pressing, their many-buckled shoes on thick carpet for shining. Who knows where the movie stars are? We're alone.

Our guidebooks are upstairs by our beds. The Palladian churches are closed. The Academia is closed. Titian's lovely *Madonna di Ca' Pesaro* and Bellini's tender *Madonna and Child with Saints* are shut behind the great doors of Santa Maria Gloriosa del Frari Church. Do Titian's boy aristocrat and Bellini's stern Saint Benedict, who have met our stares with their own, finally close their eyes? Fiore is closed. No more Connoccia Veneziano, the sweet-tasting lagoon creatures that look like mutated crayfish. Do

Forni is closed. No more apricots in bowls of ice. The outdoor market is closed. No more white peaches that explode with juice once teeth make contact. *Cuiso. Cuiso.* All distractions *cuiso.*

Now Venice begins to have its way with us. Now it opens our eyes and ears. Now it dares us to peek beneath the veil we call reality. Romance always follows this pattern, moving into the stillness left in the wake of frantic pursuit. Venice is intensely romantic because it insists on this stillness and has the power to silence even gregarious busybodies like Ruskin, who could not say enough about the place. Who kept saying it and saying it and saying it until we, his readers, are driven to jump up and down shouting, "Enough! Enough!"

He couldn't say enough until he walked into the Scuola di San Rocco, where Tintoretto's *Crucifixion* was waiting to get the best of him. "I must leave this picture to work its will on the spectator, for it is beyond all analysis and above all praise." It comes as no surprise that Ruskin's most profound romantic moment occurred when this compulsive analyst finally came face to face with beauty "beyond . . . analysis." Keats's Beauty. The Truth that defies reason and silences the tongue. Beauty that leaves us lonelier than before.

Venice is romantic because like all romantic objects of desire it will forever elude the compulsive analytic grasp.

Monty Roberts, horse trainer favored by the Queen of England, writes that if you go after a wild horse, it will walk or run away. If you gain the horse's trust, if you dare turn your back on it, stay put, and wait, chances are eventually you'll feel the heavy weight of its head upon your shoulder, feel its damp, warm breath in your ear. If you're lucky. If you wait. If you trust. If you believe. If you dare.

That daring is what separates us from the Romanticists, who trusted that in the silence of the fully experienced moment, Truth and Beauty would breathe sweetly in their ears.

When a reporter asked recent Pulitzer Prize-winning poet, Charles Wright, how he found his voice, he responded, "It eventually found me." Ah, yes, but one has to want to be found.

We are waiting to be found as we sit on the Gritti terrace and pull our shawls snug against midnight's chill. We are sentinels at the gates of our own lives.

"Once when I was in Florence," Dean whispers, "I climbed to the top of the Duomo with a girl I knew. As we stood there and stared out over the rooftops, the bells began to ring and pigeons filled the air, and there was nothing to do but passionately kiss. There were no words. We kissed and kissed and kissed and never spoke of it again." Silence.

The tide moves in from the lagoon and licks the palazzo's stony haunches. "I wonder what ever became of her?" We join Dean's sigh.

We're wrong when we refer to these experiences as "found moments." We don't find them, they find us. Such moments ride in on Beauty and remind us that Keats was right, that in knowing this, we know all we need to know.

13

THE KING OF FOREPLAY

O.K., so Venice didn't deliver important insights into Hollywood's take on romance. It's clearly time to head for the source. I take a plane to the Coast (as they say) to interview Sydney Pollack, who, Harrison Ford tells me, is a great romantic, "the king of foreplay."

The director of such films as *Three Days of the Condor, Tootsie, Out of Africa,* and *The Way We Were,* as well as the more recent *Sense and Sensibility,* with Emma Thompson, and the remake of *Sabrina,* with Ford in the Bogart role, this is a man who gets it, who knows that romance is in the longing not the humping. In his movies, hearts ache, eyes tear, hands touch, smiles are brave, and you may see a stranger across a crowded room, but you'll never see a bare bottom on a bed.

Stepping off the plane, I feel like a budding Fauvist shocked by brightness. Los Angeles's light startles those of us accustomed to the subtleties of gray. I squint against the flat glare that looks like something Cecil B. De Mille forgot to turn off.

At the airport's car-rental office, I request a sensible, mid-size, four-door sedan. The clerk looks at me and sees a project. An evangelical glint brightens his green, green-tinted contact lenses. "Hey, live a little," says he. The flat light presses against his dangling rhinestone earring. A day-old growth of blond beard stands out on his chin, Brad Pitt style. He wants to be an actor. Everyone here wants to be an actor. Wants to shine against the light.

"It's a beautiful day," says Mr. Feel Good Avis-Rent-a-Car Guru. "How about a convertible?" There's a particular bounce to L.A. talk. A perkiness. A determined defiance of the-terrible-

state-of-the-world. It's difficult to register protest in an atmosphere of such buoyancy. But I do. I'm thinking about my nervous husband back in New York, to whom I regularly make a
series of vows before leaving home. I will not talk to strangers.
I'll look both ways before crossing. And I will never, under any
circumstances, ride in a car with the top down.

But Guru takes me by the hand (they like to touch you in
L.A.) and leads me to the parking lot, where he gestures
grandly, opening both arms as though delivering an aria center
stage. "How about this?" "This" is a little red Miata. "You're kidding," say I. I want it. I can't help myself.

"I'll give you a special deal. Come on. I can tell, you're a
top-down kind of girl."

It's been so long since I've been called "girl," so long since
"Ma'am" was "Miss," that there's no saying No. A deal is made, a
credit card surrendered, and I drive off low to the ground, wind in
my hair, smog in my lungs, and, oh yes, a song in my heart. "Doo-
wha-doo-wha-doo-wha-ditty, / Talk about the girl from New
York City." Flat out against flat light that turns a landscape of
swimming pools, pink motels, and storefront acupressure salons
into so many stage sets. How could you do anything here but play
Let's Pretend?

Vrooom. Straight to the Four Seasons Hotel in Beverly Hills.
The Hot and Happening Four Seasons in Beverly Hills, where the
stars crowd the bar at night and the breakfast room in the morning. Where chances are good that you'll be pressed up close to
some movie star in the elevator and be unable to watch his movies
ever again with your former rapture now that you discover he
doesn't bathe or change his clothes over the course of three days.
If you're lucky.

"Welcome to the Four Seasons," says cheery Randy as he
opens my door. Nuts. I wanted to spring over the side.

The bellhop appears before I've figured out how to raise the
convertible top. My luggage is carted away, and I leave the
mechanics to Randy.

One of the good things about a job that frequently requires
others to pay for my travel is that I've gotten the chance to

learn something very important. Four Seasons hotels deliver hotel romance. A particular romance of Let's Pretend You're the Fairy Princess and We're Your Faithful Servants. Who taught them this? Who was the genius up there in Canadian corporate headquarters who knew that we all long for a recess from adulthood, from responsibility mingled with mundanity? Who knew that we grow weary of being working stiffs? That we want to be taken care of, just for a little while. To be cared for by a fairy godmother who's rescued us from a wicked stepmother called Real Life.

"Is this all right?" My bags are delivered to a bright room with a terrace opening to hills behind a scrim of smog, a room with a marble bathroom complete with telephone, with a bed that feels the way you imagine a cloud might feel if it weren't a cloud. "This will do just fine," say I, who feel the awakening of the Lana Turner within. Where'd I get this, "This will do just fine?"

I unpack, put on a bathing suit, and take the elevator to the fourth floor and the outdoor pool. I test the water's reality with a toe. For all I know, it could be a life-size David Hockney painting. The light's trickery makes the white lounge chairs look as though they're made of paper or acrylic on canvas. The breeze brings a breath of life. It causes a rustling in the too green leaves of potted ficus and fruit-laden lemon trees, from which, naturally, lemons and figs hang. Land of milk and honey. Land of smoke and mirrors. I test the chair with the press of a palm before lowering my full weight onto it. It holds.

This is a day of special deals and treats. Deals and treats are Hollywood's heart's blood. I've been offered, free of charge, the use of a hundred-dollar-a-day, pool-side cabana. A white canvas three-sided cabana with just enough room for a table, telephone, lounge chair, and overhead fan should I feel a swoon coming on. The canvas is gathered to a point at the top and pulled back in the front to offer a full view of pool, greenery, and other cabanas, where important men with hairy chests talk on the phone and make, you guessed it, deals.

The breeze folds and unfolds. Flap, flap, flap. A young man whose dark hair is cosmetically enhanced with copper tones interrupts my reverie to pour a glass of iced lemon water. Like magic, he reappears every time the liquid drops exactly one inch below the rim. He comes eagerly from his station, a desk at the other end of the pool. His strong legs carry him swiftly. Like all others in service here, he is cheerful, cheerful, cheerful. There's not enough he can do for me. Perhaps I'd like to see the lunch menu?

Just some iced coffee and fruit, please. I'm concerned about being drowsy for my meeting with Pollack, which has been scheduled to last exactly one hour. Nothing more, nothing less. He's a busy man. You won't catch him bare-chested in a cabana, adorned in importance and a Lycra bikini. He's far too busy searching out the perfect love story to be lulled into oblivion by the occasional, desultory splash of a swimmer, click of an overhead fan, service provided before you knew you wanted it.

I gather my courage, towel, and notes, and head downstairs to dress. The local couture code appears to require rumpled Armani, shiny Gucci. I can manage linen trousers, something I saw in a Katharine Hepburn movie.

Randy brings the car around. I'm surprised all over again to see a red, devil-may-care, no roll-over-bars Miata rather than a sturdy Volvo sedan. I give him a dollar. I want to say something grand. Something Grace Kelly would say. Something loftier than "Have a nice day." Something along the lines of "Randy. How very kind." What comes out is "Wow!"

The radio has been turned on to the station I was listening to as I came from the airport. The Four Seasons thinks of everything. I tie a scarf around my head the way I've seen Audrey Hepburn do it. I pull away to the beat of a song about the sun coming up on Santa Monica Boulevard. By the time I've gone a quarter of a mile, I'm tapping my steering wheel and singing along with Sheryl Crow, "All I want to do is have some fuu-unnnn, / I've got the feeling I'm not the only onnnne. . . ."

The hotel has provided me with a map and carefully written instructions. As promised, there on my left are the famous black cast-iron gates ordered by Cecil B. De Mille so that everyone arriving on the lot could make a "grand entrance." He was right. They create a sense of anticipation. I feel as though

I'm going to the movies. I feel as though the lights have just gone off and everyone has gotten quiet. Like the movies when I was a kid. When the lights would go out and so would the air, as though everyone was holding his breath until the curtain parted and the studio logo appeared and the music started. Then the communal exhale and a settling into seats for the duration.

These gates, "The best in L.A.," according to Rebecca, are like the curtain separating us from the magic. To be allowed inside is to have the movie begin.

Pollack's offices are in the De Mille building, part of a compound on the original Paramount lot. Nearly antique by Hollywood standards, the white stucco two-story 1926 structure looks like something that materialized off a page of Raymond Chandler. I may have to step aside for Harpo or Groucho, Rudolph Valentino, Mary Pickford, Marlene Dietrich, or Clara Bow, as I make my way up the narrow, spider-plant and palm festooned path. The lot is silent now, and yet the air is thick with the past's lingering, a past when breasts were real and lips thick with Love That Red! A past of beautiful collarbones revealed, oh my, by a bit of off-the-shoulder recklessness.

The interior walls are covered with vintage and new movie posters. Donna, Pollack's assistant, emerges exactly on schedule and ushers me to her boss's office. He stands to greet me. Sydney Pollack is big. So big that as I extend my hand to shake his, I seem to be eye level with his handmade Southwestern silver belt buckle.

Books line the shelves; birdsong and the sweet fragrance of a blooming tree waft through the open windows. We take our seats on either side of a large, tidy oak desk.

He earmarks a page and closes Joan Didion's new novel, which he admires. "I'm in the process of reading my brains out trying to find the next picture," he tells me, gesturing to neatly stacked piles of manuscripts. Pollack's a rarity. A reader in a town where the written word's greatest value is in a contract or on a menu. Here is a reader on a mission. Sydney Pollack, Mr. Romance, is looking for a love story.

And he knows what he's looking for. Not so in the early days, when "I just made what appealed to me. I had no idea that

I was a romantic and I certainly didn't set out to be one. I just told stories that felt right to me."

It was the French (but, of course) who told him that not only was he a romantic, but that he seemed to hold the secret to great romantic filmmaking. "A group of French critics did a little monograph about my work," he explains, modestly. "This was at a time when I'd made five films and was better known in that country than this one. I was truly startled to see that they emphasized the romantic nature of my films." He was particularly interested in their observation that his movies repeatedly featured "lovers who never seem to get together."

During the next five years, he found that he was frequently asked about the power of unrequited yearning, and why it was so prevalent in his movies. "I would have been lying if I'd said, 'Here's the reason.'

"But I began to ask myself the same question. Why are there so many stories in which the romance is created by the fact that the lovers don't get together? I realized that I didn't know one great love story in opera, drama, fiction in which the lovers got together. From *Tristan and Iseult* to Héloïse and Abelard to *Romeo and Juliet* to *Gone With the Wind*, to *Dr. Zhivago.*"

The realization didn't change the character of his work, but helped him to understand what he'd been doing all along, reaching into that timeless well of yearning where thirst is created and art is born.

He began to analyze what he'd been doing instinctively and discovered that among a romantic love story's essential elements are "two people you're fond of as an audience, two people you feel invested in in some way and whom you want to find the peace or happiness that seems to be eluding them."

Then you must keep them apart like the lovers on Keats's Grecian Urn. The unspanned space between them is the womb of romance. For Pollack this space is most dramatically found in the irreconcilable differences between people who love each other.

"I like to find two strong-willed people with different points of view. I look for the argument, the center of those differences. If you try to be fair to that argument and not make one right and the other wrong, you sometimes dig such a valley between them that the only truthful ending for the film is for them to part." The result is "a greater resonance. Once those differences are resolved, and the two get together, the yearning is satisfied and the story's over."

Requital doesn't live on, cling to you as you walk out of the theater into the light of day. It doesn't haunt your dreams. It doesn't make your heart ache while you're doing the laundry or cooking dinner.

Children need happily ever after, because their hearts aren't trained in the art of breaking open. Grown-ups know the passion is in the longing.

We've always known it, but once again it took the French to tell us so. It was there in the twelfth century that what has become known as "courtly love" was born. Its only requirements were two noble beings, the singer of the song, the troubadour, and the object of his desire, a lady most fair, a lady of the court, above him in station. Chances are that the songs of "courtly love" were disguised songs of desire for mystical union with the divine, inspired by the Cathars, Christian heretics who migrated from Byzantium and were firmly established in the South of France by 1160. The spiritual goal of this highly secretive, persecuted group was the release of the soul (God's province) from the body (Satan's) through renunciation of matters of the flesh. For them, there would be no earthly requital for desire. Whatever the source, powerful stories and poignant songs of unrequited love began to flourish and gave language to age-old longing, form to the amorphous desire to merge with the pure, the good, the beautiful, to be reborn into that purity through love.

What Pollack learned from his study of the oldest known love stories was "We don't value anything that we have in great supply. We're not capable of sustaining it for a long period of time. If you have chocolate every day, chocolate doesn't taste good. If you have caviar every day . . ." Try me.

He probably knows. Don't be fooled by his lack of ostentation, by the professional intensity, by the blue jeans and blue work shirt, by the absence of grandeur and pomp, Sydney Pollack is a very successful man. Studios are well pleased with his box-office record, and actors and writers who value his sensitive intelligence are keen to work with him. There's plenty of caviar and chocolate in this life.

So I have faith in his assertion, "It seems to be a human trait that you value enormously that which you cannot have. And no matter how immature that sounds, it's part of the human animal, and it's true with love stories.

"I think if you got everybody in the world to talk candidly and honestly about themselves and their lives, you'd find that most people have not married the great love of their life. The question is, do they think they didn't marry the great loves of their lives for the simply reason that they didn't marry them?" Does the power of that romance live on in memory because it is a dream and therefore elusive, whereas "they have ready access to the person they married"?

That is the question he regularly returns to in his films, preferring to focus on the great love affair that does not culminate in marriage. "Like the one in *The Way We Were*."

Oh, yes. That one. I remember the steady stream of women leaving the Paris theater in New York in 1973 having just seen Barbra Streisand and Robert Redford in that Pollack movie. They clutched crumbled tissues and stared out at the world surprised, red-eyed, careless of their mascara and disappointed in the men at their sides.

"Streisand's and Redford's characters will remember that relationship all their lives, which isn't to say that Streisand's character married a lesser man. I think of that as a very happy marriage. But it's not going to erase the mark made on her by the relationship with the Redford character."

Pollack doesn't necessarily start out determined to keep the lovers apart. "But again and again I find that I've created a situation where the only truthful way is for them to part."

He recalls his early movie *The Electric Horseman,* starring Jane Fonda and Redford. "Even in a light romantic comedy like that, there's no way it could work between those two people in the context of the world in which they lived." She an up-and-coming big-city reporter, he a down-and-out rodeo star driven to advertising breakfast cereal. "He's not going to work in New York City in a sophisticated environment. But for a time, without the distractions of the respective worlds that they come from, they have personalities that are of real interest to one another, and they create sparks when they come together." Although there is no requital of desire, the traditional troubadour trial by fire is endured, and both characters emerge with knowledge of their true or, a mystic might say, divine selves. They merge with an elusive truth rather than each other.

"It seems that I deal with similar issues in every film, even in action films like *Three Days of the Condor* or *Jeremiah Johnson*. Always at the center of the movie there is a love story."

Watch them at your peril. Nobody lives happily ever after. They live wiser. They've learned about love, they've learned about themselves, they've learned something about the other guys and what we're all doing here together. They've learned the great lessons, but they don't get the sweet innocence of happily-ever-after.

"I think that you speak best about everything else in a one-on-one relationship. Even politics. I've always said that if a woman is sitting in a room reading a newspaper and a man sits down, you have a political situation. Does he smoke? Does he ask her permission to smoke? Does he ask to borrow her newspaper? Does he say, 'Thank you' when he does? Is he rude? Is he considerate? Is she considerate? Is she friendly?" The love story anchors the film, and the characters' responses to that love reflect the film's themes. "Or, more pretentiously, you might say that they are metaphors for each other."

For instance, his film *Out of Africa*, starring Redford again and Meryl Streep, "is essentially about ownership and possession. The central question is, If I say, 'I love you,' then what of myself am I obliged to give up, and how much of myself can I keep?" Karen Blixen, played by Streep, is, "a woman who wants ownership of everything, including people." Redford's Denys Finch-Hatton, on the other hand, "is a man who flees to this place (Africa from England), because he can't stand the idea of curtailing his individuality based on the demands of a structured society or another person. So he goes to this vast uncivilized place, and there he meets this woman who is determined to own the land, the people, and him.

"Hatton believes in living side by side, not intertwined, to which Blixen responds, 'My God, in the world that you live in there would be no love at all.' 'Or the best kind,' says Redford.

"Those arguments run so deep that those people could never have been together. It so happens that historically Hatton died in a plane crash, but had he not, they never would have made it."

And yet we want it to work. They want it to work. We, the children at the movies, in the laps of the storytellers, want the happily ever after.

But Pollack is steadfast, "It's the yearning that makes the film work." The sparks have to fly, there has to be "chemistry between the two people, whatever the hell that is." The atmosphere must be charged with unsated sexual energy. "If you dissipate that, you're stuck in this no man's land of sustaining love. This might be wonderful in life, bliss in life, but in terms of storytelling it fails, because there are no opposing forces, no tension."

Tension is his films' framework. It lives in the long silences, in the unspoken emotion. It lives in the ache evoked by the beauty of the natural surroundings that will not be possessed. It is there in the space between the protagonist, an outsider, and the civilized world he or she struggles to inhabit.

"You can't steady something without opposing forces. You want to straighten a tree, you pull it in opposite directions. You pull a rope this way, and another that way, and another way, and then the tree stands strong. But if you pull in only one direction that tree is going to be very, very weak."

Consummation of love pulls everything in one direction. "You have one great moment left after lovemaking, and that's the first time the lovers meet afterward, particularly if there's an obstacle in the way of their romance, if it's adulterous or intertribal or intercultural. Any situation that makes the union somehow illicit.

This is a great moment always, one full of drama." Imagine, he suggests, that the lovers are a Muslim and a Catholic. "They sneak away at night, and now the next day they go in to work and there she is and there he is. Now you have a terrific moment. How are they going to behave? That's appealing and it's sexy and audiences can't wait to see how they're going to be that next moment. It's a great mystery to me how writers skip that moment so often. I'm always sitting down with writers, saying, 'Well, we're missing a terrific moment here. What's the next morning like?' "

What it's like is tense. "It's so fraught the first time two people make love that they don't really get to know each other any better. It's a hurdle that they've gotten beyond, and how are they now?" Once that scene has been accomplished, the romance cannot be sustained on film. "One gets into familiar territory, one gets comfortable, or not, with the other person, gets drawn more and more into the relationship. Then, in terms of storytelling, all you're left with is trying to invent the cutest way to show two people in love. You do montages, and they look like hygiene commercials, people walking through flowers. We're reduced to absolute adolescence when showing two people in love on film. Do you bite off fruit and put it in her mouth with your mouth? It's just absurd. It doesn't translate. It's like watching mothers with their babies. It's great for them but it's sort of boring for everybody else.

"I can sustain several hours of *falling* in love, and I can sustain several hours of breaking up, but if I have to go for more than five minutes in a movie of *in* love . . ." he throws his arms up in helplessness.

But are we willing to watch several hours of falling in love? The American attention span appears to be diminishing along with the ability to withstand frustration. The studios strive to satisfy a perceived audience hunger for what Pollack calls "the sensate, a thrill, a ride. A *Twister* or a *Mission Impossible*. Movies that do something to you sensorially." And leave your heart alone. It's as though we've regressed. That like children we rush to fill rather than dare to experience the gap between object and desire.

From Pollack's vantage point, "There seems to be less patience for the kind of complicated, collective experience that has to take an hour and a half to get to the high point. *Twister* is 'Look out! Here it comes!' right from the beginning, and it stays at that level of intensity. Our world has become an MTV world with little patience for narrative. When I was growing up, things were very linear. You would tell a story with a beginning, a middle, and an end. Today you'll see kids doing homework with earphones on, listening to rock music, playing with a computer, and watching television with no sound. Seven things are going on at the same time, and so the fight for attention is intense, and they do not have patience with beginnings and endings. They want the middle. They want to cut to the chase."

And the chase is inevitably graphic. "There is no point beyond which you cannot go in a movie anymore. When I first began to make movies, I was still very strongly influenced by the movies that I had seen as a kid, in which a graphic love scene would have been very rare. Now movies deliver levels of violence and sexuality which would have been impossible fifteen years ago, even ten years ago. Once you get exposed to that your nerves are a little bit raw, so to create a sensation among people whose nerves are raw requires even more sensation, and we get into a very bad circle here.

"There're too many exciting alternatives. When I say exciting I mean exciting to the nerves, to the glands, to the senses. In a certain way, we've become jaded about what it is that affects you."

He pauses and to illustrate his point turns for example to one of his favorite references, cuisine. "We know that about food, and we know that about wine, but we don't know it about life. We know better the sequence of food to serve to keep you interested. You don't ever start with chili peppers and then serve a delicate dish. You would say, 'What are you doing? You're not going to taste this after you taste that.' You don't ever start with a harsh, rough Chianti and then go to a beautiful, delicate Bordeaux. And you can't do that in life, either. Once you excite the nerves and get them buzzing, it's very hard to sit back and relax and be moved by something lyrical and delicate. The result is an entertainment business serving up greater and greater sensation to make the audience feel something."

He thinks that this perceived need for thrill rather than intense

emotional engagement was born with the drug culture of the sixties and the early seventies. "You felt you smoked a joint and all
sensation was heightened. The music sounded better, sex seemed
richer, your thoughts seemed to be more profound. Whether or
not they were is a whole other thing, but everybody was looking
for more sensate experiences. And the film business got caught in
this rat race."

The great romantic movies, he believes, came from the "middle market which has sort of disappeared, but that's where the
Casablancas and *The Best Years of Our Lives* came out of. They
weren't 'event' movies." He cheers up a bit at the thought. "Well,
actually there are a lot of great romances. *Ace in the Hole* had a terrific love story in it with Kirk Douglas and Jan Sterling. *Young Man
with a Horn* with Douglas and Doris Day. *On the Waterfront* had a
good love story. *East of Eden* with Julie Harris and James Dean,
Rebel Without a Cause with Natalie Wood and James Dean, and
that wonderful movie with Warren Beatty that Kazan did, *Splendor in the Grass*. That's a wonderful movie.

"The sixties changed absolutely everything. It changed the
way people talk, it changed what was shocking, what wasn't
shocking." He thinks that the powerful influence of that time
was a reaction to the conventional morality that had preceded
it. "The intensity of the words, the acts, the concepts came from
their forbiddenness. It was so powerful that suddenly it was as
though everyone was saying of sex, for instance, 'Hey look, this
is a normal, natural thing. Animals do it. Everyone does it. Do it
whenever you want.'

"Of course, there are really good things about that, and there
are very bad things about that. It's good that you take away the
myths and taboos that shrouded sexuality in the United States
prior to the sixties." On the other hand, what it did to the movies
is not particularly interesting. "The truth of the matter is, watching two people simulate sex in a movie is boring. But it's become
currency, and I think there's something sad about it because it's
defused the intensity of sex as something reserved for a very special place in one's life, or a very special set of circumstances, or a
special kind of relationship."

Sigh. What's he doing later today?

"It's not that I'm puritanical, just sad that sex will never be for this generation what it was for my generation, and, of course, I think it was extraordinary for my generation. Extraordinary in the sense that it represented the ultimate connection to somebody. It didn't just represent a token of having a nice night. It was something much more than that, almost magic, mystical. And that's partially because it was forbidden. Because it was not something you could just decide that you would do whenever you wanted to do it.

"We take it for granted in a way now. We just do. I can remember the fifties very vividly and, Jesus, a guy who got caught sneaking out of a girl's house who actually spent the night there, he would be very embarrassed if everybody found out. Whereas today, my daughters, for Christ's sake, have been living with guys since they were fifteen years old or something. It's a different world, and I admire it, and I feel bad for them at the same time."

And us moviegoers? Does he feel bad for us? Are we to face a screen and a world devoid of romance because we don't have the patience, courage, or attention span to sustain it? If the greed for profit, the hunger for thrills escalates in direct proportion to the demise of patience and ability to withstand frustration, if easy access to drugs allows us to numb the pain of unrequited love, will we become too cowardly for romance? Decide not to risk it? Prefer to skip that part of experience? Will those muscles in our hearts atrophy to the point that they can no longer be called into service.

I think of Barbara Hernstein Smith, my college Renaissance Poetry professor, who, one day halfway through the term, looked up from her notes, removed her glasses, and gazed out at us with a mixture of curiosity and despair. "What's the matter with you?" she asked us, a generation of long hair, hoop earrings, bell bottoms, discontent, and safely impersonal free-love rhetoric. "Why are you so afraid to risk love? So you love and you lose. So what?"

The end of the world, we thought back then. Not for us the heart of Petrarch: "I cling to life, and yet would gladly perish; /Detest myself, and yet another cherish." Not for us Henry

Howard, Earl of Surrey: "When raging love with extreme pain /
Most cruelly distrains my heart; / When that my tears, as floods
of rain / Bear witness to my woeful smart."

Perhaps it was too much heartbreak too young. Two
Kennedys, one King, one Kent State student, all gunned down. We
decided to sit it out.

Have we healed? Do we dare bring our hearts out of stor-
age?

Pollack doesn't know. And yet he sits here at his desk looking
for a love story. Chances are it will have all the elements of great
romance. Chances are it will start something like this. "His name
was Jeremiah Johnson and they say he wanted to be a mountain
man. The story goes that he was a man of proper wit and adven-
turous spirit well suited to the mountains. . . . Nobody knows
whereabouts he come from and don't seem to matter much. . . .
This here's his story."

Chances are the protagonists will be outsiders, people of deep
integrity who have lost their way. They'll fall in love, find temporary solace from loneliness, suffer great pain. Self-knowledge will
emerge from grief, the inevitability of being at odds with this
earthly life will be recognized, the lovers will go in the direction
such knowledge leads. It will never be the same direction.

Chances are this is what Pollack's looking for. He'll look
until he finds it.

MRS. ADELMAN

Back from the Coast, I find myself at the corner of Amsterdam Avenue and Seventy-ninth Street with Mrs. Adelman. Mrs. Adelman of the English accent and refinement. Mrs. Adelman of the widowhood worn wistfully. Mrs. Adelman of the typewriters.

Something there that loves a typewriter, I told my friend Fran Kiernan yesterday over lunch. "Oh, yes," said she, who has just finished writing more than a thousand pages on the life of Mary McCarthy. "Mary wrote on an Olivetti and swore by it."

Fran has spent so many years with McCarthy that they are now intimates on a first-name basis. The empathy runs deep. When Fran looks sad, it's generally because "Mary had a bad day."

Fran and typewriters go way back. Starting as an assistant on her way up to becoming fiction editor at *The New Yorker,* she typed on hand-me-downs of the illustrious. She'd use them until the keys stuck. Her last had belonged to Janet Flanner, a "Facit which had particularly good action." It was an honor to touch those keys.

We spoke of this, we who now write on computers but remain unconverted. "So," I said to her as we settled in next to the fireplace at Lumi on Lexington Avenue for soup and cheer against the cold rain of early spring, "I'm not entirely convinced. I mean, big deal, so you can cut and paste with the touch of a single key."

"When I first came to *The New Yorker,* I typed *Ancestors* for William Maxwell." We both sigh, sharing a deep admiration for this writer, for whom words of praise seem too slight. "As you know, that was a very complicated book. That's when I learned to cut and paste. He'd just do it with scissors and tape, moving things around." Yes. We stare out at the rain bouncing up a few inches as it hits and then surrenders to the pavement. Yes, those were the days. Sigh.

"I've felt for a long time that I wrote better on a typewriter. But with big projects and short deadlines . . ." I leave the rest unsaid.

"Oh, I know, I know. I never could have written this biography without a computer."

"But people did. Boswell's Johnson. Plato's Socrates. Vasari's lives of the artists."

"Hmm, yes." We eat soup in silence.

"On the other hand," I say, "yesterday I was revising an article and was appalled to find repetitions. Clunky transitions. Things that would never have happened if I'd had to retype the entire manuscript as I edited."

"Yes, but you're under time pressure."

"I'm not sure I've saved time. First draft longhand, then into the computer, then at least twenty drafts. Then reading out loud to see how it sounds. And then, what really settled it for me . . ." until that moment, I had not realized that it had been settled, "I received a friend's new book. She's an elegant writer. Her last book was pre-computer and was lovely. Here the computer was showing. Like a soignée lady walking into Le Cirque 2000 in vintage Chanel with a rip in her stocking and mascara running down her face."

"So, what are you going to do?"

"Go see Mrs. Adelman."

I tell her about Mrs. Adelman of Osners Business Machines, a dusty gray store humming with the sound of overhead fluorescent lights. A store the size of a Park Avenue apartment's walk-in closet. Mrs. Adelman of the stacks of discarded typewriters that she tends lovingly, nursing them back to health.

"One day I was in her store and fell in love with a little Olympia. It was just sitting there on the counter, looking sort of like Sylvie in midpirouette."

"Who's Sylvie?"

"I can't remember her last name. A delicate swan of a balle-rina. She's French and occasionally dances with ABT. Anyway, this typewriter reminded me of her and I reached out to touch its keys. They were facing me, after all," I added defensively, still a bit surprised by what happened. "And suddenly, there was Mrs. Adelman directly across the counter, she'd been nowhere to be seen a second ago, and there she was reaching out to stop my hand. I was shocked. I asked her why.

"'That,' she told me breathlessly, 'belongs to a famous play-wright, and he doesn't let anyone but me touch it.'"

"So, whose was it?" Fran asked. This was as close to good gossip as either of us had gotten in the months and years of soli-tary confinement with our respective subject matters.

"Well, I know it's not Wendy Wasserstein's, because she sent me there in the first place, and that's not the typewriter she works on, and Mrs. Adelman said 'He.' Maybe it's John Guare's. No, he's not that eccentric. Maybe that guy who wrote *Who's Afraid of Virginia Woolf.*"

"Edward Albee?"

"Maybe."

"How about Neil Simon?"

"That would be cool."

I'm not sure how we made up our minds. As with many life-changing decisions, you could be put on the stand under oath and still not be able to bring forth the natural progression of thought and conversation that lead to certainty. All I know is that as Fran walked me to my bike, now shiny with rain, I was promising to give her the name of the person in charge of home shopping at the Vinegar Factory, a must for writers with hungry husbands and looming deadlines, in exchange for her call to Mrs. Adelman to ask if she had any old Olivettis.

Somewhere between the soup and salad, the tea and cookies, we had achieved this balance of obligation. Writers, perhaps more than any other professionals, know as Kafka did, "The devil is in the distractions." And that's no metaphorical devil. Each time the phone rings it's like the tolling of the bell of doom. And to have to make phone calls is worse.

"I like to think," Eudora Welty once said, "that my life is taking care of itself while I sit and write. So sometimes I'm really surprised when I look up from writing and find that I haven't gone out to the Piggly Wiggly for supper things."

So Fran and I agree each to take charge of a detail of life. A northern version of Piggly Wiggly and the instruments of change.

This morning the phone rang. "Barbara, I talked to Mrs. Adelman. She has an old Olivetti and a new one. She says the old one is a better machine. I'm going over at twelve-thirty tomorrow to look at it, but you have first dibs."

"Why?"

"Because it was your idea."

I'm not at all certain about that, but agree to go have a look and "If I can't resist, we'll have joint custody."

In my excitement, I call my sister, Becky of the quick wit. It's hard to tell whether she's rolling her eyes in the fashion of her namesake, my daughter, but chances are pretty good as she asks, "Why?"

"Because I think I wrote better before the computer."

"Well, if that doesn't work," she responds, affecting a redneck drawl, "Then I'm jus' gonna send you some sharpened pencils. And if that doesn't work, I'm gonna send you a quill. And if that doesn't work, I might just send you a tablet and a chisel."

Nonetheless, here I stand with Mrs. Adelman, and it's still raining and it's still gray, and I am decidedly suffering from Wallace Stevens's "Depression before Spring": "But no queen comes / In slipper green."

"Do you want to type on a typewriter because *you* want to or because Wendy Wasserstein does?"

Does everybody in New York hang out a shingle? I admit there is a defensive tone as I assert that this is my idea, for me, for my work, and that Wendy Wasserstein might support the idea, but I'm not doing it because she does. As I continue a long-winded defense of myself, I am suddenly six years old, not having the faintest idea what the Empire State Building is, but assuring my mother that I would not jump off it, "Just because Linda Parquette did." My playmate, Linda Parquette, who must have enticed me to do something *outré*, such as wearing our mothers' Cherries in the Snow lipstick to school.

"No offense, Mrs. Adelman, but may I please see the Olivettis?"

"You know your friend is coming over to look tomorrow."

"I know. But she tells me I get to go first."

"O.K., then." She sighs and moves slowly toward the back of the shop. She and Carlos, her assistant, return with two small machines and set them on the counter. They turn each to face me the way a nurse in the nursery will hold a baby to the window for that moment when a new grandparent falls in love.

"Now, don't tell me which is the old and which is the new. I'd be prejudiced on behalf of the old." I feel it's time to show who's boss, even though it is perfectly clear that one machine is made of plastic and the other steel.

Suddenly plastic, beige plastic, the color of my computer, the color of my manuscript stand, the color of my Tupperware seems like the material of the antiromantic.

"Oh, God, yes!" was the response of my friend Elizabeth Berg, prolific, graceful novelist, when I had called her earlier in the day timidly to test my theory that computers had hurt the art of writing. "The invention of the devil," she replied. Some friends are so satisfying. "Computers are what is separating human beings from each other. . . . Listen," she'd added with excitement. There was a pause and then the distinct sound of keys that thud rather than clink, walk rather than skip. And then the sound of a bell as evocative as the church bells of Bruges. Another time. A time of simple faith that progress mattered less than art.

"That's what I just bought. That's my wonderful old Royal. I decided when spring comes I want to be able to sit out in my back yard under the trees and type."

I reminded her of the scene in the movie version of James Dickie's *Deliverance* when the actors play "Dueling Banjos." We imagined April air humming with the sound of typewriter keys hitting hammers which in turn hit rollers, air resounding with ringing bells and cranking return levers playing to each other across the airwaves between Boston and New York.

She emboldened me. I'm ready to follow the lead of anyone who can write last paragraphs like that in *Range of Motion*:

> I am living on a planet where the silk dresses of Renaissance women rustled, where people died in plagues, where Mozart sat to play, where sap runs in the spring, where children are caught in crossfire, where gold glints from rock, where religion shines its light only to lose its way, where people stop to reach a hand to help each other to cross, where much is known about the life of the ant. . . . I am living here on this planet . . . and I am listening with gratitude, and I am listening for as long as I can, and I am listening with all of my might.

Shelley could not have said it better. I'm ready.

To show Mrs. Adelman, librarian, third-grade teacher, mother, authority figure that I am playing fair and square, I start with the plastic one. Its keys are fatter and probably considered an improvement over its slender cousin's. But, even as I type, "Mrs. Adelman has a typewriter that belongs to a famous playwright and she won't let anybody touch it," my eyes are on the delicate keys of the smaller green steel version. I move onto that one. "Mrs. Adelman has a typewriter that belongs to a famous playwright and she won't let anybody touch it." No question. This is my typewriter. The bell isn't quite loud enough. A ping rather than the Royal's gong, but the return lever makes a satisfying two-note tune as it engages the gears and moves the roller up a notch, then urges it across the page with a soothing, low whine.

"Who is the famous playwright, Mrs. Adelmann?" I type. "Will you tell me if I buy this typewriter?" There's a typo. I crank back and strike a long-forgotten slash mark through the extra *n* in Adelman. Who knew I'd missed it so? The return lever is no thicker than a pen, just the right size for my finger. We're partners meant to be. A perfect Platonic fit.

"Of course you know which is the newer one," says Mrs.

Adelman perhaps tiring of the game and turning to a customer shifting restlessly behind me.

"Well, yes, but it's my favorite anyway."

"Do you mind if I help this gentleman?"

"Not at all." I am eager to ingratiate myself. I feel like a potential adoptive mother meeting with the agency. Will she approve of me? Find me deserving? Will she entrust a good typewriter to me?

"I'm in a hurry," the customer says. Big news in New York. He orders up a cartridge; Mrs. Adelman knows the size. "Thank you. I'll be back."

"Yes, I know. Next week," she says. She knows her customers. This is no Computerworld. This is no CompuServe, no miles and miles of mall. I wonder how old she is. Sixty? Seventy? When she dies (this is not the sort of woman who will retire), when she dies, will the store be gutted, the ceiling lowered, Halogen lights installed, and no-animal-testing shampoos and bubble baths, loofas, and aromatherapy candles decorously stacked on these shelves?

I continue to type. Back and forth between machines. "Mrs. Adelman has a tyupeweriter . . ." I leave the typo. In an age of perfectly turned-out pages, I suffer a nostalgia for frailty. For a misstep. For mistakes made and not immediately deleted. Mistakes made and the sky not falling. Mistakes noted rather than put-behind-us-so-we-can-get-on-with-our-lives.

Suddenly, I see the ashes. There where the hammers curve and form a small, inky valley is a thick layer of cigarette ashes. "This typewriter is very old indeed," I tell Mrs. Adelman. "This is from the olden days when people smoked while they worked. The olden days of hard smoking, hard drinking." She peers in, raises her glasses up to her forehead for a closer look, and smiles. "Hmm. I hadn't noticed that."

Now I know I have to have it. Now I am part of a chain of nervous, sweating writers, so focused, so scared that we don't even notice where the ashes fall. I see the previous owner as though his ghost has just entered the store. The long sleeves of his blue drip-dry shirt are rolled up. There are sweat stains under the arms. He's unbuttoned the two top buttons. Gray hairs curl out of the *V* of his cotton undershirt. His tie—he owns three—is carelessly tossed on the desk next to him. He doesn't notice that the ice has melted in the half-full glass of bourbon. He leans forward to erase a word and the ashes fall off the end of his cigarette. He squints against the smoke. Click, click, click, ding. I can smell him. Cigarettes, bourbon, sweat, ketchup.

"I want this one."

Mrs. Adelman pauses. Smiles. Softens. "I think this is going to work out very nicely."

I stroke its cool green metal.

"It will take some time to get it ready. I have a man who works very lovingly on these machines." Now I am really happy. I had been unaware of a vague and distant grief underlying my days. How casually I shop at RiteAid, no more neighborhood pharmacist. How easily I run into Staples and fill my plastic basket with printer paper, fax paper, disposable pens, and turn off my mind while the computer tallies it. Until this moment, I was not clear how much has been lost in the missing touch of a human hand. Handwritten receipts and recipes on index cards. A proprietor shuffling through her wares and smiling triumphantly when she finds exactly what I need. I suddenly fear for the health of the man who works "lovingly on these machines." I hope he's young and robust, but it's hard to imagine. No doubt he's ninety and has arthritic hands.

I am suddenly filled with a deep gratitude for Mrs. Adelman and this man who share a love of hands-on mechanics, the beauty of a machine that can be taken apart and reassembled and made to do its job. I think of the Chrysler Building, built in 1930 by auto maker Walter Chrysler, who erected an homage to endless possibility. The Chrysler Building with fenders and hubcaps glinting in the sun, its hubristic stretch to the sky, its spire that lets me know I'm home as I approach from Queens and foreign lands. New York where dreams come true, and people still hold on to the old ones.

"I'm glad you have this typewriter." We're friends.

Now, how to break it to Fran. "I'm a no-good pal," I begin

to write to her. Pen on pad. "How about you get it for week-ends . . . and by the way, as I left, Mrs. Adelman told me that she does have an old Olivetti in the back that she hasn't had a chance to look at yet." The next morning I walk the dog by her apartment, leave the note and some compensatory tapioca pudding.

Fran calls jubilant later in the day. "I went and met Mrs. Adelman. I was there for over half an hour trying out other machines, before she said, 'Well, there *is* something in the back you might want to try.' She was obviously waiting to size me up and determine if I was worthy. It's lovely. It's the cousin of yours. Older. Perfect. This was obviously meant to be. But it will be a month before I get it. . . ."

"I know, because she has a man who will work on it lovingly."

"And it needs more work than yours," she adds with pride.

"Oh, Fran, I forgot to tell you. As I left the shop, I asked Mrs. Adelman, 'So are you ever going to tell me whose little Olympia that was that I wanted to touch when I came in here the first time, but you wouldn't let me?' 'Oh,' she said, smiling, 'Woody Allen's.'"

15

RIVER IS BORING.

VOLGA IS BETTER.

Hooray. Another trip. Not back from the Coast two weeks and my restlessness moves in. Maybe I'm just not a backyard kind of girl. Maybe Guru Rent-a-Car was right. In my heart of hearts, I'm a top-down kind of girl. Sorry, Thoreau. Albeit this is a mere journey to my neighboring island, Brooklyn, but who could resist the chance to travel back to a time when twenty-one-year-old Grand Duke Alexis, visiting the Mississippi in 1872, wired his father Alexander II back in Saint Petersburg. "River is boring. Volga is better." Oh, yes, the Volga is better indeed. The Mississippi may be our very own romantic river. Who has not wanted to throw a raft to its vagaries and hop on board? It was the disappointed dream and blight of my childhood that I never became Huck.

But the Volga is so other. The Volga of Tolstoy, Dostoevski, Chekhov, Turgenev. The Volga of the Teaching Little Fingers to Play piano piece "The Volga Boatmen." Yo ho heave ho. The Volga that floats by not humble farmsteads or homey plantations or fishing shacks, but palaces, one for winter, one for summer, one for the royal offspring. It is this Volga, not the Volga of industry and revolution and suppression, not the Volga of Stalin and horror, that brings us out today. It is this river of romance and legend and mystery that leads us to Brooklyn and the jewels.

Nancy Newhouse, my *Times* editor, calls and tells me to get on that press bus and head straight for the recently arrived exhibition at the Brooklyn Museum. "After all, if you're writing about romance, you'll want to see the jewels of the Romanovs."

Writing about romance on a typewriter. Can't wait.

My daughter, her dog, and I run for the bus. She's going on to work, there are movie stars whose lives depend on it, but in a sweet reversal of roles she has humored me and walked me to the bus. Reversal, except I am certain that my smile never held a trace of mockery as I waved good-bye.

Fine with me. She's headed for an office, I for diamonds. And sapphires and rubies and pearls. My fellow pilgrims bring their Chaucerian eccentricities along. "Who's sitting here?" asks the best dressed of our lot. Fur hat, good boots. She eases herself into the front seat. "Actually," responds a woman across the aisle, spread vastly in variations of purple across her own seat. Purple eye shadow, purple sneakers, anklets, sweater, stretch pants. "Actually," she repeats, "the woman from the Brooklyn Museum." "Well, I don't suppose she would mind moving back," says Fur Hat, while patting the seat for her white-haired male companion. Purple looks to me for the immediate companionship of strangers sharing moral superiority. Emboldened by my responding smile, she says, "Well, excuuuuuuse me."

Museum gets on, notes that her seat has been taken, and moves to the back. She's a mere hireling and trained to do so. The bus starts and so do the giggles, the kind you hear among women about to embark on the *verboten*. The kind you hear around a dessert table. "Oh, I really shouldn't . . ." They're talking about their love of jewels. They titter as though speaking of sex, which of course they would not discuss here, aloud, among strangers.

"I understand that we are about to see the largest blue sapphire in captivity."

"Yep, 253 carats. Emperor Alexander II bought it in 1862 at the London Great Exhibition for his wife, Empress Maria Alexandrovna."

I spin around in my seat to find this know-it-all who's done her homework. Sure enough, she looks like a grown-up version of the girls in eighth grade who always finished their assignments on time and then did extra work for bonus points.

Down Fifth Avenue, we're slowly drawn away from the glamour of the spoils in Harry Winston, Tiffany, Bulgari, Cartier. "Did you know," Nancy asks, when she joins me later at the museum, "that someone traded the Cartier building for a matched strand of gray pearls?" No, indeed, I did not. "The source, Nancy. I want the source."

Today, the two great stone lions that guard the entrance to the Public Library are wearing hard hats. In this town, even the king of the jungle needs extra protection. On down Fifth Avenue in the slow momentum of morning traffic, we enter the mall ambiance of lower Fifth. Fast food, carpet, and camera stores. FIRE SALE! EVERYTHING MUST GO! Down toward the promise of the towering World Trade Center. Big things can happen to big men in a big building. Left, over the Manhattan Bridge. "No commercial traffic on the Brooklyn Bridge," the driver explains over his taped rap music.

I look out at that forbidden bridge with longing. Those spider-web strings of steel holding carloads of people who put their faith in the science of spans and arches. Below and beyond them, New York Harbor opens like arms to the sea, welcoming the tempest-tossed, the lonely, the refugees from dullness. Here, here, it seems to sing. Enter here where dreams come true. The view can make you believe in that early American dream that equated prosperity with happiness. There is such beauty in it, such promise.

I wish Walt Whitman were sitting in the seat beside me, singing songs of himself and this harbor, that bridge. The rush of bus tires across the bridge's grating take on the rhythm of his poem:

I am with you, you men and women of a generation, or
    ever so many generations hence,
Just as you feel when you look on the river and sky, so I
    felt.

Whitman is with us as we cross high above his river, a river that to him held all the romance of distant rivers, Volga included. For him, romance was experiencing the universal while observing the particular. For him, this river had the power to bind us to one another across all time and space. We are one, we who bear ancient and enduring witness to currents, tides, and reflected sky.

A man and a blackbird are one, according to Stevens. "A man, a woman, and a blackbird are one." Volga and Mississippi are one. Volga and Mississippi and East rivers are one. No, protests the young Romanov. Volga is better.

Perhaps, but today, Alexis, you, Whitman, your river, our river, and we merge as we journey toward one another across disparate routes to the beauty and folly that bind us.

Down Fulton Street, down Eastern Parkway, toward the Botanical Gardens and Museum's announcement, "Here we are." We pile out as excited and shy as schoolchildren on a class trip. "Can we eat lunch now?" Doughnuts, croissants, coffee, and press kits await us. We march in as directed. Off with the winter-worn coats, gloves thin at the fingertips, wrinkled scarves. Off with oversized backpacks that could hold a filched diadem. Elevator to fifth floor, turn left.

How to respond to what awaits us as we stand shoulder to shoulder with our peers and gaze at strands of perfectly matched sea pearls, a large chunk of uncut diamond, a tiny amber mouse with one diamond eye? How to avoid appearing ignorant or uncool about history and provenance?

Soon self-consciousness dissipates as we are lost to time.

What kind of time is this when artistry could exist on such a level, devoted solely to beauty and whimsy? I am immediately in thrall to an eighteenth-century pair of earrings in the form of bees and a matching diadem-bandeau in the form of a garland, both crowded with diamond wildflowers in pastel hues created by inserting pale-colored foil beneath the stones. Hidden within the petals are diamond bees set on springs, a mounting method known as *en tremblant* (ah, those French), so that when the viva-cious Empress Elizabeth I tossed her little head, the bees appeared to seek nectar from the stones.

Here's a diamond to be worn between breasts bared by fash-ionably low-cut bodices. The setting was designed for the sole purpose of drawing attention to the adorned's cleavage. Tantalizing. Mesmerizing. The heart of romance. So near and yet so far . . . She loves me, she loves me not. Touch me, touch me not. Desire me, oh yes, desire.

Jewels entirely befitting Peter the Great's daughter, who, upon becoming Empress seventeen years after her father's death, oversaw a rococo court of biweekly balls for eight hundred and a closet of some fifteen thousand gowns. Not to mention several thousand dancing shoes. This is the stuff that dreams are made on.

Americans, it appears, are flocking to dream along. When the exhibition opened at the San Diego Museum sixty thousand advance tickets were sold, more than at any other time in the museum's history. We of the Whitmanesque, democratic dreams have heads easily turned by romances of royalty. We who idealize log cabins guiltily lust after marble and mirrors. We of the miniskirts and bell bottoms and blue jeans are mesmerized by gowns embroidered in gold. The sturdy, modest American wife, who wears a small diamond solitaire engagement ring—"We married young and it's all we could afford"—imagines herself sporting something more along the lines of Empress Maria Feodorovna's 7.6-carat blue diamond, cleft from the same stone as the Hope diamond. I, who stand here with my hair pulled back in a rubber band, fancy tresses held in place by these Leopold Pfisterer ribbon-shaped diamond hairpins. It seems not at all ludicrous and perfectly possible. Sometimes a romantic interlude is a recess from reality that refreshes, renews, and somehow sets our spirits right.

Did they take it seriously, these Romanovs? Catherine, who celebrated the birth of grandson Alexander by playing a card game with precious stones for chips? Empress Alexandra Feodorovna who required three hours to be outfitted in her pink silk moiré gown and four pages to bear its twenty-pound train? What does it mean when we are told that Catherine the Great and Elizabeth I loved jewels? Who doesn't? What head remains unturned?

Jewels, my friend Maurice tells me, are "enticement and atonement." Something you can hold in the hand, wear round the wrist, something that carries a message beyond words.

This is my beauty worthy of beauty, Alexander II seems to say to Maria Alexandrovna.

"He must have done something very, very bad," a friend tells a woman whose husband has just given her a new diamond ring. A very large new diamond ring. Very, very bad, indeed.

"He must love you very much," says the proud mother of a newly betrothed damsel who holds out her left-hand ring finger newly lit by the Gatsby green light of emerald.

Precious and semiprecious stones have always been more than mere mineral content. Talismans, amulets, cures for body as well as soul, religious adornment, symbols of authority and power, guardians at the gate of vulnerability. Light captured and held in the hand.

The magi, those wise men from the East, believed that stones had the power to protect the newborn. Evil could be kept at bay by the proper adornment of a child with talismanic gems.

Legend has it that the first important diamonds discovered by Europeans in South Africa were found in a sorcerer's bag. Magical diamonds with the power to seduce, to intimidate, to influence faithfulness. Originally thought to have achieved its power and brilliance from a thunderbolt, a diamond endows its wearer with the properties of heavenly light. Ultimate authority, goodness, power. For Hildegard of the Rhine, the diamond was the devil's enemy. The power of light over darkness. It is little wonder that the Romanovs would choose to toss them about their wigs, wrists, and cleavages.

We hold out our fingers and wait.

16

CHASING AMAZEMENT

Like many young girls, I wanted to save France. Being burned at the stake seemed a small price to pay for being able to ride your horse everywhere.

I started hearing voices. Just like Joan. "Turn left," the voice would say when I'd walk out the door in the morning. "Not that tree, this one," the voice would say as I contemplated a site for my tree house. Just like Joan. I had a horse, I heard the voice. But there was a hitch. I had parents, and this was Connecticut.

Joan of Arc was one of the few great romantic, true-life adventures that starred a girl. Who wouldn't want it? The freedom, the beating heart heading into battle, talking back to boys and kings. It's all I wanted for a long time after my father innocently gave me the book.

It was a stunner. So much better than the *Hardy Boys* and *Nancy Drew* and *Cherry Ames Visiting Nurse* and *Trixie Beldon*. This was a real girl engaged in real derring-do.

My childhood was steeped in books of adventure. My father took me in his lap and read *Tom Sawyer* and *Huckleberry Finn* and *The Old Man and the Sea*. He did me the great courtesy of never suggesting that "This may be too old for you." He just read. And I would dream of being a boy floating on a raft and exploring caves. I'd dream of growing up to be an old man fishing alone and fighting a shark.

I think that children love adventure stories because their romance rings so true. Children understand that we are alone, absolutely alone in this world, except for the strange companionship found in silence and solitude. They know that it's less lonely just outside the border of the civilized world. Children are close enough to Wordsworth's remembering, to Plato's reminiscence, to sense that home is where the wilderness is.

It became clear to me, with the onset of puberty, that high adventure was not to be my lot. Don't talk to strangers. Don't accept rides in cars with strangers. Don't go into the woods alone. Be home before dark. The perimeters closed in. I've been fighting them ever since.

I remain an avid reader of adventure tales, vicariously thrilling to every attempt at Everest, the Poles, solo flights, solo sails. I still dream of hitting the road.

"Hey, how about it?" I ask my husband. "How about I put the dog in the car and head west?" I start singing, "This land is your land, this land is my land, / From California to the New York island, / From the redwood forest to the . . ."

"Are you kidding? Alone in the car on lonely roads?"

"I wouldn't be alone. I'd have the dog."

"Oh, a lot of protection that would be."

I hate it when he does that. When he underestimates my dog. First I couldn't be Joan of Arc, now it looks as though I'm not going to be John Steinbeck.

Naturally, when I read *Travels with Charlie*, that became my obsession. Heading west. The great American romance, the peculiarly American romance. Is it born in the blood of those of us conceived on this soil?

It seems to be the case in my family, what with great, great, great uncle so and so who got scalped, my great grandmother who got as far as Ohio, and my grandfather who finally made it all the way to California. My father, bound to New England, could be caught casting his gaze westward when closing a book or staring at an atlas.

One summer, he put us in the car and headed off across the country, telling us the history of things, picking up pine cones the size of our baby brother, being amazed by the Rockies. He wanted us to join him in his awe. We wanted a motel with a swimming pool.

We stood beside bubbling mud, watched Old Faithful be faithful, camped out in canyons, watched a man be clawed by a bear, and feared our father might make us move to Texas because he loved the open spaces. He loved driving through that state at night, all windows open, singing, "The stars at night, are big and bright, boom, boom, boom, boom, / Deep in the heart of Texas! Remind me of, the one I love, boom, boom, boom, boom. . . ."

My little sister was hot and sweaty and sat too close in the backseat. How come our mother couldn't keep the lemonade cold? Why did everything start to taste like the waxed paper it was wrapped in? Our golden retriever shared the backseat and panted and drooled all the way to California. That was that trip.

The next was worse because I was thirteen. In a car with my family. Enough said.

But something took. It was the excitement in my father's eye. His eagerness to get going each morning. His amazement at the scenes we were inhabiting. I've been chasing his amazement ever since.

"But it just seems destined to be," I protest to my husband. "What are the odds against that chance encounter?"

I'm referring to one of life's mini-adventures that leaves you a bit breathless, wiping your eyes, and reliving it in your mind, testing its reality. I'm used to being stopped by strangers who want to talk about the dog. "What kind is he?" "How old is he?" "May we pet him?" "We used to have a standard poodle." "He's gorgeous." Walking down the street with Gabriel can be like walking down the street with Leonardo DiCaprio, so I wasn't surprised when, earlier in the day, the dog and I were stopped by an attractive older woman who asked the usual questions.

"How old is he?"

"Ten."

"Isn't he in lovely shape?"

"Thank you."

"That's such a wonderful breed. Standard poodles. And of course the black ones are the best of the bunch. We had one just like that."

Smile.

"He went everywhere with us, Charlie did. We just couldn't stand to leave him behind. He was a wonderful, wonderful dog.

"Once my husband wanted me to go across the country with him, to camp out, see all the sights, and then write about it. I just wasn't up to it but I didn't want him to make the trip all alone so I said, 'John, why don't you and Charlie go instead?' So they did. It was a wonderful trip."

I had been half-listening and was now on full alert. Could this possibly be? Do things like this really happen? "Your dog's name was Charlie?"

"Yes."

"As in *Travels with* . . . ?"

"Yes."

"Are you Mrs. Steinbeck?"

"Why, yes, dear, I am. They had such a wonderful trip . . ."

Why are the boys having all the fun? Charlie and John. Orville and Wilbur. Lewis and Clark. A friend's husband is taking a month off from work to follow Lewis's and Clark's trail. Alone. "Hey," I say to her. "I want to do that."

William Least Heat Moon. Peter Matthiessen. Paul Theroux. They do that sort of thing in real life. Girls do it in fiction.

"Someday I want to write a novel about a woman who's driving home on the Connecticut Turnpike and when she gets to her exit she just keeps driving," says a writer friend of mine who lives in Connecticut. Well, Elizabeth Berg did write a novel like that. Why is the romance of adventure, of hitting the road, relegated to let's-pretend for women?

Because it's not safe, that's why. Have you seen the movie *Breakdown*? Well, my husband did. And it's not safe because who will look after the children and the pets and the husbands? And don't tell me this is the late twentieth century and women can do anything they want to do. They can't. And neither can men.

But I want to live my romance. I've done the Thoreau trip from my front door to my gate. I've spent months along the small pond of Central Park. And I've got to tell you, they do not make Balboa's adventure seem small by comparison. I want to head for the Pacific and stand there in silence and great surmise.

(If I can see past the shorefront hotels.) I want to eat the best cherry pie this side of the Mississippi at some country fair. I want to return to the live-bait and beer stores in Mississippi, where I've sat at counters and been served plates of whatever was for lunch, usually fried chicken, mashed potatoes, and gravy eaten next to jars of jumping black crickets and squirming grub worms. I want to hear the things people are talking about in those places. The poetry Woody Guthrie heard.

When I was trying to find Fallingwater and called information in southwestern Pennsylvania, "This-is-Dotty-how-can-I-help-you," asked me to hold on "for a sec. I just ate one of them peppermint patties and its gone and got stuck on the roof of my mouth." Thwack. A slight popping sound, "There. Now, what can I do for you, hon?"

I want to hear the music of those accents, witness that sweetness of purpose, meet the Dottys who call you "hon," because they assume you're just as sweet as can be.

Sentimental? Nostalgic? Or truly romantic? That's what I want to find out. I want to get off the Internet and Interstate, and then if America turns out to be one big mall interrupted by occasional theme parks and government-protected sanctuaries, then yes, this would be both nostalgic and sentimental. But I think the romance is in the journey. Is in whatever it was that made the Romanticists head for adventure: Byron to fight in Greece. Goethe to find himself in Italy. We like to think that there is something out there for us to love. That will awaken our love. That will show us just where we belong in the scheme of things. That will remind us of how very small we are when compared with the spread of the natural world, that will reconnect us to whatever we lost in our sleep and our forgetting.

It's no accident that the romantic hero traveled past the borders of his known world, met adventure, fought monsters, returned home against all odds, and then left again. Out there was where he learned what was to be learned. When Odysseus returns home, we know it's only temporary. The world is his schoolroom. It's there for the taking. I want to take my share.

17

BEHOLDING

Yet I remain right here testing Thoreau's theory that the great adventures lie between out doors and the gate. Right here, even though yesterday it was spring in Paris. It was spring in Paris, and the chestnut trees must have been in pink bloom, the air heavy with their sweet perfume, causing hearts to ache with the sadnesses of all springs past. It was spring in Paris, it was Sunday, and I imagine that lovers sighed and stayed in bed and parents took children to the park and students sat in cafés and tourists headed for Place Vendôme.

It was spring in Paris, and according to a front-page story in today's *New York Times*, "'The Sevres Road,' by the nineteenth-century painter Camille Corot, was stolen from the Louvre . . . early yesterday afternoon. The canvas, measuring 13.4 by 19.3 inches was apparently cut from its frame. The police closed the museum as soon as the theft was discovered by a guard, and officers searched departing visitors. Corot, who died in 1875, is known as a master of landscape painting."

It's hard to imagine. In broad daylight, in a museum full of visitors, how did anyone cut the painting neatly from its frame and walk back into the light of day?

Hard to imagine until I think of the power of art, of how, when a painting and observer connect, it's as if the artist's soul reaches out of the canvas, grabs hold, and won't let go. It steals your heart. Perhaps this was a case of stealing back.

I understand the impulse. How big a leap is actual theft from Rebecca's fantasy, "Now's your chance, Mom," when, during our visit to the Prado, the guards turned off the alarms so that the panels of Bosch's *Earthly Delights* could be closed for us?

Once when I'd reached one of those end-of-my-rope periods, I determined to take four days off from my life. What would nourish, strengthen, and heal? I pondered this, narrowing the field to wilderness hikes, cathedrals, museums. Nature and art, two things I could count on to fill me with joy, exaltation, Plato's divine enthusiasm. Either experience would send me home refreshed and ready to resume work.

The Prado. I would return for a second visit. I would go for the sole purpose of visiting Van der Weyden's *Descent from the Cross* and Velázquez's *The Maids of Honor*, known affectionately and familiarly as *Las Meninas*. I would look at these paintings all day, go out to dine alone at ten in the evening, and walk home at midnight through ancient streets. Solitude, beauty, delighted palate. Perfect.

I booked a flight for the next day, said good-bye to husband and dog, and though I couldn't find a vacancy, departed with a light heart and the spontaneous traveler's belief that there's always a room at the last minute.

I arrived in Madrid, went straight to the Northern Renaissance galleries of the Prado, and immediately burst into tears upon seeing the Van der Weyden painting. "It's still here," I thought with relief. As if what? The painting had been a figment of my imagination? Been stolen by someone overcome by the desire to possess what had possessed, to love back, to return the embrace, to cut the painting from its frame, and carry it home as a groom might carry a new bride?

Nonsense, I told myself and went to stand in front of *Las Meninas*, to puzzle over its riddles. Was this a painting of Velázquez at work on a self-portrait, using us as the mirror in which he sees himself reflected? A reversal of the usual role in which we stare into a painting and find ourselves? Or was he painting the pretty little princess poised nearby, staring out at us as the artist does? Was he painting the queen and king whom we see reflected in a mirror behind him? Or is that a mirror? Perhaps that too is a painting?

I was vaguely aware of other viewers behind, in front and beside me, stopping, commenting, moving on. "Ahhh," little Spanish children said, "*Las Meninas!*" "You see . . ." husbands would explain to their wives, "he is painting the little girl because she's dressed up." My legs began to ache, I sat down on the cold marble floor until a guard asked me to stand up, I looked at my watch. Two hours had passed. In no time.

I determined to return with a large mirror and prop it against the wall opposite the painting to see what the artist would have seen had he been looking out at a mirror as he painted a self-portrait.

No, say the guards. "Eez not possible." A wag of the finger, a shake of the head, "No meers. No meers." Of course, it was just my way of taking possession. My theory. With this theory, I stake my claim. With these words, I thee wed. I'm here, Velázquez, I'm here. No different from staring at owls and hawks. I want a connection the subject matter won't allow. I want a balm for the ache of yearning.

"I can imagine that one could lose sight of limits the way I lost sight of time as I stood and stared at *Las Meninas*," I tell my husband as we read the story of the Louvre theft. One could reach out in a sort of mystical trance and remove the Corot canvas from its frame, roll it up, slip it into a purse, and exit into the chestnuts' embracing scent.

He is appalled. "The idea is romantic, but the deed is ugly," says he. "I'd want to wring the neck of anyone who did that to a beautiful painting." He hasn't had his coffee, he's a bit cranky, but I understand his point. It's a point at which we often divide.

Given the power of art, without sound or overt gesture, to move into our souls and push all other considerations aside, I prefer to think that the theft was an expression of high, albeit illegal, romance rather than the work of a highly organized ring. I prefer a thief who had no intention of stealing that painting and didn't think of it as stealing but was suddenly possessed by a god, by divine enthusiasm. It happens all the time. We go in search of the sublime and it claims us before we reach our planned destination. It can take our breath away. It can rob us of reason. "I am not thinking, madame; I am moved."

"*What are you doing with that painting?*" my friend Jennifer's sister asks her. "You're *Jewish*." Furthermore, "Why are you keeping a crucifixion scene on your desk?" In front of the children.

It's a postcard from the Prado. A reproduction of Van der Weyden's *Descent from the Cross*. "When I saw this painting," Jennifer, a curator, explains to me, "for the first time, I understood the power of art. It absolutely levels us. There are no divisions. It's not about religion, it's not about class, it's not about gender. It's all about the human heart. This painting is about loss and grief and despair, about an intensely passionate moment in time."

She and I returned from our separate trips with the same postcard. We staked our claims within the boundaries of the law. Could those boundaries be blurred by passion? They are all the time. That's why they're in the law books as Crimes of Passion. They're the crimes that interest us the most.

Of course it's extreme, a flight of fancy, to imagine art theft as the result of romantic impulse, but I think it's a flight that helps us understand art's power and why that power frightens us. If we allow ourselves to stand in front of a painting and simply let it be, if we shed our theories, our guidebooks, our audio tours like so many lovers shedding layers of clothing, if we bring ourselves naked to the brink of experience, then we surrender control. Is it possible to see, *really* see, art any other way? I'm afraid not. I'm afraid few of us would dare.

Which is why I like to imagine that someone, on her way to see the pinky Renoirs, was stopped in her tracks by *The Sèvres Road,* a poetic, painterly ode to the pastoral. I like to imagine someone caught off guard and riveted by those deep greens, the golden road of packed earth leading to some vaguely discerned destination merging with the sky.

I like to imagine her eyes moving through meadow and pastureland, past the man on horseback, past the woman rushing home to prepare the noon meal. I like to think that as she stared at those top-heavy trees and slender fences, the hanging branches and azure air, she was making her own pilgrimage toward that place where landscape surrenders to the seduction of white clouds in beckoning blue, to that point of astonishment where earth and heaven meet.

Perhaps she restrained her eager eyes, holding them back from their instinctive rush to that point of surrender. Perhaps she waited, heightening the moment, visually caressing color centimeter by centimeter before the final rush to green merger between earth, sky, and eye.

It's entirely possible. It's called falling in love. We don't expect it to happen like this. But then we never do. The time's not right. There are complications. Impediments. Distractions. Rules and regulations. Tribal taboos. How much easier to move on, to be satisfied by prettiness, one painting after another. Corot. Courbet. Rousseau. One-glance stands, no commitments.

So much easier than withstanding the shock of having our hearts snatched from slumber. Who wouldn't prefer the snooze alarm, a pillow over the head? In spite of all our laments, our reports of searching high and low for romance, in spite of claiming we can't live without it, the truth is we'd just as soon sleep through, thank you.

Which is why my fantasy is completely unlikely. No doubt there was a plan, a getaway car, a fence, a reckless dealer, a greedy collector. "But the crime has been committed, the deed done," I protest to my husband. "So who would not prefer a scenario in which the act was not heartless but heartful, a dance in the dark, a search for the sublime?" He shrugs and continues reading the op-ed page. He is unconvinced, but I prefer a circle of passion, from Corot's eye, to the road, to his palette, to the canvas, and then more than a hundred years later to the eye and soul of the observor. A mandala, a glimpse of eternity.

Twelfth-century troupadour Giraud de Borneil claimed, "The eyes are the scouts of the heart. The eyes go forth to find an image to recommend to the heart. And when the eyes have found such an image, if the heart is a gentle heart then love is born." I prefer the gentle heart to a greedy thief. I prefer the traditional Chinese view of art, in which a painting's vital energy radiates to the observing eye and heart, to the more Western belief that the eyes may go scouting, but the image they find does not respond in kind.

Entirely possible, Amherst professor Joel Upton responds when I call to share my musings on the theft. Anything can happen "when we behold art rather than just looking at it, when we give up all fear of losing control and stand before a painting and view it on its own terms, using that as an occasion for insight not just analysis."

I'm ambivalent about this. I'm a bit scared every time. How much calmer my life was in the days before Rebecca introduced me to Upton. She'd called from college to say, "You've got to come up and sit in on one of his classes. It will change your life." So it did. He turned the coolly removed observation of art into a driving occupation ever fraught with the possibility of calamity. Those with ears to hear will hear, those with eyes to see will see, but do we have the emotional energy to behold paintings, not as something remote from our lives, but about them? To sense that a painting has revealed, not only our inner lives, but connected us to every human heart ever moved by such beauty? To behold a painting can be the most heartbreakingly romantic experience on earth.

In the summer, my family and I leave the city for a little seaside community, where the residents gather on the beach at night to watch the sun go down. When it makes its final exit, spreading its glow along the sea's horizon, there is a round of applause. "Oh, that was the best ever!" "Do you think so? I thought last year's sunsets were far more spectacular." Each time it's a surprise. A surprise that the colors are so showy? A surprise that it's set again? As opposed to what? Changing its mind and rising instead? More applause. There's no encore and people zip up their windbreakers and head home to open the wine and drop lobsters into deep pots of water they'd set to boil before this sunset excursion.

If we listened to Joel Upton we would break into that kind of applause when we stood in front of Petrus Christus's *Virgin and Child in a Chamber* or Rogier Van der Weyden's *Descent from the*

Cross or Jan Van Eyck's *Mystic Lamb*. We would do it each time, surprised that the painting is still there, that it still has the power to move. Each time would be different, so that we would come back again and again and again. "Excuse me, this is not a place for public spectacle," museum directors would reprimand and bring the Kleenex. Why not? What better place? And next time, bring a picnic, choose a painting, and sit down on the floor in front of it.

If we listen to Joel Upton, we could never enter a museum casually again. Never meet friends there before going on to lunch, never visit every famous painting in every famous museum of any given foreign city. If we listen to Joel Upton, we'd choose one painting, or let it choose us, and then we would behold it and then we'd have to go home, put ice packs on our heads and take a long nap.

Several years ago when Joel's children were young, he and his wife, Sara, took them to Musée de l'Hôtel Dieu in Beaune to see Van der Weyden's eighteen-foot-long *Last Judgment*. His five-year-old daughter, Meg, stared and stared at the painting, then suddenly bolted and disappeared. A frantic search ensued, and she was eventually found sitting outside on the steps, pulling at her long hair. Her astounded father realized that she had been overwhelmed by the panel at the far right depicting a man lifting a woman by the hair to pull her from the pit of hell. "Now that," says Upton, "is beholding."

I think of two businessmen in button-down shirts, highly polished shoes, Brooks Brothers suits, whom I saw standing in front of Vermeer's *Girl with Pearl Earring* at the exhibition in Washington, D.C. They looked as though they'd just run up from the Pentagon during their lunch hour. Or the CIA. Or some Federal office of Budget or Traffic Control. I was intrigued that they'd bothered.

They stood stiffly. They made casual banter. Then the one in gray gabardine became very quiet. After about four minutes he turned to the other man and said, "Looks like someone I wish I knew." There were tears in his eyes. He tried to smile but the tears kept coming.

Then I thought of Rebecca's take on art, "Keep your eyes

open because you never know. . . ." You never know when you might be looking eye to eye with miracle. Blink and it's gone. Blink and you've missed it.

I think of a visit to the Clark Museum in Williamstown, Massachusetts, with my Bennington Writers' Workshop students. Their assignment was to cruise through the galleries until "something calls to you." Then I asked them to look at that particular painting or sculpture for an hour and write about the experience for the next day's class.

Each wrote a deeply personal essay in response to the work she had seen. For one, it was nostalgia for a time when two women could sit quietly in sunshine and have a long, perhaps aimless talk uninterrupted by the dailiness of life. Just like the nineteenth-century women in the painting. For another, a woman with a red parasol personified a longing for wholeness to which the writer was finally able to give expression. In the course of her hour of "beholding," she had fallen in love with the stranger in the painting. As she read her essay to the class, she began to cry. Just like my man in Washington. When one of the students asked why she was crying, she looked mystified. "I really don't know," said she. I believed her.

This is what Upton wants from us. If we want to see "what a painting has to tell us," we must do more than "look." We must "behold," which, if I understand him correctly, requires that we come before a work of art without the usual armor of distraction, time pressure, perfect control. That we shed defenses and dare offer ourselves to the canvas as vulnerably and completely as the canvas offers itself to us. That we be as available to possible pillage and plunder. That we dare plaster ourselves against the air of some gallery and meet a painting on its own defenseless terms. So defenseless it could be neatly sliced from its frame, as neatly as the viewer's heart from her chest.

Part IV

TEACHERS

18

JUST SITTING THERE
WAITING TO BE USED

———·•·———

Barbara Cook is conducting a Master Class at the Juilliard School of Music. Barbara Cook, former ingenue lead, Barbara Cook of the blond, blond hair and a voice that resembles the ring of raindrops hitting a galvanized pail, Barbara Cook now older, sadder, wiser, and heftier, who, when singing "Oh What a Beautiful Morning," sounds like one emerging from long grief to the shock of joy.

I stood in line forty-five minutes this morning, waiting with the others who now fill Juilliard's auditorium. We all want to see what Cook has to teach this college's exquisitely trained and groomed seniors. I look around. Every seat is taken. How did they all know about this? What is the underground that connects music lovers to the choice, unadvertised events? Are there beat drums only they can hear?

I've been curious about Cook ever since I heard her sing three years ago at Café Carlyle. I hadn't been prepared for copious tears that soaked my own handkerchief and then my husband's. I had thought we were just having a romantic night out. What in the world was this woman doing to me? How did she make a song zing straight to the heart, practically bypassing the ears? How did she deliver meaning that the soul absorbed before the words were consciously registered? How in the world did she do that?

I once asked Charity Hume, a teacher in a private Manhattan

boys' school, how she was able to stand in front of a roomful of restless, hormone-frenzied, pubescent boys, who would rather be out of these ties and into the park, how she was able to stand there, capture their attention, and then seduce them into learning. Well, she guessed it was as if they were falling in love.

"When we fall in love it is an awakening. What teachers do is to awaken us to ourselves."

"Of course, what teachers really do is listen, listen, listen. Even if the kid's just asking to go to the john." The oldest trick in the book of *The Art of Seduction*. The chapter mothers once made certain their young daughters knew by rote. Listen to a guy as though your life depended on it. There was a time when it did.

The gifted teacher is a seductor, working the magic that will make a student fall in love with her subject. Working the same magic that Andrea Marcovicci finds in the declaration behind all great love songs. "I am better for having loved." The successfully seductive teacher causes the student to fall in love with the subject. Thus afflicted, the student also falls in love with herself in conjunction with the subject. They awaken each other. A love story.

Today I watch Barbara Cook rouse six sleeping beauties. Gently, one at a time, she lifts the veil that separates the student singer from the heart of the song. She's like a groom lifting his new bride's veil in an old-fashioned wedding, a ritual that reveals the pair to each other as though for the first time. Even if they've been living together for twelve years, even if they've known each other since childhood.

This Master Class becomes part of a stream of ancient, enduring rituals and tales that serve to dramatize our capacity to be reborn into something wonderful and strange. A potion-induced slumber is awakened, a veil is lifted, a voice is found. Barbara Cook is midwife to the hearts and souls of these slumbering youths. Start fresh, she tells them. Shed all preconceptions. Forget what is "expected" of you. She never says anything as tired as "This is the first day of the rest of your life," she simply delivers them to it.

Helen Houghton, Rebecca's ninth-grade English teacher, who inspired her to learn hundreds of lines of poetry by heart, so that they could be hers forever to be drawn upon for inspiration, strength, and companionship, once told me that she saw teaching as an act of "informing and transforming." She compared learning to a conversion experience, a shedding of an old skin. Rebirth. "The teacher's obligation is to allow the student to inform herself about herself. To encourage her to clean out the muck so that the truth can shine through." Every student has a genius for this, said she. "You just have to have faith in that genius and give the student the courage to be equally faithful."

Today's teacher stands here on stage in a black silk tunic billowing over matching pants with an elasticized waist. She paces, marking her territory, delivering her voice to each corner of the stage. This is her world, her universe, we as an audience feel ourselves dissolving into it.

The blue of her eyes is bright enough to be seen from my seat twenty rows back from center stage. Her blond tresses loop the loop before tumbling to her shoulders. Her pert nose and softly rounded cheeks are reminiscent of the Southern cheerleader we found so fetching in *Candide* and *The Music Man*.

She introduces long-time pal and accompanist Wally Harper, who smiles and nods. She peers into the audience and looks for the students who will perform today. "Where are they?" She asks. Six hands appear above the seats in the front row.

She beams, turning the warmth of her attention in their direction, like a proud mama overseeing a large brood. She assures them, "This is not a performance." Good luck there, Barbara. We're the audience, and we're restless. We cough, we stir in our seats, we cross and uncross our legs. The scratch of wool, the swish of silk, the rustle of polyester. We crackle the cellophane wrappers of our throat lozenges.

The students smell each other's fear, the sweat mingling with dry-cleaning fluid and floral deodorants.

"And because this isn't a performance," she continues, smiling, "I will ask you to do things that you wouldn't ordinarily do in a performance." Pause. Panic.

"O.K.?"

They nod.

Good girls and boys.

"O.K., then." She looks down at a sheet of names she holds on a clipboard. "Shelley Watson." Shelley, dressed to the nines, walks on stage full of chipper self-assurance. "Hi, there, Shelley. What are you going to sing for us today?"

"Cry Me a River."

"O.K., darlin,' let's hear it."

Do we ever. She belts that song right out into the stands. Ethel Merman is back among us. When she's finished, she's clearly pleased. So are we. The applause is enthusiastic.

"Sweetheart," Cook croons softly as she approaches her. "Let's talk about what that song means." Pause. She puts her hand up and places it on the slim shoulder. "Why don't you just speak the words to me as though you were telling me a story. This guy sounds like a real son-of-a-bitch."

To illustrate her point, Cook begins to speak and paraphrase the lyrics. "'*Now* you say you love me, you son-of-a-bitch, after you've put me through all this crap." She asks Shelley, "Tell me what being 'so untrue' means. Did you walk in and find him in bed with someone else?"

The student looks perplexed, then giggles. "O.K., I'll try it." She starts to speak. "First you say you love me . . ." The song begins to take on a depth of sadness that had been lost beneath the hearty defiance of musical delivery.

When she has finished speaking the words of the song, Cook walks back to the side of the stage. "O.K. Now sing it. Show us how much this hurts. And, sweetheart, try it quietly." She adds, "What I'm saying may not be right, but it's the sort of thing I use to help myself."

Watson's whole expression changes. Her posture takes on an attitude of defeat that clings to a gossamer thread of courage. The take-that-Buster attitude is replaced by a more complicated consideration of what it means to love the wrong guy, and to continue loving even after it becomes clear he's no good. Gone are the hundred times we've heard this song before. Gone the fledgling torch singer. The audience is very quiet and remains so for a moment before the applause.

"How interesting," Cook muses as she walks over to the young woman, who seems in awe of what has just happened, as though someone else just sang that song. "Shelley, can you tell me how it was that you determined to sing it the way you did the first time?"

"I thought that's what the audience expected."

"Ah," Cook responds with a been-there-done-that sort of smile. She moves closer to the twenty-year-old student, who rocks a bit unsteadily on her very high, very lamé shoes. The flowing black tunic almost envelopes the smaller woman. As Cook speaks, the tone is that of a South that nostalgia makes me wish the Yankees hadn't vanquished. A voice without threat or criticism, a voice thick with gentle, sweet encouragement that creates a sense of intimacy.

"We feel we're 'expected' to do things such and such a way," she says looking directly at the student, seeming to forget the audience. "And if we do it the way we're expected long enough, it becomes a habit."

"Empty yourself of all those expectations," she dares the young woman. "Get rid of all that so you can feel the truth of who you are."

You could almost miss the earth-shattering, asteroid-crashing power of the radical thought that Cook has just set afloat on stage as delicately as a bubble blown through a child's plastic wand. If this young woman who listens attentively and fidgets because she can't take notes and is nervous she might not remember, if this clearly talented young woman fully understands what is being asked of her, she might consider another, less perilous profession. Banking, maybe. Venture capitalism.

Is she really prepared to don battle fatigues, lace up heavy boots, strap on a pith helmet, take up weapons, step lightly lest there be land mines, clear the brush of blinding preconceptions, crawl stealthily toward her target, and put a bead on her self?

And what about us, the happy audience smug in our senior authority, shaking our heads in ready agreement, yes, yes, of course, that's what she should do. When was the last time we did that? When was the last time we dared?

James Martin is next. He walks on stage smiling, working hard at appearing self-assured.

"So, James, what will you be singing for us?"

"'Isn't It Romantic' by Rodgers and Hart from *Love Me Tonight*." He says it the way people picked from the audience of talk shows introduce themselves, "Frank Steadman from North Bend, Indiana." All on one strong note they hope will disguise an unnerving attack of excitement, exhibitionism, and fear.

"*Love Me Tonight*," Cook responds and walks off to the right side of the stage, leaving James in the spotlight. "Sounds good to me," she adds. The audience laughs.

He pulls himself up tall, this less than tall young man in an olive-green suit. He folds his small hands, one at a time, each neatly over the other like freshly ironed handkerchiefs in a drawer.

He sings, "'I've never met you, / Yet never doubt, dear, / I can't forget you, / I've thought . . .'"

"James, one sec." Wally stops playing as Cook walks from her place. No tapping stick, no clicking high heels, no Callas fling of a shawl. Once she's next to him she reassures, "You sing beautifully, but I think that overarticulation creates a barrier, something we have to get through to get to you." A barrier most likely provided by and gratefully accepted from the coach of the folded-hands posture.

She begins to reminisce as though she and James are sitting on a park bench and the rest of us are minding our own business. "When I was in rehearsal for *Candide*, Leonard Bernstein called a meeting to discuss articulation. 'Oh, dear,' I thought, 'I must be being sloppy.' But no, he wanted less articulation. You see, what we're about is communicating. So sing as you would talk, because the ear is used to catching that."

What we are about is communicating. And not. And getting tongue-tied and feeling our hearts swell with unsaid words, our throats close around emotion that can't find its translation. What we are about is communicating, but can we get the words out? And if we do, will anybody listen?

Cook looks down at the sheet of paper in her hand. "I see that you are in your first year as a Young Artist with the Juilliard Opera Center." She sounds impressed. He forgets the momentary shame of having been interrupted at the very beginning of his song. "I know that opera coaches tell you otherwise," she continues, "but, for this kind of song I'd like you just to try something for me. Pretend you're around a poker table talking to your friends." She notes his earnest face, his studious intensity, and hooks her arm through his. ". . . Or a chess table, James."

"Bridge," says he.

"Or bridge. Make it more colloquial." She's making it easier for James to be brave.

She continues to hold his arm in hers, pats it, and suggests that he give it a try. They remain like this as he speaks the lyrics. "Isn't it romantic? / Music in the night, / A dream that can be heard. / Isn't it romantic? / Moving shadows write, the oldest magic word . . ." She occasionally interrupts to ask what he means, just like someone on the other side of the poker, the chess, the bridge table. It becomes clear that some of the meaning is lost on one more experienced at cards than love.

When she thinks he's beginning to get an inkling of what Hart had to say on the subject, she invites him to sing, stopping him at "I know the way you kiss." More "Wow!" than interruption, she exclaims, "Now that's gold! That's a phrase just sitting there waiting to be used. I choose which songs I'm going to sing based on phrases like that." Just waiting to be used. Like all the rest of us. Waiting to be turned to song.

"O.K., sing it again." She pats his arm and retreats to the side of the stage. James's posture relaxes. We stop noticing him more than the song. We cease marveling at his technique. He's a crystal-clear vessel. When he sings, "I know how you kiss," Cook, well pleased, bursts into happy laughter that sounds like the youthful fly and tumble of voice she once brought to her role of Marion, Lady Librarian.

He keeps singing, no interruptions, and when he's through, teacher, seductress, lady librarian, angel walks to his side, saying, "Beautiful, beautiful, beautiful." She hugs him. He grins and lowers his head and hunches his shoulders like a third grader who's just gotten a gold star on his homework and been called to the front of the room to "share it with the whole class."

Still holding him, she says, "I think you have to think more deeply. You don't have to worry about the notes, just think about every single phrase." She thanks him and sounds genuinely grateful.

It's Kate Jennings Grant's turn. Tall, dark, and slender, she bends slightly at the waist as she shakes Cook's hand. As pliant as a young, green willow reaching for a spring. Cook puts her arm around Kate's small waist and reassuringly confides, "You know, I used to be scared to death when I went to auditions. I would sit there thinking that everyone sang better, that everyone was prettier. They certainly were slimmer." Laughter from the audience. "Then one day it occurred to me that if I could reveal *my feelings* about this [song], then I would forget about competing. I started to try to understand the meaning of each phrase." She pauses. "When we're young we feel we're not enough . . . we think, 'They want to hear Barbra Streisand' so we put on a lot of stuff that's not ours. Most of the time, we feel we have to hide, but on stage safety lies in revelation. Safety lies where we're vulnerable. When we are being honest and revealing we're putting ourselves in touch with the universal core in all of us."

Releasing the young woman to her own fate, Cook walks to the side of the stage and waves her hand as though shedding the enormity of what she has just said. Brushes it aside as though she hasn't just opened her hand and held out the gem of a lifetime's mining. An offering from one who clearly has found it less than safe to be vulnerable, but knowing that life depends on it, that truth and beauty depend on it, offers the gift within the "safety" of performance.

"But this is just my side of the story," she says dismissively, "There are lots of sides. If you don't buy it, O.K. I'm just trying to plant a seed. Then it will grow and be fed by other teachers."

She invites Kate to begin singing her selection, Jerome Kern's and Ira Gershwin's "Long Ago and Far Away." Kate seems so tender and young to those of us long past our raw, thin-skinned twenties. She sings in a gentle soprano strengthened by smoky undertones. Cook stands, holding her glasses in her hand. She watches and listens and doesn't interrupt.

The song ends. We are enthralled. Cook begins the praises as she walks toward the young woman. She pulls up a chair and absently pats the back of it as she thinks for a moment. "You know, Kate, what I'd like is for you to sit down here and sing it again. Sing it more quietly and pensively. Sing it for yourself alone, not as though you're performing." Kate sits down; Cook takes one steps back. "Let's see what happens, honey."

The student leans into one side of the chair as though surrendering the weight of her soul to it. She gazes off to a far corner of the room. She seems so terribly alone up there in spite of the fact that the teacher remains close. Her song is almost a whisper, although it carries through the hall. Wally Harper slows the tempo to support this quieter approach. It is clear that she is singing for herself and hearing the words in a new way, in her way. The audience is silent. Riveted.

I realize that although I'd been moved by the beauty of her first version, my mind had wandered, I had been watching for responses from Cook and the audience. Now my attention narrows down to encompass only the words sung by a beautiful young woman who has tears in her eyes. They begin to flow. As she nears the conclusion, "Chills run up and down my spine,/ Aladdin's lamp is mine . . ." her sobs break through the notes. She struggles to continue, swallows, takes a deep breath, "The dream I dreamed was not denied me. . . ." Her head bows, she can't go on, she turns around and looks pleadingly up at Cook, who leans down over the chair and takes the young woman in her arms. "You see," she tells her, "we *are* enough. We are whole and complete and perfect right now."

Whole and perfect and complete when the song sings the singer, when the poem writes itself, when the building rises organically from its site. When we get out of our own way.

After Kate leaves the stage Cook tells us, "You know, I conduct these Master Classes around the world, and the courage of the students never fails to move me." She looks down to the young men and women in the front row, holds her arms out to them and sighs, "I appreciate it."

She calls on Sean Arbuckle, who is going to sing the Gershwins' "They Can't Take That Away from Me." He's a handsome, dark–haired young man. He moves to the piano, leans slightly into it, and begins. There seems no reason for Sean not to be starring on Broadway right now, with his good looks, clear tenor, and assured presentation. But, ah, that seems to be the problem. Here comes Cook out of her corner, here she is easing the blow of interruption by taking his arm in hers. "Now 'fond,' that is not a hot word." The audience laughs, Sean smiles, waiting for the magic that will transform him as it did Kate. "You have to go for the most powerful choice. Sex is a powerful choice. You're not say-ing, 'I miss your fond caress.'" She grins, letting him know that, of course, 'fond' is not really what is meant here. She asks for the next words, "'The way you wear your hat,'" he supplies. "Ah," says Cook, letting go of his arm and moving forward on the stage, opening her arms, "No one *ever* thought to wear a hat this way." She turns to him, "We need to see how you *feel* about this person."

She brings the chair to Sean and asks him to sit there. He begins again, Harper grins at the piano, Cook shows her delight by smiling and clasping her hands, the audience sighs when they hear him sing, "'The way you sip your tea.'" We can see her, we can see that the way she sips is delicate, endearing, is somehow her way alone, that he has fallen in love with these little things about her, the parts of the other we love so inexplicably.

"We may never, ever meet again on the bumpy road to love. . . ." You can feel a sigh whisper through those in the audi-ence who are no longer traveling that road.

The change in both song and singer is astonishing. "They can't take that away from me" becomes a brave statement full of doubt and heartache. Cook approaches and reaches for him like a mother bear taking a cub to its breast. "It's just amazing, isn't it?" she asks.

"It's the magic chair," he responds.

"It's so thrilling. It's like giving someone permission to be. You can do that for yourself," she assures, hugging him again. As he's walking off stage, she calls after him, "Thank you for letting us in."

A man sitting in front of me removes a white monogrammed

handkerchief from his breast pocket and holds it to his eyes. "I've *never* heard that song sung that way," he whispers to his companion. "Never."

The next student, Danon Kirschenmann, is advised, "Don't sing 'After You' from the outside in. I want you to find a way to inform the words." She rubs his back, steps to the side, and listens to his moving delivery, clearly informed by Kate's, Shelley's, James's, and Sean's lessons that have come before his. When he concludes, Cook opens her arms wide and exclaims, "It never ceases to amaze me. If you really show us your humanity, there's no way to be wrong." She pauses and adds, "Until it's wrong to be human."

Claire Lautier's sweet soprano is slightly reminiscent of Cook's own some thirty years ago. She delicately approaches "If Love Were All" before Cook interrupts midway and motions to the chair, asking her to sit there. "Start over for me, darlin'." She stands behind with her hands on Claire's shoulders for the entire song. As the young woman nears the end, a tear moves its way down her cheek and is soon joined by others as she finishes "If Love Were All."

The audience is crying. Cook is cooing, "That was so gentle. So sweet. I'm just amazed by the courage of you young people, by the way you trust me. I really appreciate it."

Now only Harper and Cook remain on stage. Two old friends. "I hope that it helps," she concludes. "But if it doesn't, forget it." The students laugh. The audience applauds.

The audience shouts for the teacher to sing. They clap, they whistle. She holds up her hand, says something to Wally, and agrees. "O.K. Now let's see if I can put this into practice. It's a lot harder to do it than to talk about it, you know."

But she knows what she's talking about and she knows what she's singing about. She catches us up in her song as though it were a net cast into a river. We swim right in and for the next three minutes it's the only world we know. And it's beautiful.

In her essay "The Teaching of Literature," Flannery O'Connor asserts that a teacher's first obligation is to the truth of the subject being taught. If she is teaching literature, it is to show that the novel concerns itself with the central mystery of our position on earth, the "ultimate mystery as we find it embodied in the concrete world of sense experience." A mystery comprised of yearning, loss, union, bliss, truth, and beauty.

Each time we immerse our senses in the "concrete world," they emerge dripping with the elements of mystery. The closer we approach, the more saturated we become. The romantic teacher urges her students to approach closer than they dare. Her goal is to transform the student from stone (the "perfect" performers who first sang for Barbara Cook) to sponge (the young woman whose deep sobs stopped the singing altogether).

Here's how Joel Upton "teaches" his Amherst College students about Van Eyck's *Mystic Lamb*. He enters the lecture hall without a word. He puts Barber's *Adagio for Strings* on the CD player. He turns off the lights, turns on the projector, and inserts a slide of the fifteenth-century masterpiece. The wall is covered with the deep blues, vibrant reds, fertile greens of the drapery. A mythic landscape with Flemish towers in the background is crowded with the multitudes of Revelation: "And behold, a great multitude which no one could number, of all nations, tribes, peoples, and tongues, standing before the throne and before the Lamb, clothed with white robes, with palm branches in their hands."

The music begins to muffle the projector's low hum. "I'll see you after class," says Upton, who then disappears for the next hour and a half. You call this teaching?

In peak learning experiences, the teacher succeeds in piercing the veil between student and subject. This is what happened when Barbara Cook's students became one with their song, one with song and the heart of the songwriter. Who is to say how many of Joel Upton's students sitting in the dark are having this experience with Jan Van Eyck? What I can tell you is that there were few dry eyes when the lights came on, and the silence continued in spite of the fact that the professor had returned to the room, turned on the lights, turned off the music and the slide projector. The silence continued and the students continued to stare straight ahead as though the painting were still before them. Then someone's stomach gave a mighty roar and we were reminded that it was long past lunchtime.

". . . Most experiences are unsayable," Rainer Maria Rilke writes in his first letter to a young poet. "They happen in a space that no world has ever entered and more unsayable than all other things are works of art, those mysterious existences, whose life endures beside our own small, transitory life."

This is rarely understood in our chattering world, eager for explanation and diversion. Upton is humble enough to know that the power of art is "unsayable" and that the only way to teach is to encourage watchful silence.

The ultimate knowledge: when to shut up.

The romantic teacher asks of his students a certain vulnerability. He urges them to probe below surfaces, to have faith that the world wants to be beautiful and wants to teach. Then he dares them to take on faith that the world is our most romantic teacher of all.

This is what Joel Upton is asking of his class the following week when I sit in to listen to him speak to a group of nine about Vermeer's *Girl with Pearl Earring*, the painting that had so moved the Washington businessman when it had visited briefly from its home in The Hague.

He addresses those of us who have gathered in a small room on the lower floor of Mead Art Building. "I want you to interrogate a painting. I want you to see beyond its surface, to push against it in the context of other paintings and other ideas. I want you to hold the work in a vulnerable embrace, to behold it and then to use your beholding as an occasion for insight.

"You don't need an expert to tell you what a painting is saying. You simply need the courage to probe its mystery and to give up control."

Before projecting the slide, he adds, "Prepare to be changed."

We meet Vermeer's model's unflinching gaze with our own. After a while her serenity seems to permeate the atmosphere of the classroom.

"Why," asks Upton, "does she so captivate?" He notes that the painting is indescribable no matter how hard we try to describe it. "Try to feel romantically," he urges, "see this painting as a point of separation between love and love's object."

As I look I begin to experience the pain of a moment whose loss is grieved in the same moment that it is captured. What do the students see? Do they know yet about the depths of loss in love?

Upton says that, when observing this painting, "Art historians should remain mute." An echo of Wittgenstein: "Whereof one cannot speak, thereof one must remain silent."

But we were born to blab, especially of the things whereof we cannot speak. We talk around it if necessary. We talk against the nervousness that begins to enter Upton's frequent long pauses.

"If in your gazing upon her, you fall in love with her, I am certain she loves you." I look up from my notes to see if he is as serious as he sounds. I look at his students to see if they are smirking. He is serious and they don't smirk.

I am unsettled. This well-known and highly respected art historian, with scholarly honors and publications, not to mention a Ph.D. and years of study, teaching, observation, and travel under his belt, is taking us beyond perspective and depth and orthogonals and vanishing points, the reference points on art's compass. Upton is an ancient sailor sailing off the chart of the known world. Here there be dragons. Here there be yearning and heartache. Here there be romance.

"Look," he says, drawing a diagram on the board. "We are capable of looking at the world the artist was looking at and looking at the artist." His diagram shows one line going from the observing eye to the painting. Another from the observing eye, looping up over the frame to the artist himself as the artist stands before the painting. A complex unity.

And he has taken it further with his statement that the girl loves us, the observer. That somehow, through the connection with the artist, we become one, and therefore the object of the model's love as she in turn is the object of the artist's.

I'm reminded of a poem by the Persian mystic Rumi:

> Look! This is love—to fly toward the heavens,
> To tear a hundred veils in ev'ry wink,
> To tear a hundred veils at the beginning,
> To travel in the end without a foot,
> And to regard this world as something hidden
> And not to see with one's own seeing eye!
> I said: "O heart, may it for you be blessed
> To enter in the circle of the lovers,
> To look from far beyond the range of eyesight.

After class, Upton and I sit in the student lounge and drink coffee next to wall-length windows framing a view of distant blue Berkshire Mountains. I ask him whether his students can conceptualize not seeing "with one's own seeing eye." Isn't that an eye that is opened by time and experience? "And, O.K.," I venture, "heartache?"

He nods. "I'm perfectly frank with my students that this class won't make sense to them until they're forty."

So why does he bother?

"Because I want them to know that there's more to love than those stupid things they watch on TV or at the movies. Love is a blend of the sacred and profane, and in class I try to get them to learn that visually, through paintings." He wants them to know "All things are interrelated."

He sets them on the course Proust set for himself, the work of finding the connection between unlike things.

"It's so hard," a friend of mine muses the next day after I've told her about the class and my conversation with Upton. She remembers being the age of those students and wonders if they're able to learn the lessons he offers. "At that age you've got so much to think about. Your love life, your grades, what happens after college. Your makeup."

And at that age being asked to be vulnerable is the same as being asked to surrender the tools you've counted on to hold yourself together in a world that you're beginning to fear may have chaos at its center. You might, just might, dare, if the challenger has done the same and lived to tell the tale, then you might trust the hand that reaches for yours. But this is a high-risk venture. What if you lose control?

From Barbara Cook's class, we see the answer to that. You might break down and cry before an audience of hundreds. You might learn something about the human heart. You might catch a glimpse of our universal interconnection. For a brief moment, you might be aware that from artist to viewer, from lyricist to singer, from teacher to student, a common web of silver strings is woven. It holds us safely in its embrace.

Part V

JERUSALEM, MY HAPPY HOME, AND OTHER DREAMS OF ROMANCE

19

WHEN I GET TO HEAVEN,
GONNA PUT ON MY SHOES

Since romance is born into the space between reach and grasp, it is little wonder that death provides a fertile womb.

Although Lao-tzu declared in the sixth century B.C., "There is no difference between the quick and the dead, they are one channel of vitality," though we visit séances and seers who "speak" to the dead, death remains "the land from which none returns." It does not yield to our urgent pleas for order out of chaos, nor does it answer our wailing, "Why?" We fill in the blanks with the myths that bind us together in this life as we ponder the next. We address so much poetry, philosophy, and art to the mystery that I imagine if there is a "hereafter" and if the dead can "see" we must appear like so many ants scurrying about, building tiny mounds of sand we call monuments to the dead. Are we that absurd? Are we that determined?

Yes. The irony is that we believe our lives depend on such scurrying. Consider the energy we put into gaining and maintaining faith that life does not end with death. Consider the power of that faith when it results in Rembrandt's capturing Jesus midsentence in *The Risen Christ at Emmaus*, or in the upward burst of energy in Titian's *Assumption* as angels, who know the way, return Mary to God. Consider the quiet, patient face of Jesus as he holds his arms out to his mother in Van der Goes's *Death of the Virgin*. Consider the fear, trembling, and redemption of Mozart's *Requiem* or the aching tenderness of

Fauré's *Pie Jesu*. Consider the power of a faith that inspired deaf Beethoven to utter, "I shall hear in heaven."

Romance, the journey out of homesickness, finds a satisfaction in the concept of death as homecoming. "Swing low, sweet chariot, / Coming for to carry me home. . . ." "Going home, going home, / I'm a going home. . . ."The slaves' state of alienation and homelessness became the great muse for the American poetry of the hereafter as a point of return.

We give familiar names to this heavenly home, this "place" out of time and space, this "nonwhere," as it was known to twelfth-century Persian mystic Sohrawardi. In a favorite ninteenth-century American folk hymn "Land of Rest," we call it Jerusalem. "Jerusalem, my happy home, / When shall I come to thee? / When shall my sorrows have an end? Thy joys when shall I see?" We envision it as the location of ultimate insight. "Through many dangers, toils, and snares, / I have already come; / 'Tis grace that brought me safe thus far, / And grace will lead me home."

The description of Paradise, in the highly visual book of Revelation, suggests a "place" part fairy tale, part Magrit. Jan Van Eyck was challenged to translate it into blazing color in his Ghent altarpiece. "And I John saw the holy city, new Jerusalem. . . . the street of the city was pure gold, as it were transparent glass . . . And the city had no need of the sun, neither of the moon, to shine in it: for the glory of God did lighten it, and the Lamb is the light thereof."

Who wouldn't yearn for such dreams of glory? Freud said we did and then recanted, but he was onto something. Perhaps the terminology was too stark, *thanatos*, the wish for death. Perhaps if he had called it an eternal longing to return to some mysterious source, we would have been more receptive. For we have sensed that as we come from mystery so we return. We think of this vague, unsettled longing, not as cold instinct, but as soulful yearning for an amorphous home and reunion with the source of our life. We decorate the mystery like so many Elsie de Wolfes. We drape the hereafter in luxuriant, human trappings. We make it almost irresistible.

In the Koran, Paradise is that place where "true servants of

Allah shall be well provided for, feasting on fruit, and honored in the gardens of delight. Reclining face to face upon soft couches, they shall be served with a goblet filled at a gushing fountain, white, and delicious to those who drink it. . . . They shall sit with bashful, dark-eyed virgins, as chaste as the sheltered eggs of ostriches."

A first-century Buddhist "Description of the Happy Land" promises a place of deep, wide rivers, converging and flowing calmly, their water "fragrant with manifold agreeable odours, in them there are bunches of flowers to which various jewels adhere, and they resound with various sweet sounds. And the sound which issues from these great rivers is as pleasant as that of a musical instrument, which consists of hundreds of thousands of kotis of parts, and which, skillfully played, emits a heavenly music."

The myths hold out the possibility that in this great hereafter we will be reunited with those we have loved. "If you get there before I do, / Coming for to carry me home, / Tell all my friends I'm coming too, / Coming for to carry me home." So deep is this dream of reunion that it seems stamped into our souls. I was taken aback when I heard myself say to a dying friend, "When you get there, tell Bobby I love him." A message to be carried to my dead brother, a request delivered as spontaneously and naturally as though she were on the way to a party Bobby was hosting. "When I get to heaven," says the Reverend Mark Anschutz, a Yale-educated theologian, well schooled in the ways of Episcopal restraint, "first thing I'm going to do is go find my mother and pick up my dogs." He tells me this over dinner, in a tone so matter-of-fact that he could be saying, "And, for dessert, I'll have strawberry shortcake."

Not only *that,* writes Bunyan in *Pilgrim's Progress,* not only do we reunite with all those we've loved, but with new, improved versions. "There, also, we shall meet with thousands and thousands that have gone before us to that place; none of them are hurtful, but loving and holy, every one walking in the sight of God."

Not that it's easy to get there. The Egytians considered the journey so hazardous that they buried the traveler with detailed instructions from the *Book of the Dead,* a map for the soul to find its way. Led by two hawks, the deceased would be reborn as though rising "out of the egg in the hidden land" and would become one with the divine Soul, the source of all creation. "I am Yesterday, Today, and Tomorrow. . . . I am the divine hidden Soul who createth the gods. . . .

"When we've been there ten thousand years, bright shining as the sun, we've no less days to sing God's praise than when we'd first begun."

One morning, a few years ago, my husband awakened amazed by a dream. "Everybody was there!" he woke me to announce. "Mozart! Shakespeare! All I had to do was ask for music and they'd play it. All I had to do was ask for a sonnet and Shakespeare would recite it!" There are those who would tell you the way was being prepared for him. There are others, like his wife, who would respond, "Sounds like heaven to me," and roll over and go back to sleep.

Whatever the response, it is another example that romance is not learned, it has a life of its own. It shines through my husband's dream, my message to my brother, and through dear Corot's utterance, "I hope with all my heart there will be painting in Heaven." It is there in the poetry of unschooled slaves who sang, "I want to be ready, I want to be ready, I want to be ready, ready to put on my long, white robe."

And for some, it would seem that death offers the most elusive of all treasures, reunion with the lost self. The Gnostic "Hymn of the Pearl" presents one who toils here below while his alter self remains in Paradise. When the wayfarer returns to his heavenly home, the Robe of Glory comes to meet him. "Its splendor I had forgotten, having left it as a child in my Father's house. As I now beheld the robe, it seemed to me suddenly to become a mirror image of myself: myself entire I saw in it, and it entire I saw in myself, that we were two in separateness, and yet again one in the sameness of our forms." Several centuries later, Wordsworth would concur. Our poetic selves do not forget our otherworldly selves. They keep their sights set on "That immortal sea / Which brought us thither."

The Romanticists believed that in moments of heightened awareness we could sense that spark of the divine, our birthright. "Everything, everything is a brief exchange / Between the earthly and the divine," writes contemporary poet Vickie Karp. The Sufis said so eight centuries earlier. For them, death was the ultimate exchange, a return to a generative matrix from which all life flowed. A complete circle, a spark of divinity that we carry with us at birth and return to its source at death.

If we share what Jung referred to as a universal unconscious, and if it is revealed in dreams, religion, myth, art, and literature, then we share life's loneliness, that ancient awareness that we are separated from a vital part of ourselves. For some, this loneliness is too much to bear. They confuse the promise in the romance with fact, and stake their lives on it. In the suicidal moment, according to Jorge Luis Borges, they become as invulnerable as gods:

> He will smooth back his hair, adjust his tie (as fits a young poet, he
> > was always a bit of a dandy), and try to imagine that the other
> > man—the one in the mirror—performs the actions and that he,
> > the double, repeats them. His hand will not falter at the end.
> > Obediently, magically, he will have pressed the weapon to his
> > head.
> It was in this way, I suppose, that things happened.

I, too, have been forced to such imaginings of late. A beautiful boy I knew, Keatsian in sensibility and Pythagorean in insight, took his own life. "Why, why?" Those who loved him, and they were many, ask the inevitable question and are met with the inevitable void. All that's left is the imagining.

His eyes were brown. A deeper brown than most. Merry on their glistening surface, dark in depths beyond our view and admiration. His smile was slow and sweet. His ways gentle. He listened with such attentiveness that silences in conversations with him hummed. Curly of hair, lanky of limb, and dear to know.

One early March morning before the sun came up and before fellow-student revelers at a college house party headed back to their dorms, my friend took his leave and went to the beach. A beach whose beauty had been robbed by the everyday detritus of alcohol and drugs. But he loved to watch the sun come up there. To watch the unfolding of that "old dependency of day and night." To sit among discarded beer cans and pint whiskey bottles, tossed aside still wrapped in brown paper bags clinging like an embrace. He'd sit in the rubble, his jeans absorbing the damp of the ebbing tide, and he'd wait for the sun to rise. Sit in the rubble and keep his eyes on that red orb emerging from the sea like an egg being laid upside down by a divinity with a keen sense of beauty and the absurd.

He did this every once in a while, I'm told, came to the beach to watch night break camp and move out, came to sit and ponder imponderable mathematical equations, mysteries of atoms, and the meaning of life.

"I've heard that reading poetry actually changes our brains on a cellular level," he once told me. Then he smiled, mocking even the hint of pedantry. "Well, that's what a friend said, anyway. He's majoring in the English Romanticists."

My friend's brain was changing on a cellular level. The more he watched that sun come up, the more he stared at equations on classroom blackboards, the more he contemplated the meaning of it all, the keener his hearing for the Pythagorean celestial harmonies. When he went to the beach, he heard the music.

So how to explain the March morning when he left the party, sober as usual, entreated by his friends to stay, as usual, and headed for the beach with a knife in his pocket? A knife he'd bought two weeks before. How to explain getting on the subway, riding the thirty minutes to the sea, walking down to the sand, sitting and sensing the dewy dampness settle on his lashes and tightening his hair's coiled curls? How did he decide as he sat, his thighs and buttocks itching with the briny ooze of damp sand seeping into his jeans, how did he decide that this morning he wouldn't wait for the sun? That ruby-encrusted Fabergé egg of the gods.

How to explain the decision to take the knife from his pocket and insert it into his own throat?

Some days later, as his seventeen-year-old cousin watched a rainbow spread its span across a blue, blue bay, he asked, "How could he decide not to stick around to find out what happens next?"

He did. It was just a different "next." Chances are that like Keats, like all romantics, he lived his life "half in love with easeful Death." Then one day it became more than half.

Death is to the romantic what Mont Sainte-Victoire was to Cézanne, Rouen Cathedral to Monet. If we stare long enough, approach enough times, will we eventually merge and become one, and in the oneness gain knowledge that flames our yearning even though we're not certain what it is we want to know? Will our blood commingling with heaven at last offer Wallace Stevens's "requital to desire"?

Since the beginning of time, our love of death as rebirth into new life has been at odds with our love of life as it is right here and now. Death as the ultimate creation calls sweetly to the romantic, who turns instead to poetry, stories, song, art, earthly love. Until he doesn't. Until such expressions seem but flimsy representations substituting for the ultimate creation into new life, the chance to be born anew into embracing light. The merging of desire and the end of all desire.

My friend studied physics. He knew what physicists, philosophers, poets, and mystics know. That our eyes deceive us. That reality is illusion. That form is empty and emptiness form. Love thy neighbor as thyself because thy neighbor is thyself. Life is a series of events enfolding and unfolding, and nothing ever dies. Energy to mass, mass to energy. "Time, like an ever-rolling stream, / Bears all its sons away." "The past," writes physicist David Bohm, "is active in the present as a kind of implicate order." On these commandments hang all the laws and the prophets.

Rage for order. The romantic engages in "The maker's rage to order words of the sea." To give words to what is beyond words. To give heavenly music an earthly song, a cantilevered edifice. To give emptiness form. A mere illusion, says the Buddha. Form only exists because we habitually say it's so. Because we suffer from Einstein's "optical delusion."

When this rage for order falters, it can lead to the kind of despair Tolstoy experienced when he was unable to write. "One can live only so long as one is intoxicated, drunk with life, but when one grows sober one cannot fail to see that it is all a stupid cheat. What is truest about it is that there is nothing even funny or silly in it, it is cruel and stupid, purely and simply." He hung a hangman's noose in his attic, just in case.

We sing our stubborn song against the "stupid cheat." We sing emptiness into form as the aborigines sang the world into being. As the Hopis sing up the sun. As the Lord of Genesis sang light into the void. Rage for order causes us to sing the language of the gods even as we know there's no such language.

And as we sing being into illusion, so we sing death into being. We believe our songs. And for a reason. Our songs resonate with a truth beyond our knowing.

To sing that there is more to death than nothingness, to sing that there is a rebirth into something pure and divine, to sing that there is a final merger with the good, the beautiful, the true is simply to sing the song of the ages. Of course, it makes no sense, but our songs have never been about sense. They are lyrical, poetic truths, not historical.

Wallace Stevens's singer on the beach at Key West:

> was the single artificer of the world
> In which she sang. And when she sang, the sea,
> Whatever self it had, became the self
> That was her song, for she was the maker.

Keats knew that only art could satisfy our rage for order, and that such satisfaction was temporary. If we find this truth too hard to bear, then we become infatuated with that final order, that final union. Then we lower ourselves into Hart Crane's sea and hold our breath as he did and wait for it to embrace us, to take us into its darkness and bear us up to light. It must be so. The Church teaches us this from the moment our small bald heads are touched with holy water and we "die into Christ." And yet it is the great Christian romance. "Therefore, if anyone is in Christ, he is a new creation; old things have passed away; behold, all things have become new." A Christian interpretation of pre-Christian myths of rebirth into light and purity. The soul returning home.

Similarly, Jewish mystics speak of the angel Michael bringing the dying "home."

The Persian savior Manes's soul laments: "I came out of light and the gods. Here in exile am I from them kept apart."

We are born as soul bearers seeking lost light. For the Hindu mystic, that light can be experienced in this life through death, not of the body but of the ego. The yearning itself is the light. The yearning itself leads to the light. To yearn is to return home. But to live in yearning is to live in pain. Who would chose it? Who does not understand Keats's desire "To cease upon the midnight with no pain."

His ode was an echo of songs of the Celts, the Cathars, the Cabalists, the Sufis. An echo of Plato's "reminiscence of Beauty," which makes the soul yearn for what we've known only in dreams. An echo of Wordsworth, who knew that from birth we are trained out of those dreams.

But we are the reminiscing animal. There is no stopping us. In vague remembrance, longing is born. Longing that knows no earthly satisfaction save for the evanescence of the mystical, poetic, musical, artistic moment, when we're given a brief taste of that madeleine of ancient memory.

We are the artificers of the world, that is our lot. When it's no longer enough, we sit on a rubble-strewn beach and watch our blood flow out with the tide to commingle with heaven and requite our desire.

Can we stand the poet's awareness that the singer in Key

West and the world of which she sings exists only through her song? What if she falls silent?

What if we do? If we stop singing, we end up on a littered beach with a knife in our pocket. If we share the poet's awareness, our hearts could break from the strain. If they break open, we'll paint and design and sing again, stubbornly giving form to the pain, knowing full well that it is all illusion, "that there never was a world for her/Except the one she sang and, singing, made."

To recognize that is to recognize mortal loneliness. To know that loneliness is the mother of truth and beauty is to share the heart of the twelfth-century troubadour, for whom earthly, carnal love offered no requital to desire. To know that is to sing boldly, like him, into the loneliness, to embrace the paradox of the mystery, what is beyond our earthly grasp is its only satisfaction.

Wordsworth wandered lonely as a cloud. The desert fathers led hermetic lives. Keats lay dying far from home, in rooms filled with the music of a fountain's flow. From their loneliness came insight verging on what the Buddha called enlightenment. They sensed what cosmologists now tell us: We are made from the leftovers of stars. Afterthoughts in a universe of afterthoughts.

To be in an earthly frenzy of passion, to engage in the Tristan and Iseult love of love, is to dramatize ourselves at center stage, shutting our minds to the humbling knowledge that we are merely made of the leftovers. Just so many shepherd's pies.

My friend repeatedly asked family and friends, "What does it mean? What does any of it mean?" I think he knew full well what it means. It means nothing. We're given the leftovers, we yearn for more. We attempt to make beauty out of what we're given, we sing against the emptiness, we dance in the void. We are absurd in our dancing and singing.

But who can stand the thought? Not my friend. My friend who wearied of singing his song by the sea. Who wearied of singing the world into being and drew the sharp point of his new knife across his neck.

"I did drugs with Timothy Leary up there in Millbrook in the sixties," a woman tells me. "And then I discovered that God wasn't in LSD." She has to go now. "I've got to go get ready for the Dalai Lama, who's coming to town."

The Dalai Lama, who writes that the subject matter of the wisdom sutras, as taught by the Buddha, explores "levels of transcendent experience associated with the realization of emptiness." That a realization of emptiness comes from the practice of compassion, altruism, and the slow-growing awareness that nothing has intrinsic identity, that form is a result of our projections.

Sounds pretty sixties to me.

"You will be with me this day in Paradise," the man on the cross promises the neighbor who hangs next to him, crucified for crimes.

The criminal and the saint are one. Student and teacher are one. A man, a woman, and a blackbird are one. And death, according to Wallace Stevens, is the mother of beauty.

> She says, "But in contentment I still feel
> The need of some imperishable bliss."
> Death is the mother of beauty; hence from her,
> Alone, shall come fulfilment to our dreams
> And our desires. Although she strews the leaves
> Of sure obliteration on our paths.

When the ancient Celt returns from the land of the dead singing songs of longing for that place of immortals he's left behind, he sounds like the Williams College economics professor I recently met who told me of his "near death" experience. "I had a heart attack while I was playing squash. By the time they got me to the local hospital I was declared dead." His heart as known by cardiologists may have shut down, but the heart of the poets was opening. "I walked into a great light and felt surrounded by love. It was a homecoming.

"I thought of the Zen poet Suzuki, who upon visiting Niagara Falls said, 'How lonely those drops of water must be before they can rejoin the river below.' That was how I felt, that I had rejoined the river below, returned to my source." Upon being revived and returning to "real" life, he was overcome by a sense of loss and grief. For months, he longed to leave the loneliness of this life and return to that other, where he had experienced complete peace and fulfillment.

It almost destroyed his marriage. "After all," his wife says of the moment when the heart monitor registered her husband's death, "I was living the worst moment of my life, and he was living the best of his."

His children found it hard to forgive him for his glowing message. "Don't worry. When I die, I will always be with you." Thanks just the same. Give us a dad who comes to the soccer matches in his old, worn pea jacket with leather-patched elbows, the dad who yells at us when we've been on the phone too long.

But his ear was now tuned to the whisperings born into the human heart from the moment it took its first beat. The troubadours sang its song throughout the South of France, courting death with the same passion and in the same poetry with which they courted their ladies fair. "Far more it pleaseth me to die / Than easy mean delight to feel," wrote Almeric de Belenoi. This hunger for enduring love, *joie d'amour,* was a hunger for death itself, a mystical union with the pure feminine from which one is reborn into "newness of life."

Christian mystic Saint John of the Cross sang that the frenzy of unrequited passion created a fire that burned the body until the soul was released. We are hypnotically led to that fire.

As the troubadours sang, the builders of cathedrals stretched their spires ever upward like lovers' arms reaching for heaven. The blood of their labors commingling, virginal seeking requital for desire.

The troubadours, coming from a history dating from the third century, when Persian influences spread into Europe, bringing the poetry of the Sufi mystics, recast the romance of mystical union in terms of knightly quests. They poeticized the struggle of day and night, the reconciliation of darkness and light. The darkness of the here and now, the light hinted at by day, promised by dawn, but only experienced in its entirety in death, which unites the yearning heart with its desire, thus putting an end to all desire. "You will be with me this day in Paradise."

The ages sing us a song of ultimate union. To merge with the feminine, to be completely whole, a man must die. Must enter mother sea, mother sky. Only then will his soul, which Plato proclaimed feminine, only then can that blessed virgin, that lady most fair imprisoned in our bodies, be released into Paradise.

Death, the mother of beauty, will give birth to Plato's remembered beauty, to Keats's Beauty as Truth. Or so they tell us through the ages raging, raging for order.

We desire an end to desire, the end of ecstasy's path where ecstasy ends. "This wild desire / Is bound to be my death, no matter if I stay or go. / For she who could deliver me, no pity will she show," the troubadour sings, though he knows release will come only in death, for the mortal lady will no pity show. Not if she is pure. Not if her image is created as the natural evolution of mystical thought. Not if union with the "lady" is the final union of male and female, human and godhead.

Through earthly love we seek the rebirth promised by mystical love. We claim to be born anew, we claim we can bring our lovers to new life. "He's changed a lot since she married him." "When I find my true love, I won't be lonely anymore." We cling to these beliefs and grow very, very old. Earthly love makes its demands. Yes, our lovers may deliver us, but they demand a ransom for deliverance.

Did my friend ponder these things as he sat on the beach, determined to beat the sun this day to Paradise? My friend sitting on the beach, soaking up the salt, sensing the brine of creation sting his buttocks and thighs. My friend sitting in his assiduously sought solitude, waiting for the music of the spheres to begin its harmonious blending. My friend leaning into the harmony, pressing against it, bleeding into it until his note too was played.

His blood mingled with brine, his soul flew forth and sang its lost song.

The Romanticists would tell us this is how it was. I don't know.

Part VI

DARLIN', SAVE THE LAST DANCE FOR ME

20

NOW WE KNOW SHE
DREAMS, BUT DOES SHE
DREAM OF ME?

——·••·——

We live in a quantum universe in which, according to physicist David Lindley, we are unable "to obtain . . . all the information about an object that [we] might want to know." Even though we know more than we ever knew before. Even though we know that neutrinos, world-famous, ever-elusive, subatomic particles with no electric charge, actually have mass! Even though we know that no matter how far we travel toward or away from light, we remain the same infinite distance away. 299,792,458 meters per second to be precise. Even though we'd recognize the DNA of the gene that causes tuberculosis if we met it on a street corner. Even though we know she dreams and Dr. Rodolfo Llinas has seen it happen on his magnetoencephalograph machine.

We're smarter than ever. Our brains are expanding with the universe. And so are the mystery and the yearning. Even in contentment we feel the need for imperishable bliss. Call it homesickness. Call it romance.

We live in a quantum, ever-changing, unknowable universe. We hold our binoculars, our light sensors, our telescopes and microscopes to it, and yet nobody's ever laid eyes on a neutrino; nobody can define light quanta though every rascal thinks he can; and we still don't know if she dreams of me. And Dr. Visscher, dear Dr. Visscher, apiarian troubadour, will never ever know what it is to be a bee.

This spring the new brood of red-tailed hawks has left the nest. Except for one. He sits and waits. We sit and stare. One week passes. Why? Why? Why? We wonder aloud and in the same breath offer answers. "He's scared." "He's the runt of the litter." "He's injured." "It's a female and she's too smart to leave." Even as we say it we know that we don't have a clue.

The knowledge that will sate our hunger is beyond our grasp. Like infinity, it remains the same infinite distance away. And yet we press ahead.

Mystery expands with the universe, and even neutrino detectors can only register neutrino debris, not the particle itself. Even though we build a water tank the size of Chartres Cathedral, fill it to brimming, and bury it one mile beneath a Japanese mountain. Even though in that mass of buried water a neutrino collides with an atom and the resulting debris emits shock waves of blue light measured by scientists who shout, "Alleluia! Neutrinos have mass! Neutrinos have mass!" Even then we're left with a hunger to know. "Hey, what do these guys *look* like?"

Imagine. There are an average of three hundred neutrinos in every teaspoon of space. That spoon you're using to stir your coffee, that will do nicely. Take it out, look at it. Look very carefully. See any neutrinos there? Have you ever seen one?

Imagine. A neutrino can penetrate six trillion miles of lead and come out the other side unscathed, not a hair out of place, not a nail chipped. Ever felt one? Nobody has. Not even the scientists who now jump up and down in their hiking boots and raise glasses of mineral water in celebration of their discovery. A breakthrough in science. "The Universe May Never Be the Same," the *Times* headline tells us. Rock-a-my-soul-in-the-bosom-of-Abraham.

Scientist Enrico Fermi had never seen nor felt nor smelled one either, but he sensed they were there, and sixty-eight years ago, acting on faith alone, he gave these elusive subatomic particles their name, Italian for "little neutral one."

Fermi, like Adam, was merely naming the animals, doing what comes naturally, giving mystery form. Doing what we were born to do.

So now, thanks to Fermi, they have a name. And now, thanks to the latest developments in quantum mechanics, we know they come in three flavors: the electron neutrino, the muon neutrino (associated with the muon particle, a zaftig electron), and the tau neutrino (associated with the muon's obese cousin).

But as Lindley informs us, all the information is not in. There are other flavors to be revealed. For that the neutrino stalkers will have to bury the beating human heart in their water tank the size of Chartres Cathedral one mile deep beneath a Japanese mountain. Then they'll discover a fourth flavor. The yearning neutrino. It's the mass we're made of.

But that's not all. The light sensors will eventually register another. What's this? The physicists will scratch their heads, take off their glasses, and rub their eyes; they'll push each other out of the way for a closer look. "Could there be a fifth flavor of neutrino? No. Impossible." But look. There it is. And the fifth shall be called the bull-headed neutrino! And it has mass! And it is ours.

Neutrinos essential to the romantic life. Without neutrinos of yearning and neutrinos of bull-headedness we would fail to penetrate the six million miles of lead that exist between us and eternity.

Embrace me, you sweet embraceable you. Nonsense. Our universe is ever changing, the world at its very core is shifting beneath our feet. It is untouchable, unembraceable. It will not be held. It will not be ours. It will not love us back.

But that didn't stop Fermi from loving the neutrino, the cave painter from loving the deer, Thoreau from loving his oak, the Central Park birders from loving their owl, Rousseau from loving the radiant green of underlit leaves.

When Lindley asserts that the one sure thing that quantum mechanics can tell us is "that at the most fundamental level, the world is not wholly knowable," he echoes Zeami's twelfth-century refrain:

the world so unsure, unknowable
the world so unsure, unknowable
who knows—our griefs may hold
our greatest hopes.

And yet we won't take No for an answer. We wander the earth with outstretched hands, creatures of yearning taking specimens from the wild for closer study. We remove animals from the wilderness, domesticate them, and call them pets. We pluck the wildflowers of meadows and transplant them within the binding walls of our own Sissinghursts. We hold a hawk in the focus of binoculars.

It's in our nature to do so. It's our gift that we can. We press ahead even as we know that merger and union, that imperishable bliss, will elude. For all our scouting, peering, studying, embracing, we won't know what strange impulse makes our dog cry out in sleep and jerk his limbs as though running with an ancient pack. We'll never plumb the deep mystery of soil's grateful opening to rain or a leaf's exaltation of the sun. We'll never hear the sigh of a winter bough submitting to snow.

And yet we know they call to us like Wendell Berry's swallows and redbirds:

> Meet us in the air
> over the water,
> sing the swallows.

> Meet me, meet me,
> the redbird sings,
> here here here here.

Here here here here is all we have for sure. But that doesn't stop our stubborn insistence on connecting to one another across time, space, species, and gender. It doesn't diminish our conviction that inspiration, intuition, imagination, and dreams are the vehicles for such connection. It doesn't stop us from listening for the music of the spheres.

And so we'll watch, we'll listen. Just so many strings waiting to be played.

SELECTED BIBLIOGRAPHY

Abrams, M. H. *The Mirror and the Lamp.* New York: Norton, 1953.

Ackerman, Diane. *A Natural History of Love.* New York: Vintage Books, 1995.

Adams, Henry. *Mont-Saint-Michel and Chartres.* New York: Penguin Books, 1986.

Albanese, Catherine L. *Nature Religion in America: From the Algonkian Indians to the New Age.* Chicago: University of Chicago Press, 1991.

Bachelard, Gaston. *The Poetics of Space: The Classic Look at How We Experience Intimate Places.* Boston: Beacon Press, 1994.

Barfield, Owen. *Romanticism Comes of Age.* Middletown, CT.: Wesleyan University Press, 1986.

Barlow, Elizabeth. *The Central Park Book.* New York: Central Park Task Force, 1977.

Barzun, Jacques. *Romanticism and the Modern Ego.* Boston: Little, Brown and Company, 1943.

____. *Teacher in America.* Indianapolis: Indiana University Press, 1981.

____. *The Energies of Art: Studies of Authors, Classic and Modern.* New York: Harper, 1956.

Bataille, Georges. *Lascaux; or the Birth of Art: Prehistoric Painting.* Lausanne: Skira, 1955.

Bédier, Joseph. *The Romance of Tristan & Iseult.* New York: Vintage Books, 1994.

Berg, Elizabeth. *Range of Motion.* New York: Random House, 1995.

Bernanos, Georges. *Diary of a Country Priest.* New York: Macmillan, 1937.

Bernard of Clairvaux, Saint. *Bernard of Clairvaux: Selected Works.* Mahwah, NJ: Paulist Press, 1987.

Berry, Wendell. *Collected Poems.* New York: North Point Press, 1995.

Bersani, Leo. *The Culture of Redemption.* Cambridge, Mass: Harvard University Press, 1990.

Blake, William. *The Poetical Works.* London: Oxford University Press, 1958.

Bowra, Maurice. *The Romantic Imagination.* Oxford: Oxford University Press, 1961.

Brians, Paul, ed. *Bawdy Tales from the Courts of Medieval France.* New York: Harper & Row, 1972.

Brooks, H. Allen. *American Buildings and Their Architects.* Garden City, NY, 1972.

Brown, Norman. *Life Against Death; the Psychoanalytical Meaning of History.* Middletown, CT: Wesleyan University Press, 1959.

Bull, John. *The Audubon Society Field Guide to North American Birds, Eastern Region.* New York: Knopf, 1977.

——. *Birds of the New York Area.* New York: Harper & Row, 1964.

Bullett, Gerald, ed. *Silver Poets of the Sixteenth Century.* London: J. M. Dent & Sons, 1964.

Campbell, Joseph. *The Hero with a Thousand Faces.* Princeton, NJ: Princeton University Press, 1973.

——. *Transformations of Myth Through Time.* New York: Harper & Row, 1990.

Cather, Willa. *Song of the Lark.* Boston: Houghton, Mifflin, 1943.

Chauvet, Jean-Marie, Éliette Brunel Deschamps, and Christian Hillaire. *Dawn of Art: The Chauvet Cave.* New York: Abrams, 1996.

Clark, Kenneth. *The Romantic Rebellion.* London, 1973.

Darwin, Charles. *The Expression of the Emotions in Man and Animals.* London, Oxford University Press, 1998.

——. *Voyage of the Beagle.* New York: Penguin Books, 1989.

De Rougemont, Denis. *Love in the Western World.* Princeton, NJ: Princeton University Press, 1983.

Dillard, Annie. *Pilgrim at Tinker Creek.* New York: Harper's Magazine Press, 1974.

——. *Teaching a Stone to Talk: Expeditions and Encounters.* New York: Harper & Row, 1980.

Duby, Georges. *The Age of Cathedrals: Art & Society, 980–1420,* 1981.

Edinger, Edward F. *Ego and Archetype.* Baltimore: Penguin Books, 1974.

Egyptian Book of the Dead, trans. Charles Davis. New York: G. P. Putnam, 1894.

Eliot, T. S. *Four Quartets: The Centenary Edition, 1888-1988.* Orlando, FL: Harcourt Brace Jovanovich, 1971.

Emerson, Ralph Waldo. *Complete Works.* Boston: Houghton, Mifflin, 1903–1922.

Enge, Schröer, and Wiesenhofer, Claßen. *Garden Architecture in Europe 1450–1800: From the Villa Garden of the Italian Renaissance to the English Landscape Garden.* Germany: Benedikt Taschen, 1992.

Ferris, Timothy. *Coming of Age in the Milky Way.* New York: Anchor Books, 1989.

Fisher, Helen. *Anatomy of Love.* New York: W. W. Norton, 1995.

Fitzgerald, F. Scott. *The Great Gatsby.* New York: Scribner, 1995.

____. *The Crack Up,* New York: Laughlin, 1949.

Flexner, James Thomas. *The Light of Distant Skies: American Painting 1760-1835.* Boston, 1954.

Forster, E. M. *Howards End.* New York: Bantam Books, 1985.

Frankl, Paul. *The Gothic: Literary Sources and Interpretations through Eight Centuries.* Princeton, NJ: Princeton University Pressk, 1960.

Frazer, James George, *The New Golden Bough.* New York: Criterion Books, 1959.

Frost, Robert. *The Complete Poems of Robert Frost.* New York: Holt, Rinehart and Winston, 1961.

Frye, Northrop, ed. *Romanticism Reconsidered.* New York, 1963.

Gadamer, Hans-Georg. *The Relevance of the Beautiful and Other Essays.* Cambridge, MA: Cambridge University Press, 1986.

García Márquez, Gabriel. *Love in the Time of Cholera.* New York: Knopf, 1988.

Gill, Stephen, ed. *William Wordsworth.* Oxford: Oxford University Press, 1984.

Gilson, Etienne. *The Spirit of Medieval Philosophy.* Notre Dame, IN: University of Notre Dame Press, 1991.

Gleckner, Robert F., and Gerald E. Enscoe, *Romanticism: Points of View.* Englewood Cliffs, NJ: Prentice-Hall, 1962.

Goethe, Johann Wolfgang von. *Faust, A Tragedy.* Boston: Ticknor and Fields, 1857.

____. *Italian Journey 1786–1788.* San Francisco: North Point Press, 1982.

Graff, M. M. *Central Park, Prospect Park: A New Perspective.* New York: Greensward Foundation, 1985.

Hayden, John O., ed. *William Wordsworth: Selected Prose.* New York: Penguin Books, 1988.

Heisenberg, Werner. *Encounters with Einstein.* Princeton, NJ: Princeton University Press, 1939.

Hesiod. *Works.* Cambridge, MA: Harvard University Press, 1982.

Hitchcock, Henry-Russell. *Architecture: Nineteenth and Twentieth Centuries.* Pelican History of Art, rev. ed. London: Harmondsworth, 1971.

Hoffmann, Donald. *Frank Lloyd Wright's Fallingwater: The House and Its History.* New York: Dover, 1993.

——. *Frank Lloyd Wright: Architecture and Nature.* New York, 1986.

Hofmann, Werner. *The Earthly Paradise.* New York, 1961.

Holmes, Oliver Wendell. *Ralph Waldo Emerson.* New York: Chelsea House, 1980.

Honour, Hugh. *Romanticism.* New York: Harper & Row, 1979.

——. *Venice: A Companion Guide.* New York: David McKay, 1971.

——. and Fleming, John. *Henry James in Venice.* New York: Little, Brown, 1991.

——. *The Venetian Hours of Henry James, Whistler and Sargent.* Canada: Bulfinch Press Book, 1991.

Hugo, Victor. *Notre-Dame de Paris.* New York: Penguin Books, 1978.

Huizinga, J. *The Waning of the Middle Ages: A Study of the Forms of Life, Thought and Art in France and the Netherlands in the Dawn of the Renaissance.* New York: Anchor Books, 1949.

James, Henry. *The Painter's Eye: Notes and Essays on the Pictorial Arts.* London: Rupert & Hart-Davis, 1956.

Jammes, André, and Eugenia Parry Janis. *The Art of French Calotype.* Princeton, NJ: Princeton University Press, 1983.

John of the Cross, Saint. *The Poems of St. John of the Cross.* Chicago: University of Chicago Press, 1979.

Kinkead, Eugene. *Central Park, 1857–1995: The Birth, Decline, and Renewal of a National Treasure.* New York: Norton, 1990.

Krober, Karl. *Romantic Landscape Vision: Constable and Wordsworth.* Madison, WI: 1975.

Lanchester, John. *The Debt to Pleasure.* New York: Owl Books, 1997.

Lawrence, D. H. *Etruscan Places.* New York: Compass Books, 1957.

Lethaby, William. *Architecture, Mysticism and Myth.* New York: George Braziller, 1975.

Levine, Philip, ed. *The Essential Keats.* New York: The Ecco Press, 1987.

London, Jack. *Call of the Wild.* New York: Dutton, 1974.

Marx, Leo. *The Machine in the Garden; Technology and the Pastoral Ideal in America.* New York: Oxford University Press, 1964.

Masson, Jeffrey Moussaieff, and Susan McCarthy. *When Elephants Weep.* New York: Delacourt Press, 1995.

Mazonowicz, Douglas. *In Search of Cave Art.* Rohnert Park, CA: Gallery of Prehistoric Paintings, 1973.

____. *Voices from the Stone Age: A Search for Cave and Canyon Art*. New York: Crowell, 1974.

Montaigne, Michel de. *Montaigne's Travel Journal*. San Francisco: North Point Press, 1983.

Morris, Richard. *The Edges of Science: Crossing the Boundary from Physics to Metaphysics*. New York: Prentice Hall, 1990.

Motion, Andrew. *Keats*. New York: Farrar, Straus and Giroux, 1997.

Murray, Peter. *The Architecture of the Italian Renaissance*. New York: Schocken Books, 1963.

Nate, Kevin. *Frank Lloyd Wright in Japan*. New York: 1993.

O'Connor, Flannery. *Mystery and Manners*. New York: Farrar, Straus and Giroux, 1961.

____. *The Habit of Being. Letters of Flannery O'Connor*: New York: Vintage Books, 1980.

Olmsted, Frederick Law. *Creating Central Park, 1857–1861,* Baltimore: Johns Hopkins University Press, 1983.

Ovid (Publius Ovidius Naso). *Metamorphoses,* trans. R. Humphries. Bloomington, IN: Indiana University Press, 1955.

Pagels, Heinz R. *The Cosmic Code: Quantum Physics as the Language of Nature*. Great Britain: Pelican Books, 1984.

Palladio, Andrea. *The Four Books of Architecture*. New York: Dover, 1965.

Panofsky, Erwin. *Early Netherland Painting, 2 vols*. New York: Icon Editions, Harper & Row, 1971.

Peckham, Morse. *Beyond the Tragic Vision: The Quest for Identity in the Nineteenth Century*. New York: George Braziller, 1962.

____. *The Triumph of Romanticism*. Columbia: University of South Carolina Press, 1970.

Person, Ethel S. *Dreams of Love and Fateful Encounters. The Power of Romantic Passion*. New York: Penguin Books, 1989.

Petroff, Elizabeth Avilda. *Body and Soul: Essays on Medieval Women and Mysticism*. Oxford: Oxford University Press, 1994.

Plato. *Gorgias*. New York: Penguin Books, 1986.

Plato. *Symposium* in *The Republic and Other Works*, trans. B. Jowett. Garden City, NY: Dolphin, 1960.

Plutarch. *Makers of Rome*, trans. Ian Scott-Kilvert. London: Harmondsworth, 1965.

Pound, Ezra, and Noel Stock, trans. *Love Poems of Ancient Egypt*. New York: New Directions, 1962.

Raphael, Max. *Prehistoric Cave Paintings.* New York: Pantheon, 1945.

Richardson, Robert D., Jr. *Ralph Waldo Emerson: Selected Essays, Lectures, and Poems.* New York: Bantam Books, 1990.

Rilke, Rainer Maria. *Letters on Cézanne.* New York: Fromm International Publishing Corporation, 1985.

Rosenblum, Robert. *Modern Painting and the Northern Romantic Tradition.* New York and London, 1975.

Rosenthal, M. L., ed. *William Butler Yeats: Selected Poems and Three Plays.* New York: Collier Books, 1962.

Rosenzweig, Roy. *The Park and the People: A History of Central Park.* Ithaca, NY: Cornell University Press, 1992.

Rumi. Trans. by Annemarie Schimmel. *Look! This Is Love, Poems of Rumi.* Boston and London: Shambala, 1996.

Ruspoli, Mario. *The Cave of Lascaux.* New York: Abrams, 1986.

Russell, Mary Doria. *The Sparrow.* New York: Villard, 1996.

Schama, Simon. *Landscape and Memory.* New York: Knopf, 1995.

Schenk, H. G. *The Mind of the European Romantics.* London: 1966.

Scully, Vincent. *Architecture: The Natural and the Manmade.* New York: St. Martin's Press, 1991.

——. *American Architecture and Urbanism.* New York: Henry Holt, 1988.

——. *The Earth, the Temple, and the Gods.* New Haven, CT: Yale University Press, 1962.

——. *Frank Lloyd Wright.* New York: George Braziller, 1960.

Secrest, Meryle. *Frank Lloyd Wright.* New York: Knopf, 1992.

Shakespeare. *The Tempest.* New York: Washington Square Press, 1961.

Shelley, Percy Bysshe. *Shelley's Poetry and Prose.* New York: Norton, 1977.

Sims Warren, Gwendolin. *Ev'ry Time I Feel the Spirit: 101 Best-Loved Psalms, Gospel Hymns, and Spiritual Songs of the African-American Church.* New York: Henry Holt, 1997.

Smith, Norris Kelly. *Here I Stand: Perspective from Another Point of View.* New York: Columbia University Press, 1994.

Snyder, James. *Bosch in Perspective.* Englewood Cliffs, NJ: Prentice-Hall, 1973.

——. *Medieval Art: Painting, Sculpture, Architecture, 4–14th Century.* New York: Harry N. Abrams, 1988.

——. *Northern Renaissance Art: Painting, Sculpture, The Graphic Arts from 1350–1575.* New York: Harry N. Abrams, 1985.

Stevens, Wallace. *The Collected Poems of Wallace Stevens.* New York: Knopf, 1969.

Stoddard, Whitney S. *Art and Architecture in Medieval France*. New York: Icon, 1972.

Sutherland, Donald. *On Romanticism*. New York: New York University Press, 1971.

Talbot, Michael. *The Holographic Universe*. New York: Harper Perennial, 1992.

Tanizaki, Jun'ichiro. *In Praise of Shadows*. Stony Creek, CT: Leete's Island Books, 1977.

Teilhard de Chardin, Pierre. *The Phenomenon of Man*. New York: Harper, 1959.

Thoreau, Henry David. *Journal*. Princeton, NJ: Princeton University Press, 1981.

_____. *Great Short Works of Henry David Thoreau*. New York: Harper Perennial, 1993.

Thorlby, Anthony. *The Romantic Movement*. London, 1966.

Tuchman, Barbara. *A Distant Mirror*. New York: Knopf, 1978.

Underhill, Evelyn. *Mysticism: A Study in the Nature and Development of Man's Spiritual Consciousness*. New York: Penguin, 1974.

Upton, Joel. *Petrus Christus: His Place in 15th Century Flemish Painting*. University Park: Pennsylvania State University Press.

Vermeersch, Valentin. *The Flemish Primitives*. Belgium, 1989.

Wellek, René. *A History of Modern Criticism: The Romantic Age*. New Haven, CT: Yale University Press, 1991.

Welty, Eudora. *The Eye of the Story*. New York: Vintage, 1979.

Whitman, Walt. *Leaves of Grass*. New York: New American Library, 1955.

Wilczek, Frank, and Betsy Devine. *Longing for the Harmonies: Themes and Variations from Modern Physics*. New York: W. W. Norton, 1988.

Williams, John, ed. *English Renaissance Poetry: A Collection of Shorter Poems from Skelton to Jonson*. New York: Anchor Books, 1963.

Windels, Fernand. *The Lascaux Cave Painting*. New York: Viking Press, 1950.

Wright, Frank Lloyd. *An Autobiography*. New York: Horizon Press, 1977.

_____. *In the Realm of Ideas*. IL: Southern Illinois University Press, 1988.

_____. *An American Architecture*. New York: Horizon Press, 1955.

_____. *Man in Possession of His Earth*. Garden City, NY: Doubleday, 1962.

_____. *Frank Lloyd Wright, Architect*. New York: Museum of Modern Art, 1994.

——. *The Future of Architecture*. New York: Horizon Press, 1953.

——. *Letters to Apprentices*. Fresno: Press at California State University, Fresno, 1982.

——. *Letters to Architects*. Fresno: Press at California State University, Fresno, 1984.

——. *Letters to Clients*. Fresno: Press at California State University, Fresno, 1986.

——. *Master Architect. Conversations with Frank Lloyd Wright*. New York: Wiley, 1984.

——. *Natural Houses*. New York: Horizon, 1954.

Wundram, Manfred Pape, Thomas. *Palladio 1508–1580: Architect between the Renaissance and Baroque*. Germany: Benedikt Taschen, 1992.

Zajonc, Arthur. *Catching the Light: The Entwined History of Light and Mind*. New York: Bantam Books, 1993.